# WHITE WITCH DOCTOR

## DR. JOHN A. HUNT

Printed in Canada

For information address:
Durban House Publishing Company, Inc.
7502 Greenville Avenue, Suite 500, Dallas, Texas 75231
214.890.4050

Library of Congress Cataloging-in-Publication Data
John A. Hunt, 1930

White Witchdoctor / by John A. Hunt

Library of Congress Catalog Card Number: 00-2002115650

p. cm.

ISBN 1-930754-33-7

First Edition

10 9 8 7 6 5 4 3 2 1

Visit our Web site at
http://www.durbanhouse.com

Book design by:
Strasbourg-MOOF, GmBH

THIS BOOK IS DEDICATED TO TWO IMPORTANT GROUPS OF PEOPLE:

TO MY WIFE, ANN,
& MY CHILDREN, DAVID, PETER AND DEBORAH,
WHO ALL LIVED THROUGH THE EVENTS DESCRIBED HERE
& GAVE ME THEIR LOVING SUPPORT AT ALL TIMES.

IT IS DEDICATED ALSO TO THE PEOPLE OF SOWETO,
BARAGWANATH HOSPITAL & SOUTH AFRICA. MAY THE
GRAND HOPES & UNTOLD PROMISE OF OUR WONDERFUL
COUNTRY BE FULFILLED.

# ACKNOWLEDGEMENTS

I am indebted to a large number of people who have helped in many ways during the genesis of this unusual book. The first is Dr. Patrick Grace, during whose "Life Writing" class at the Huntington Museum of Art the idea was born. He has been by turns a teacher, coach, editor and literary agent. Without him this book would never have seen the light of day. The members of the writing class have helped enormously by patiently listening to what I have read and offering me their gentle suggestions.

Several people have read chapters or the whole book and given valuable advice and encouragement. They include my wife Ann and adult children David, Peter and Debbie. Physicians giving their help include Doctors Bonnie Beaver, Arthur Mcunu, Venki Raman and Dev Rellan in Huntington. Doctors John Chapell, Saul Issroff, Michel Rivlin and Bernie Tabatznik have been of untold help because they have also been 'Bara Boys' and understand the scenario better than most.

My editor, Bob Middlemiss has helped form twenty chapters into a book. John Lewis, my publisher told me that Bob was the best in the world and I have found that to be true in fullest measure. Both these gentlemen have been easy to deal with and very receptive to new ideas, making the book production process very simple.

Ann Hunt deserves a second and rather special mention. She conceived both the name for the book and the idea for the cover design.

To everyone mentioned and others whom I may have forgotten, I am profoundly and eternally grateful.

# DISCLAIMER

WHITE WITCHDOCTOR is a true story based on my recollections of life in South Africa and my career at Baragwanath Hospital, Soweto, Johannesburg, the largest hospital in the southern hemisphere—and arguably in the world. For reader interest, the chapters are written and arranged by subject, not chronology. Some clinical events are unique, while others are examples of the many such cases we saw at the hospital.

To preserve privacy, all names have been changed with the exception of public figures, politicians, and others in the public domain. One favorite patient, Zephania Ndlazi, retains his name, as his story and pictures went round the world on television and other media. I chose pseudonyms randomly from my memory, genealogy, television and elsewhere, trying only to keep some flavor of South Africa at the time.

For political and historical knowledge, I have relied heavily on the works mentioned in the bibliography, including Internet Web sites and newspapers. My thanks go to all the authors for their insights, as my high school history courses consisted of relearning the Great Trek every year and memorizing a series of dates from Britain and Europe. The last two chapters reflect my total re-education during the writing of the book, causing me to develop a vastly modified and more objective viewpoint. I only hope that reading these chapters can give as much value to my readers as I received from writing them.

I apologize for any errors that may be found. While inadvertent, these are my own entirely, based on faulty memory or my interpretation of facts or opinions presented by others.

No patient's feet echo down the corridor towards my office, and no patient awaits me in the examination room next door. It is one of those infrequent quiet times, an oasis of calm, when I can sit behind my desk and watch the afternoon sun slant across the room, shimmering on my diplomas. My name shows up clearly in the light. But they do not refer to me as the White Witchdoctor, as my memorable patient, Zephania Ndlazi, would have it. Just my name: John Hunt.

I look across at the credenza, my safe harbor for things I will keep forever. As I sit there, memories flood back. They mingle with vignettes of America, my adopted country, and my home here in West Virginia. All are part of my life, which straddles South Africa and America, two countries, two ways of life, two calls for allegiance. I owe so much to my new country. It has been good to my family, giving us a home when we needed one, a way to earn a living and educate our children, and an avenue of service to others.

But South Africa is in my bones—deeply embedded, as only Africa can be. I look at family photos on top of the credenza. There too is a drawing done by my infant son many years ago. They are echoes of this other land.

Looking through my window, I see a little bit of America, so different and yet so similar. But always the pull of South Africa. I look again at the credenza, get up and walk over to it. I know what I'm seeking. I take out boxes of South African newspapers and photographs and the carousels of my prized medical slides. I hold a slide to the light, remembering, the small rectangle drawing me back into Baragwanath Hospital. The image is of Zephania Ndlazi's leg and his toothless smile. Bittersweet memories flood in.

Then I pick up a yellowing copy of the Sunday Times. Under banner headlines, it covers the Soweto riots, starting June 16, 1976. A Wednesday. That day Hector Peterson, at age thirteen, had been the first victim of police fire. The photo of his body held in the arms of an older boy is there. It went around the world, raising awareness of South Africa's problems. There is now a memorial to him and a public holiday—Youth Day—dedicated to all the children who rose up against the inferior 'Bantu' educational system and who died in trying to overthrow Apartheid.

Several pages of photographs reveal the horror of that day. Burning overturned buses. Schools in flames. Bodies lying in the streets. Rioters being chased by policemen. Soldiers in armored cars… It was the largest outbreak of violence South Africa had ever experienced. The police could not control it. Like a forest fire, it leaped from place to place for the rest of the year.

Far down the corridor I hear someone's tread, but it retreats. I am again, at least for the moment, alone with my thoughts. June 16, 1976 had been an historic and fateful day for South Africa. Baragwanath Hospital had played a pivotal role. But it was a day of decision, which prompted me to write to friendly Professors of Surgery in the United States, seeking their help. They were generously forthcoming.

Tough decisions would lie ahead for the family: whether to stay or to leave our beloved country, family, friends, neighbors, security, lifestyle, sunshine, home and schools. Even Rags, our Jack Russell terrier, had his say. The children would not go without him.

Almost exactly two years later, I stepped into my new job as Chief of Surgery at a V.A. Medical Center and to a new life in America.

That night in bed as my wife, Ann, slept, I found myself thinking about Hector Peterson and Zephania Ndlazi. Hector, I had not known, but I cared for many of his fallen and injured friends on that fateful day. Zephania I knew well. He was black, tall and thin. Upbeat and cheerful, he was almost toothless, which did not help his broken English. He had been brought to the hospital with his severed leg under his arm and asked for it to be put back on. In performing the surgery we made history that day—he and I. That Zephania had dubbed me the White Witchdoctor was a well-appreciated accolade, but a small footnote to history.

Before I fell asleep, the idea of writing a book about it all firmed in my mind. This would bring cohesive resolution to my twin worlds. I'm sure both Zephania and Hector Peterson would approve.

"Urgent!…Urgent Direct!…Urgent!"

The shouted warning came repeatedly from a strapping Zulu porter with colorful, large, wooden disks in his earlobes.[1] They flapped up and down as he ran. He was rushing a patient on an ancient gurney at terrifying speed along a cement corridor and up the ramp toward the back door of the operating theater block.[2] The well-known cry[3] sent all in his path jumping aside to allow the trolley to pass. The gurney announced its own coming, an oval wheel rattling and complaining all the way. The half-naked patient reeked of Shebeen-brewed alcohol. He was covered in semi-dried blood and vomit. He lay ominously still.

A young female house surgeon[4] and a male medical student ran alongside the trolley, trying to reach the theaters before the patient.

It was Friday—payday—at 7 o'clock in the evening, and the serious drinking had begun in Soweto. The Shebeens[5] were full and the fighting had started. These Shebeens were privately owned drinking joints, often with hard-eyed black women, known as 'Shebeen Queens,' in charge of brewing and selling the Bantu beer[6,7] and other special drinks. They did the brewing in four-gallon or larger paraffin[8] cans. The other drinks were often adulterated with a wide variety of additives, including methylated spirits, silver polish, laboratory alcohol, and berries from weeds that grew in the veld[9]. These mixtures made up drinks with unusual names like 'Skokiaan,' 'Pineapple,' 'Dynamite,' and many more, equally exciting and exotic. The Shebeens vied with each other over the 'quality' of their hooch, and some actually provided credit. So, even at this time, when European style alcohol had been made legal for Africans, the Shebeens remained popular.

One Shebeen had been written up in the South African Medical Journal. Their brews were so potent that the patrons did not make trouble at the end of the evening. They were simply laid out under the bushes. If they were lucky they woke up the next day. It was said that the liquor was adulterated with calcium carbide, a chemical used to make acetylene gas for old-fashioned miner's headlamps or for welding. It was also used illegally to blast fish to the surface in rivers.

At Baragwanath, meanwhile, a long night lay ahead. Fortunately, Unit Five had managed to sneak away and have some supper before it became too busy—not too common on a Friday 'intake'[10] night.

The trolley crashed through the double doors of the theater block.

"Stab Heart!—He was alive in Casualty," the houseman and the student shouted, as they rushed down the main corridor.

The sudden uproar galvanized the nursing staff. They rushed out into the hallway. Maria, a plump scrub nurse with a cheerful round face, grabbed a shiny, two-foot round drum of sterile instruments and started running towards one of the thirteen operating rooms. Her burden bounced up and down on her belly.

"Not that way!" she called. "Theater three."

The porter stopped in his tracks and tried to turn the corner. The dead weight of the patient slid him obliquely off the stretcher until feet and buttocks hit the ground. House surgeon and student caught the dead man in mid-slide and pulled him back onto the trolley.

As head of surgical Unit Five, I was on duty with the Unit. Casualty had just called to tell me about the case. Still dressed in white coat and street clothes, I rushed round the corner to see what was going on.

"Mr. Hunt,[11] he's a precordial stab.[12] I know he looks dead right now, but we saw him alive," the young house surgeon panted.

"Thanks a lot, Adele! You always bring trouble," I teased her.

"Don't shoot the messenger," she retorted.

I shouted: "Call the anesthetist!"[13]

A probationer nurse[14] dashed out of the operating room to look for him in the upstairs lounge. Another nurse called from the phone outside the theater.

I pushed the operating table out of the way and positioned the patient on the gurney in the center of the theater, under the big round operating light. I felt for the carotid pulse[15] in the neck and found nothing. The patient was not breathing, so he was clinically dead. I flashed my penlight into the man's eyes and saw the pupils were large, but not yet wide open and fixed, so death was still occurring.[16] I knew my team had seen him alive. I was determined to save this life.

"O.K., let's go!" I called out.

A staff nurse grabbed a bottle of Betadine[17] disinfecting solution from a shelf and emptied its brown contents liberally over the patient's chest and abdomen, letting it overflow on all sides. She hastily scrubbed the chest with a brush and sponge. Maria opened the drum and covered a small shiny table with a green towel. Before she could set out any instruments I called out: "Knife please, Sister."

I took the scalpel with my bare hands, as there was no time to change clothes, scrub up or put on gloves. The delay would have destroyed any chance of saving the patient. He would be one more added to Soweto's horrendous murder toll. The crime would also change from common assault to murder—a sad end to a simple drunken brawl.

As word of the case spread through the building, the room started filling with nurses and medical staff. Many had been through this before. Everyone got busy with an appropriate job. The junior doctors and the student each grabbed an arm or a leg. They started cutting down to find collapsed major veins in order to start IV lines. They placed large bore needles into the veins and set up bicarbonate or saline drips. A student nurse went to the recovery room to fetch any O-Negative[18] blood left over in the 'fridge' from the last big case. Mercifully, she found two bottles.

I counted the ribs by eye. We needed no anesthesia since the patient was already dead. I slashed across the left chest, an inch below the nipple. There was no bleeding from skin or muscles, confirming arrest of the heart. As the knife entered the chest cavity, dark blood and clot welled out. I suctioned it clear, using the straight-through[19] suction tube that I had made for such cases. I pushed my fingers into the wound and forced the ribs apart, but only achieved two or three inches before grimacing in pain.

"Finochietto retractor," I called.

Sister Maria handed me a big U-shaped instrument with two jaws like deformed flat hands. I placed this self-retaining retractor[20] into the wound. As I cranked the handle, the jaws forced the ribs widely apart, finally causing an audible 'craack.' The student winced and caught his breath.

"Don't worry, Geoff," I said. "We need proper access to work. We'll close with very strong sutures round the ribs to splint the breaks and control his pain. We'll also inject Xylocaine[21] in the wound edges later."

Peter Jones, the surgical registrar,[22] made sure the intravenous lines were all running. He checked the fluids being given and asked Adele to add more sodium bicarbonate. He asked a staff nurse to place a blood pump and a fluid warmer on the intravenous line for the cold blood. He then slipped on some gloves and joined me in the operation.

With the chest now wide open, we could see clearly. The heart was quite still, and the pericardial sac[23] around it bulged with the contained blood, because the stab wound in the sac was blocked by clot. The heart could not contract due to the tension of the blood collected around it in the closed pericardium. So the patient had no blood pressure and hence no circulation. This starved both his brain and his heart of blood and oxygen, and made him technically dead. I carefully made a small nick in the tense pericardium with the tip of a scalpel and then inserted the blade of a pair of curved scissors through the hole and slit the thin tissue up and down for over six inches.

"Peter, do you see the phrenic nerve[24] there, running along the sac?" I asked. "You must avoid cutting it or you paralyze the diaphragm."

As I cut, blood and clot poured out of the slit under pressure. Peter suctioned the blood out, helping us to see the heart lying motionless inside the sac. I took the soft organ between my hands and started to compress it firmly and rhythmically, once per second, while we looked for the hole made by the attacker's knife.

The heart slowly started to respond to the massage and transfusion with weak contractions. After I had worked with the heart for half a minute or so, blood started oozing out of a hole in the muscle. We could see the stab wound in the front of the left ventricle, near a big coronary artery. Soon, the contractions became stronger and more rhythmical. Blood squirted with each beat, in a strong, pulsating, dark red jet, hitting my clean white coat and running down in broad red streaks.

"Put your finger over the hole," I told the registrar.

The spurting stopped, but there was still some strong oozing around Peter's finger, as the heart moved with every beat.

"Have you noticed the sickly sweet smell of the blood?" I asked. "I never know if that's what the stuff really smells like, or if it's the alcohol that does it.

"Suture, Sister Maria," I said.

The scrubnurse handed me a loaded needle-holder. I substituted my left forefinger for Peter's and carefully placed the curved needle into the muscle beneath my finger and right through both sides of the wound. I included a good half circle of tissue, taking great care to avoid blocking the coronary vessel. This would have stopped the heart. I caught the needle-tip on the other side of the cut with the needle-holder and pulled some of the thread through. Jones again covered the hole while I made a surgeon's knot[25] and gently cinched it down on the heart beating under his finger.

"Peter, you have to be careful with these stitches," I said. "The knot should be firm, but not so tight that it cuts through the heart muscle—like a wire through cheese."

I then placed and tied a second suture. The bleeding stopped completely.

"Cut, about three millimeters long," I said.

Peter Jones snipped both stitches with long scissors. The heart was settling down into a rapid, even beat, with no more bleeding. We suctioned the chest cavity clear and I handed the needle driver to Peter, who placed a stitch in the long incision in the pericardium. As he was about to place another suture, I cautioned him:

"You mustn't close it too tight in case there's more bleeding. That could cause another cardiac tamponade.[26] So one stitch is enough, perhaps two. You just want to prevent the heart dislocating out of the sac, while leaving enough space for blood to drain out. Do you think you could do a stab heart now, Peter? What do you think, Sister Maria?"

"I think so," she said. "We'll see. There'll be plenty more while he's here."

While we were operating, probably two or three minutes, Fritz Brenner the anesthetist had arrived and intubated[27] the dead man.

He had not needed anesthetic or relaxant drugs. The airway was now secure, and Brenner was over-ventilating the man with 100% oxygen to make up for his 'oxygen debt.'[28] This was helping his revitalization. The intravenous lines supplied life-giving bicarbonate in saline solution to correct the severe acidosis that was always present in these cases. The patient was getting blood under pressure to replace some of his loss, restore the blood volume, and provide oxygen-carrying capacity. The EKG monitor was now connected and showed a fast but regular rhythm.

All in all, things were going nicely and the patient was alive again. Everyone began to relax. The nurses chattered softly. I often heard the exclamations *Hau!*[29] and *Modimo!*[30] in their excited talking.

Suddenly, the patient began wildly thrashing around on the gurney. Before anyone could stop him, he put his left hand into his chest wound. His right hand reached up and grabbed the endotracheal tube, which was connected to his oxygen supply. He ripped it out of his throat, complete with its inflated balloon, and then lay still for a moment. Nurses grabbed his hands and tied them down to the sides of the gurney.

"I am complaining!" the patient yelled.

"What are you complaining about?" Fritz Brenner asked.

"I am complaining. I want to piss!" cried the man.

"You're just damned lucky you can complain, or piss for that matter," muttered Fritz.

A nurse placed a stainless steel urine bottle under the drapes. A loud tinkling followed, accompanied by a sigh of relief.

"Hang on, John," Fritz Brenner said. "Stop operating for a bit and I'll get him controlled in a few secs."

Brenner now made sure the man's airway was adequate without his tube, and set up oxygen through a facemask. He rapidly injected an anesthetic agent and a muscle relaxant[31] into a vein. The patient stopped breathing, had a few muscle spasms, and then relaxed completely. Brenner quickly placed a laryngoscope through the patient's mouth, lifted his tongue, and slid a new endotracheal tube into his throat. He then re-connected the positive pressure ventilation.[32] But this time he added anesthesia to the oxygen supply.

"It's OK now, you guys," Brenner said. "The emergency's over. I've got him intubated, anesthetized and paralyzed. He shouldn't give you any more trouble. But at least we know he's alive and kicking!"

"Thanks a lot, Fritz," I said. "We'll get done as fast as we can." We started to close the wound, pausing to inject Xylocaine from large syringes into the nerves and tissues near the broken ribs. The wound edges were starting to bleed heavily, since the patient's blood pressure and circulation had been restored. Peter had to tie off the main intercostal[33] artery and vein and was able to use the electrocautery machine[34] to coagulate the remaining bleeders. Blue smoke and the smell of frying meat filled the air—just like a steakhouse, I always thought.

"Intercostal drain," Peter Jones asked.

The scrubnurse handed him a thick plastic tube, about two feet long, with two big side-holes. Jones perforated the lower chest wall with a scalpel blade and pulled the tube through this opening, leaving the drainage holes inside the chest. He stitched the tube in place and connected it to an 'underwater seal'[35] drainage bottle on the floor. We carefully washed out the chest cavity and the wound edges with an antibiotic solution.

"Pericostal suture,[36] number 2 Vicryl. Remember Sister, those really thick ones," Peter said.

Sister Maria handed him a very large curved needle, armed with a blue suture, almost as thick as parcel string.

"That rope should really hold his ribs together," Peter said to the students.

I was now called away to Casualty. Before leaving the operating room I scrubbed the dried blood from my hands and said: "Make sure he gets plenty of antibiotics. Maybe we should take some too, Peter! His chest was filthy and so was his hand. Admittedly, we did splash him with Betadine. I'm amazed how little infection you see with these emergency cases. But what we won't know until much later is whether the knife made an internal hole in the heart, or even lacerated a valve. He should have proper follow-up, though we probably won't see him again until he gets his next stab wound. Let's hope Unit Three's on intake that day."

While the registrar finished up, I found a new white coat and started walking up to Casualty. As I went, I thought of the contrast between this work and what I had done during my registrar training in Kent, England, where our first son was born. I had also been busy there. After five on every second day I was on duty for three hospitals. I was up all night many times. But I was at least taking care of patients with what I thought were 'legitimate' diseases, such as acute appendicitis, strangulated hernia, or bleeding peptic ulcer. I didn't see much trauma, certainly not of this gravity or in these numbers. But I did do a lot of surgery and gained excellent experience. One year at Christmas the operating theater nurses gave me a record of 'Mack the Knife.' The familiar tune now drummed in my head.

I remembered one morning at dawn, going home to the farmhouse where we lived. I passed a bus shelter and saw a blackbird picking strips of moss off the shingled roof, looking underneath for breakfast. The discarded moss formed a little pile on the ground in front of the shelter. I had reached home, kissed my wife and son, and fallen into bed for a few hours, before getting up to return to work. As I drove back at about nine o'clock, the bird was still digging away. The pile of moss was much bigger.

At about that time the National Health Service performed a countrywide salary review. They at long last recognized that the junior medical staff in the hospitals did most of the work, but did not get a living wage. The senior staff often did not even get out of bed at night. In the big adjustment that followed, Registrars' salaries more than doubled, and I got some good back pay. Our little family was solvent for the first time in our young lives.

After my return to South Africa and Baragwanath, I had been totally amazed by the vast difference in disease and work patterns and the enormous volume of trauma. To my great dismay, I was confronted with a stab in the heart on my first intake at Bara. A part-time senior surgeon, whom I admired, came to watch the proceedings in the operating room. Sensing this rookie surgeon's hesitation, he spoke, kindly but firmly:

"What are you waiting for, man? Get on with it."

I then opened the chest and did the case by myself, with a successful result. I was very grateful for the moral support of a respected senior colleague.

I remembered that year at Christmas, writing to my old bosses in Kent about my first year back at Bara. They wrote back in total disbelief. I frankly could not blame them. What I had just now seen and done was beyond the bounds of ordinary human imagination. Even for surgeons.

[1] <u>Ear decorations</u>: Many African men, particularly Zulus, carried enormous wooden discs in their earlobes, which had been slowly stretched for the purpose, to a diameter of up to four inches. The discs were very decorative and beautiful, with intricate geometric patterns in bright contrasting colors.

[2] <u>Operating Theater</u>: Operating Room. British usage.

[3] <u>Urgent Direct</u>: A desperately ill patient could be admitted anywhere in the hospital in record time, with the stamp "Urgent Direct!" on his blank set of records and a red sticker on his forehead. The porters knew what this meant and ran down the corridors for dear life, yelling loudly all the way.

[4] <u>Houseman or House Surgeon</u>: A compulsory pre-registration post, equivalent to the American 'Intern.'

[5] <u>Shebeens</u>: An Irish word, of Gaelic origin, meaning an unlicensed or illegal drinking establishment. It was used in Soweto in exactly the same context.

[6] <u>Bantu</u>: The correct and politically correct generic name for indigenous black Africans in South Africa. It referred also to their languages, e.g. "The Bantu-speaking people of South Africa." It replaced the somewhat pejorative word "Kaffir," long used for blacks in South Africa.

[7] <u>Bantu beer</u>: Traditional beer, brewed usually from millet or "Kaffircorn," but almost any substrate would do, even fermented bread. The beer is thick, with unfiltered residue and a slightly sickly sweet odor. South African Breweries, said to be the second largest brewery in the world, also brewed it commercially. It is often sold in plastic or cardboard cartons, like milk.

[8] <u>Paraffin</u>: Kerosene. Much used as a cooking and heating fuel in South Africa, particularly in poorer areas.

[9] <u>Veld</u>: Afrikaans word. The generally used term for South African grasslands or countryside.

[10] <u>Intake day</u>: The 24-hour day of duty for a medical unit of any kind in the hospital. There were five surgical units, each on intake in rotation every fifth day, e.g. Friday, Wednesday, Monday, and Saturday, ad infinitum.

[11] <u>Mister</u>: In British tradition, a surgeon is called Mister. It stems from the days of 'Barber-Surgeons.'

[12] <u>Precordial stab</u>: A chest stab wound in the area in front of the heart. Must always be taken seriously.

[13] <u>Anesthetist</u>: A doctor, the same as an American Anesthesiologist. In South Africa, Nurse Anesthetists were unknown. Doctors did all the work, as in Great Britain.

[14] <u>Probationer Nurse</u>: A student nurse. The numbers of stripes on belts or caps indicated levels of training. The course was three years, equivalent to the American R.N. Training equal to that of white nurses in S.A.

[15] <u>Carotid pulse</u>: The carotid artery in the neck is easy to feel from the front. It carries most of the blood to the brain. Absence of this pulse is serious, signifying death in most cases.

16 <u>Pupils and death</u>: The size of the pupils is invariably used to confirm death in clinical medicine. Both pupils being wide open and not contracting when a light is shone indicates death, or at least brain death.

17 <u>Betadine</u>: A complex modern formulation of iodine, used for rapid sterilization of the skin in surgery.

18 <u>O-Negative</u>: Group O, Rh-negative blood is relatively safe to use in anybody in a grave emergency, without a direct cross-match being done. Thus it is called 'universal donor' blood. The chances of an incompatibility reaction should be less than the chances of dying without the transfusion.

19 <u>Straight through suction tube</u>: Simply a thin-walled straight metal tube, with a small hole near the tip, to prevent blockage. The tube was as thick as the inside of the flexible connecting tube, so the maximum amount of blood could be removed in seconds.

20 <u>Self-retaining retractor</u>: These instruments come in a wide variety of sizes and shapes, largely U-shaped. They are placed in wounds and cranked open. The jaws keep the incision open without surgical effort, so freeing up surgeons' or assistants' hands.

21 <u>Xylocaine</u>: Proprietary name for Lidocaine, a modern local anesthetic, now almost universally used.

22 <u>Surgical Registrar</u>: Trainee surgeon, equivalent to the American 'Resident.'

23 <u>Pericardial sac</u>: This is a membranous sac around the heart, fitting it quite closely. It is very thin and shiny on the inside. A tiny amount of fluid helps lubricate the heart as it beats within this cover. The two phrenic nerves run down, one on each side of this sac.

24 <u>Phrenic nerves</u>: These two nerves run down from the neck to the diaphragm, causing it to go up and down rhythmically, so producing breathing. Cutting the nerves paralyzes the diaphragm.

25 <u>A surgeon's knot</u>: Is like a regular Boy Scout 'reef knot' but with a second turn on the first layer. This helps hold it without slipping, while the second layer is added. Surgeons often add one or two more layers to the knot to make it even more secure.

26 <u>Cardiac tamponade</u>: Compression of the heart by fluid contained in the pericardial sac. The heart is unable to pump, so the patient may die, as in this case. Cutting open the sac and letting out the blood relieved the tamponade. Cardiac massage was required to start the heart contracting again.

27 <u>Intubated</u>: Placed a breathing tube through the mouth, between his vocal cords and into his trachea. Used to provide an airway and connect to a mechanical ventilator or a bag for manual over-breathing.

28 <u>Oxygen debt</u>: The patient had not been breathing for a prolonged period and his tissues had built up a great need for oxygen—oxygen debt. This takes time to return to normal and is assisted by the temporary use of 100% oxygen and manual over-breathing.

29 Hau: Pronounced 'how,' essentially the same as 'wow.' An exclamation used in several Bantu languages.

30 Modimo: 'God.' Often used as an exclamation. The mo sound is pronounced as in more and the i like an e.

31 Muscle relaxant: A series of drugs used in anesthesia to control breathing and muscle tension. In this case a fast-acting agent was used, to allow rapid re-intubation and re-connection of the positive pressure breathing.

32 Positive pressure ventilation: When the chest is open the lung collapses, making oxygenation difficult. It can only be tolerated for a few minutes. Positive pressure breathing must be restored quite soon.

33 Intercostal: Between the ribs.

34 Electrocautery: An electronic machine that supplies a modified electric current. This allows the surgeon to use a hand-held pencil-type applicator to either cut or coagulate tissues and stop any bleeding.

35 Underwater seal: A simple system to prevent air from re-entering the pleural space. A glass tube runs through the stopper of a bottle and has its tip under water. The chest drainage tube connects to it. Blood and air can get out, but the water prevents air getting back up the tube and into the chest.

36 Pericostal suture: A suture placed around adjacent ribs, on either side of the wound, to hold the ribs firmly together.

When I reached Casualty, there was the usual chaos to be expected at 8 o'clock on a Friday night. The 'Pit' was overflowing with patients. The junior surgical staff had given this derisive name to an open room in Casualty where the intake surgeons worked. The other members of Unit Five, two housemen and some students, were already busy there, helped by two African nurses and an interpreter.

About 30 feet away, across an open waiting area, was the 'Resuscitation Room'.[1] This was also the surgeons' responsibility. The room was constantly staffed by experienced operating room nurses. It had recently been built to a design I had made, taking in a wide verandah and part of a courtyard. It was a large hall with ten separate cubicles. These could be curtained off for privacy and to accommodate minor procedures, such as catheterization or the placing of chest tubes.

In one corner, across from the entrance, there was an operating room light in the ceiling. There were drums[2] of sterile instruments and packs of towels and other supplies lining the shelves. This area was often used as a full blown operating theater for grave emergencies, especially stab wounds in the heart or neck. I always enjoyed reading the Afrikaans version of the name—'Opwekkings Kamer,' painted on the door, along with the English one. It translated as 'Waking Up Room.' The Resuscitation Room saved many lives. It also saved operating theater time and prevented congestion and overload

The Casualty Officers (doctors) sat in a large open space nearer the entrance of the hospital. African nurses and interpreters also formed a vital part of their team. There were scores of people waiting to be seen. They sat in rows on benches, lay groaning on stretchers, or sat patiently, slumped over in wheelchairs. Anyone in obvious trouble when they entered the front door bypassed Casualty and went straight to the surgeons.

This was not the time for niceties. I knew that the doctors were seeing cases at the rate of one a minute. I once timed myself when I worked there. There was only enough time to slap a stethoscope on the chest and listen for air entry, to see if limbs moved or if the patient was conscious, or breathing, or had a pulse. Notes on the 'Casualty cards'[3] were brief:

'Stab L. chest, 3rd space, half inch. BS present. Pulse OK.'

'Rx. Suture, 2 cc Cryst. X-ray.' Doctor's signature or initials.

The nurses then wheeled the patient to the large room next door, where four orderlies worked at separate stations, cleaning and suturing wounds and giving penicillin injections. The next stop was X-ray, in another building just outside the back door of Casualty. If the orderlies were too busy, the patients went straight to X-ray and returned later for stitching.

When the sequence was complete, they would rejoin a queue of patients on stretchers waiting to see the doctors again. If the X-ray was normal, the doctor wrote: 'X-ray OK. Sutures 1 week,' and signed off. The patient was ready to go home. Patients with abnormal X-rays or who were not fit to leave would usually be sent to the 'Pit' or to Resuscitation.

Orderlies were very smart. They had little formal schooling, but years of practical experience in this room. They attended to the wounds and well-positioned fractures and gave the antibiotic injections required for the many injuries and other conditions needing penicillin. There was just too much work for a doctor to cut loose and give local anesthetic into each laceration. It had long ago been decided that the pain from a couple of stitches would be the same as that from a few injections. So the orderlies cleaned the cuts with antiseptic and sutured them if they had clean edges, or called a doctor for anything unusual.

I was always amazed at how well the orderlies handled the injuries and the patients. If something was wrong, such as bone edges sticking through the skin near a fracture or under a scalp laceration, or grass or gravel in the wound, they knew the treatment changed. They then consulted a Casualty doctor, who might send the case to the surgeons—which was what the orderly preferred, but was too polite to say. The results from their suturing were excellent, both in appearance and the absence of infection. I could vouch for that, since I saw many of these patients in my surgical follow-up clinic.

The orderlies also applied the plaster casts for all good-position fractures, again using their intuition to call a doctor for anything suspicious. One or more members of their team attended all orthopedic Fracture Clinics, to do the cast changes. These clinics ran very smoothly, despite the huge numbers. There were few better cast-makers than these men.

Another major class of cases being seen in Casualty that night was 'blunt' head injuries. These were usually inflicted by crude weapons, such as sticks, stones, clubs, iron bars, or golf clubs. A favorite was the 'knobkierie,'[4]—a cross between a club and a walking stick. There was usually a wound involved, so the routine was much the same as for stab wounds. The interpreter took the story while the doctor did a quick neurological exam—move limbs, count fingers, examine pupils with a penlight and check sensation and reflexes. If there was no obvious neurological deficit, the patient went for suture, Crysticillin and X-ray, before returning to the doctor. Doubtful cases were sent on to the surgeons.

Since the doctors on duty in Casualty that night were success-fully handling all the simple cases and the triage, Unit Five could concentrate on the problems. When I reached the 'Pit,' the housemen immediately showed me a few cases.

"Mr. Hunt, this guy has been stabbed in the neck, well clear of the big vessels," Naomi Sher, a young pregnant doctor, said. "But I'm worried that they got his spinal cord."

I saw a half-inch wound on the back of the patient's neck, above the shoulders.

"What happened to you?" I asked.

"My friend stick me with a long knife, because I owe him fifty cents."

"With friends like that, who needs enemies?" I asked, for about the hundredth time in my career.

"Can you move your foot?" I asked.

"Aiko." (No).

The patient's feet lay still, like logs. His arms also didn't move, except for a twitch in the thumb and index finger on the right. When I raised his left arm, it fell back onto the mattress with a dull thud. When I gently used a straight pin to test sensation, there was no response below the shoulders. But his neck had good feeling and strong muscles.

"One more for the paraplegic ward,"[5] I told Naomi. "Teach the student to pass a Foley catheter, unless he knows," and the student nodded vigorously. "Then write proper orders for an air mattress and frequent turning—they develop bedsores[6] in no time, and they get depressed when they realize the truth. That makes them slow to learn the correct turning routine, so the skin soon breaks down and they are in big trouble."

"Boss Hunt, you remember me—Caiphus—I use to work in the garden," said the patient.

"Yes, Caiphus, I remember you now. It must have been four or five years ago. I'm very sorry you have this trouble. We will look after you."

I patted his head gently and then turned away, frustrated and angry with his assailant and this violent society. The only saving grace for Caiphus that night was that he did not yet know what faced him, nor yet how long and hard was the road that lay ahead.

The next man had a large ulcer on his shin. It was crusted and oozing yellow serum. Dirty rags hung off the leg. Both ankles were swollen over the tops of his old boots. Several weeks before he had received an injury to the leg, which did not heal. His home conditions were appalling; in fact, like so many patients, he was homeless. His clothes were old, ill fitting, dirty and smelly. His skin was dry, like fine emery paper, and nearly black, unlike brown, glossy, healthy African skin. He had either pure malnutrition, or alcoholism leading to it, since alcoholics usually do not have enough money for both food and drink.

"We have a problem," I said. "Under better circumstances, he would go home and raise the foot of the bed on high blocks and put on Eusol[7] dressings twice a day. That's not going to happen here, so we must admit him for the same treatment. Make sure to feed him up with plenty of protein and Vitamins B and C. Work him up properly and do his RPR test[8] to rule out syphilis. Consult the medical folks tomorrow, to help us rule out a cardiac or renal cause for his edema. The social workers might also be able to find him a home, or at least get him some assistance."

The place was now really filling up, with patients lying on trolleys in long lines everywhere. There must have been over a hundred patients in Casualty, together with many hangers-on and family members. There were a few police uniforms to be seen, with a couple of the patients under guard. Waiting was the name of the game—for the Casualty doctors, both coming and going, for the orderlies, for X-ray and for the 'Pit.' There were rows of patients still sitting on benches, patiently waiting their turn. The milling mass of humanity and the constant groaning and drunken yelling made this look and sound like a medieval madhouse.

The smells were rank and indescribable. Blood, urine, stool, and vomited home-brewed beer were everywhere. The worn-out linoleum or vinyl floor was slippery and treacherous. A cleaner was working slowly and methodically, using a mop and pail to try and get rid of some of the mess. I thought his job must be never-ending, like painting the bridges over the San Francisco Bay or the Firth of Forth in Scotland.

Suddenly, there was a commotion. The cleaner rose from the floor with his head dripping in vomit. He picked up his pail of slops and upended it on the head of a patient on a stretcher, who had just leaned over and thrown up on him. No one blamed the cleaner.

Often, at busy times like this, I would go to help the Casualty officers. But tonight I was occupied enough where I was. A patient on a stretcher was suddenly peeled off from Casualty and rushed across to the 'Resuscitation room.' I saw the porter rushing the trolley into the room, so I ran across from the 'Pit' to assess the problem.

The patient had a two-inch wound in the left side of his head. It was bleeding profusely, but that was not the main concern. His left pupil was dilated to twice the size of its fellow. His right leg did not move, but the knee reflex was increased. His right arm moved only slightly, and his grip was weak. He could barely talk. I thought his level of consciousness was reduced, even allowing for his obvious alcohol intake.

"Get the Neuro registrar," I said. "This man needs his head opened right now. We must get an X-ray of his skull stat. Sister, call theatre and tell them to prepare for an emergency craniotomy.[9] They may have to 'crash'[10] one of the other operating schedules if there aren't enough anesthetists. I think you'd also better call X-ray—the registrar might want to do an angiogram[11] on the way to surgery.

"Staff Nurse, put a big sterile pad and bandage over the wound for now.

"There are a couple of possibilities," I said, turning to the student. "The first is an extradural hematoma. Do you know what that is?"

"Blood and clot outside the membranes around the brain," he answered.

"Correct," I said. "It's often caused by a fracture across the middle meningeal artery, which runs through the bone, about where that wound is. The fracture tears it open, causing a rapid bleed and serious compression of the brain. The second possibility is a depressed fracture of the skull, like pushing in the side of a ping-pong ball, or cracking a hard-boiled egg. It's an open wound, so this would be a *compound* depressed fracture,[12] causing concern about infection, or a spicule of bone penetrating the brain and leading to epilepsy later. His reduced level of consciousness is due to concussion, together with pressure, from whatever cause. The motor cortex[13] controlling his arm and leg is suffering, while his pupil change is due to pressure on the third cranial nerve[14] in the skull."

"What's going to happen to him?" the student asked.

"At this point he can probably be saved, but if the bleeding and increased pressure go on much longer, he may not make it. If the pressure spreads to the other side, both pupils will become fixed and dilated[15] and he'll probably die, or become a vegetable.

"You might want to go and watch the angiogram and the surgery, if we're not too busy," I said. "Elevating a depressed fracture is a kind of neat operation. If he has an extradural hematoma from the middle meningeal artery, the bleeding could be quite dramatic until they get it controlled."

"I'd love to do that, Mr. Hunt. I love neurology," the student said.

"I did too, as a student," I said. "I had to operate on one of these cases in an emergency during my early training. There was no neurosurgeon for 10 miles, across south London. A young boy had fallen out of an apple tree, with an injury like this one. He was going downhill rapidly. I did surgery to save his life, armed only with 'book knowledge.'

"Before the surgery, I looked at one of my British textbooks. It carried a historical account of plugging the hole in the bone with a sterile piece of matchstick. When I got inside the skull, the middle meningeal artery was bleeding horrendously. I tried using the electro-cautery to stop the hemorrhage and bone wax to try and plug the hole, but the artery went right on bleeding. I actually had to get the nurses to sterilize a wooden matchstick. It was a perfect fit and closed the hole perfectly, just as the book said.

"It was a great case, with a full and satisfying recovery, which really stroked my ego. It still didn't convert me to doing neurosurgery as a career!"

The night went on much as it had begun. Cases started to taper off at about 5 o'clock. The head injury was done, with a good result. It proved to be an extradural hemorrhage. The student loved assisting at the surgery. The other students got to place intravenous lines and draw blood. They also learned to put in chest drainage tubes and pass urinary catheters, proving to be of immense help to the overburdened house surgeons.

I spent most of my time in Casualty and the 'Pit,' where I could do 'the greatest good for the greatest number.' I was confident that Peter Jones, who had been with me for three months already, could handle most things in the theaters by now. I only had to scrub three more times, to cope with the heavy load and do extra cases. The operations included two penetrating stabs in the belly and one in the neck, where I had to assist Jones. These are among the most difficult and demanding surgical cases.

The 'septic theatre' ran till after midnight. One house surgeon worked there the whole time, opening abscess after stinking abscess. The mess and smell made this the worst job. On intake day the housemen always spun a coin or drew straws to see who would do it.

There had been a bad car accident in Soweto and the orthopedic surgeons used one of the theaters for most of the night. I had to help them in one case to repair the femoral artery in a patient with a fracture of the thighbone. Peter Jones had to help with a blunt abdominal injury. The neurosurgical registrar looked in on another case but did no surgery.

Periodically, when things quieted a bit, I would leave Casualty and take a tour through the operating theater block and the 40 bedded surgical admissions ward, to make sure everything was under control. As I did so I remembered how bad intakes had been when I first arrived at Bara, and how successful this unit had been in making life more bearable for both staff and patients. A few years before, the space had been converted from a general surgical ward, which was the closest one to Casualty and the theater block. It allowed the new admissions an extra day in hospital. It also gave the surgeons an orderly place to work on our busy intake days. This without disturbing our existing patients.

Each general surgical unit had 40 male and 20 female beds. Before 'intake day,' which was every fifth day forever, the surgeons discharged as many patients as possible from our wards to make room for new ones. Due to the chronic overload, we seldom made more than half a dozen empty beds, which could not cope with the scores of cases often admitted, especially on Saturday nights. This caused terrible congestion and difficult working conditions in the wards. The existing patients got no rest and the new ones had nowhere to sleep.

So the five general surgeons, supported by the sub-specialists, evolved the concept of a surgical admission ward and the authorities developed it. This unit provided constant high intensity nursing. Daily at 8 a.m. or earlier, the surgical unit finishing its intake day did rounds on their new patients and cleared out the ward for the next day's unit. After 'post intake rounds,' the nurses moved everyone out, to go home or to their new wards. They then cleaned and made up the 40 beds for the new day. New admissions rarely came in before noon, by which time the ward was clean and ready to take them. Surgical cases then started to stream in. By 8 a.m. next day, there would be up to a hundred new patients admitted.

On Saturday morning we had breakfast together in the doctors' dining room before starting intake rounds at 8 a.m. when the next unit started their duty. Peter Jones was still operating on a stab abdomen. I started work with everyone who was available, evaluating each patient for admission, discharge, or triage to another unit, such as neurosurgery, ENT, orthopedics, or urology. Meanwhile, a house surgeon started work in Ward Five, trying to empty a few more beds for the influx of new patients.

This Friday's intake had been about average, with sixty-four patients in the admission ward. They filled the forty beds and others lay on thin mattresses on the floor, or on gurneys between the beds. The chaos, blood and groaning was only slightly less than we saw in the 'Pit' and Casualty the night before. But at least there was some order to it, and we knew we could manage the task ahead with plenty of nursing help.

Many men sat on a row of wooden chairs down the center of the ward, connected by latex tubes to chest drainage bottles, which stood on the floor nearby. Each bottle held its load of blood drained from the chest. Some of the underwater tubes emitted bubbles with each breath. Today there were eleven such patients, but I had often seen more than twenty. The men all waited patiently for us to decide their fate.

We examined the lungs of each man with a stab chest and inspected his bottle for bubbling or excess blood drainage. If everything was stable and the lung was expanded, we removed the tube, applied a dressing and gave the patient a return appointment for a follow-up X-ray on our next Outpatient day. If the tubes were still bubbling or there was too much blood draining, the patients were sent to Ward Five for observation and physical therapy.

We evaluated all the other patients, made decisions, wrote treatment plans, and sent them to their destinations. Those patients who were in stable condition and were sober enough to walk went home. We sent patients who needed sub-specialty care on to the appropriate wards or Outpatient services. Often, the orthopedic surgeons or others would also do rounds, hoping to discharge patients. The maxillo-facial surgeons also joined in, looking mostly for patients with fractured mandibles, of which there were usually many on a big weekend intake.

Sometimes during these post-intake rounds, we would find a seriously injured patient who had deteriorated since being seen in the 'Pit,' and then would have to go to the theater for surgery. Luckily, today that was not the case. We made twenty-five permanent admissions for general surgery, to go to the sixteen available beds in Ward Five. This would mean nine people sleeping on the floor, on mattresses or on gurneys, or chairs between the beds. Hopefully, in five days, most of them would have gone home, to make space yet again for Wednesday's 'intake.'

At two o'clock, after thirty hours straight without sleep, it was home and fall into bed for the members of Unit Five.

[1] <u>Resuscitation Room</u>: Called a 'Shock room' in some American hospitals. This was right in the Casualty area, across from the 'Pit,' where the surgical unit on duty spent the night. All shocked or severely ill surgical patients were taken there, often directly from the ambulance. The room was fully equipped and staffed for all emergencies, including major and minor surgery.

[2] <u>Drums</u>: Stainless steel or heavy chrome-plated drums, with perforated double walls, were used to pre-pack sets of surgical instruments and supplies. They were sterilized in an autoclave and then kept in storage for use as required.

[3] <u>Casualty card</u>: Every patient coming through Casualty received a cardboard envelope containing a ruled white card about 11 by 8 inches in size. At the top were the identification and demographic data, with space below for medical notes. New cards could be added. These envelopes and cards followed the patient to all Outpatient activities, forming a permanent record. They were re-issued by the clerks at every visit.

[4] <u>Knobkierie</u>: An Afrikaans word for a piece of tree branch with a bulbous end, used either as a club or a walking stick. Frequently shortened to 'Kierie.'

[5] <u>Paraplegic Ward</u>: An entire 40-beddded ward was devoted to paralyzed patients, mostly paraplegics, with paralysis of legs, not arms. Under the care of the neurosurgeon, they were long-stay patients. Their numbers grew so fast that there were also 5 'overflow' paraplegics in most other wards of the hospital.

[6] <u>Bedsores</u>: The same as 'pressure sores' or 'decubitus ulcers.' A paralyzed patient tends to lie without moving for prolonged periods. The skin that is compressed has no blood supply at the time and eventually breaks down, aided and abetted by urine or stool. The wounds become infected and go deeper and deeper, becoming difficult to treat without major plastic surgery.

[7] <u>Eusol</u>: 'Edinburgh University Solution,' sodium hypochlorite. A strong bleach and oxidizer. Is diluted for use in wound dressings. Large quantities used at Bara.

[8] <u>RPR test</u>: The lab test then current for diagnosing syphilis. The earlier test was the WR or Wasserman Reaction. Syphilis was a possible cause for the leg ulcer in this patient.

[9] <u>Craniotomy</u>: An operation to open the skull and attend to the brain or its coverings.

[10] <u>Crash</u>: To break into the middle of another operating schedule because of the urgency of the case.

[11] <u>Angiogram</u>: An X-Ray of the arteries to the head, in this patient. The operator, in this case, the registrar, sticks a needle into the carotid artery and injects radio-opaque, iodine-containing dye, to show the vessels and brain anatomy. He looks for 'shift' of midline structures to tell if there's a clot or bleed. This was years before CAT scans and MRIs made this work much more simple.

[12] <u>Compound depressed fracture</u>: Compound means that the bone fracture is complicated by a break in the skin over it, with potential for serious infection to enter the bone and the brain.

13 Motor cortex: An area on the surface of the brain that controls muscular movement, in this case of the arm and the leg. Either the blood clot or the bone is pressing on this area.

14 Third cranial nerve: There are twelve cranial nerves coming from inside the skull and controlling things like vision, smell and hearing. The third nerve controls some eye muscles and pupil size. Early pressure on the nerve causes the pupil to get bigger, until it is finally paralyzed wide open. It becomes 'fixed and dilated.'

15 Both pupils fixed and dilated: A sign of brain death. See # 14, above.

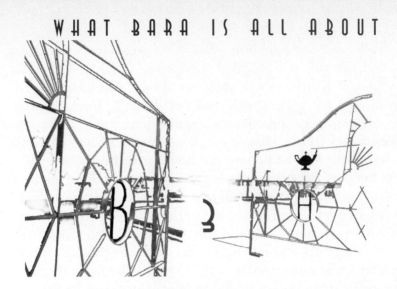

It was 8:30a.m. as I waited for Professor Davis at the desk of the Carlton Hotel in downtown Johannesburg. I had been given the pleasant chore of conducting an overseas visitor around Baragwanath hospital. The Professor, a noted London surgeon and a member of Council of the Royal College of Surgeons, was visiting South Africa to evaluate the teaching and experience being given to surgical trainees.

I really enjoyed showing off Baragwanath Hospital to visitors. I had done it often since I was a junior registrar and I was proud of the hospital. I was glad to undertake the task and felt I could do the subject justice. Since I was also a Fellow of both the Royal Colleges of Surgeons of England and Edinburgh, I should be well able to discuss surgical education with the visitor.

A tall, straight gray-haired man in a charcoal pinstripe suit emerged from the elevator with an expectant smile. I remembered him well and went forward to greet him.

"Good morning, sir, did you enjoy dinner last night?"

"Wonderful food and wine. Professor du Toit is an excellent host. I loved that KWV select wine. I know it's South African. Just hope I can get it in London."

"I'm sure you can. It's usually reserved for export only. I don't know where the Boss gets it, but I know he comes from the Cape, and still has connections there. I think your next visit is to Cape Town. You should ask Prof Louw while you're there."

I led the way to a black and white Ford Cortina GT and we got in.

"Sorry about the car," I said. "At least it's British in concept."

We headed carefully into a busy Commissioner Street, going west. The sidewalk was crowded with people of many skin colors, hurrying in both directions, on their way to work. The broad, asphalt-surfaced road was packed with traffic of all kinds, from the oldest broken-down wreck, sputtering and pouring blue smoke, to the most modern luxury vehicle, complete with uniformed African chauffeur. Bicycles, many with baskets on the front for deliveries, wove their way in between the other vehicles. Africans were calling loudly to each other across the street, adding to the din of the big city. Small black 'paper boys' darted in and out of the traffic, trying to sell their newspapers to passing drivers: "Daily Mail, Rand Daily Mail!" they cried, their thin legs and tattered clothes contrasting starkly with the tall glass-fronted skyscrapers and the elegant fashions on display in the expensive stores, aimed at affluent white people and tourists.

We turned left, toward Booysens, on our way to the hospital. I pointed out a huge old Ford sedan, packed with African men, far more people than it was intended to carry.

"Look at that car. There's another, and another. They're called 'Soweto taxis.' The owners love these big American monsters because they can pack in more paying passengers. Most of them don't have a taxi license, but do a thriving illicit trade. They're then called 'pirate taxis.' The bus company and the licensed taxi drivers get upset, because the 'pirates' stop illegally at the bus and taxi stops and grab large loads of their passengers."

"They're really full," Professor Davis said. "Their springs are flat from the load."

As we headed south, I pointed out the old steel tramlines, still visible in the road, flush with the tarmac surface, or in some places, running alongside the highway.

"When I came to Johannesburg as a student, we used rickety, double-decker trams, which ran on these tracks," I said. "During my time here, double-decker trolley-buses have replaced the tramcars on the same routes. They use parallel overhead wires for power. Now some diesel-powered buses serve the newer white suburbs.

"Baragwanath hospital and the Black area called Soweto, where we're going, are served by 'PUTCO' buses. These are long, green, single-deckers, run by a private company called Public Utilities Transport Co. You'll probably notice some of them on the road and we'll see their big terminus at Bara later."

"What's that big yellow pile on the right that looks like an Egyptian Pyramid?"

We were driving past a long, sloping, yellow hard sand wall, about 70 or 100 feet high, and probably 2,000 feet long. There were deep furrows gouging the surface from years of erosion by rainfall. The sides were otherwise bare, except where a few scattered clumps of coarse grass eked out a precarious existence.

"It's a 'mine dump', or a 'slimes dam'," I answered.

"Mine Dump?"

"Yes. The gold-bearing rock is brought to the surface, where it's milled or ground into fine sand. It then passes through a wet extraction process using cyanide. Afterwards, the slurry is piped into these rectangular enclosures, or 'simes dams.' It remains there for years, to dry out by evaporation, and to prevent the cyanide entering the environment. The piles grow ever higher, until the mine management decides they need a new dump."

I smiled across at Davis. "You may have heard the old saying: 'The Streets in Johannesburg are paved with gold.' Well, that may indeed be true these days."

"Why's that?"

"The old extraction process left behind a fair amount of gold. It's still present in the sand today. Some of the older dumps in the city area are being used as landfill for constructing roads or bridges. We may even now be traveling on a 'Golden Road.'"

I slowed for an erratic bicycle. "Until recently, there was not much other use for these heaps of sand. But research has led to success in planting grass and reclaiming the dumps for wildlife. I've seen pictures of animals thriving.

"Look over there on the left," I said. "That square derrick sits on a working goldmine, on the edge of the city—the oldest active mine in this area. It's called City Deep.

"In the same direction, far beyond the derrick, are three other dumps. A company called ERGO bought the properties from the mines. They have a great business plan. The old extraction process left behind not only gold, but also valuable metals, such as uranium, and several useful chemicals. Today, they are using more effective and cost-efficient methods to re-process the sand and extract the gold and byproducts. They can make a very tidy profit. The area is ripe for development, so once the three dumps are consolidated, they should get a good price for the cleared land."

ACROSS A PORTION OF SOUTHERN JOHANNESBURG
SHOWING A WHITE MINE DUMP.

DERRICK OF CITY DEEP MINE AGAINST BACKDROP
OF MODERN JOHANNESBURG BUILDINGS.

As we passed Robertsham on the left, I showed him the neat, bungalow-style, middle class homes in this fairly new white suburb. Each one was surrounded by a well-kept quarter acre garden, with smooth lawns, flowers and shrubbery and a garden fence. This would stand in sharp contrast to what we would soon see in Soweto, with its tiny four-room box-shaped houses sitting on pocket handkerchief-sized pieces of land.

We turned right at 'Uncle Charlie's,' a service station and road-house. It had been a landmark there since I was a boy.

"I see some planes taking off," Davis said.

"That's Baragwanath Airport, which is now a private airfield with hangars and facilities for small planes, pilot training, aerial photography, gliding schools, joyrides, parachuting—it's very popular."

"It sounds like a great facility," Davis said.

"Many people think the word Baragwanath is African in origin," I said. "But it is named after John Albert Baragwanath, a Cornish immigrant prospector in the early days. The name means 'bread and wheat' in the Cornish dialect. He was after gold discovered in the 1890s near Langlaagte, not far from here. He later ran the Wayside Inn, on the Potchefstroom Road, where the Hospital now stands."

"Everything seems to come back to gold," Professor Davis said.

I laughed. "The lure and mystique of Africa.

"During World War Two, this airport was a Royal Air Force training base. The Hospital was built rapidly during the war to handle casualties from the Middle and Far East commands of the British armed forces. Toward the end of the war it handled mostly Tuberculosis cases. It's common knowledge that the current chief of medicine at Baragwanath, an ex Royal Air Force officer, was a patient there himself during the war, suffering from both TB and diabetes. I think he was cured of the TB by Streptomycin.[1] When I was his houseman they were still his favorite diseases."

"So how did the new hospital come about?" Davis watched a private plane glide down towards the airport.

"In 1948, after the war, the South African government bought the hospital for a million pounds. Baragwanath Hospital was then taken over by the Transvaal Provincial Administration to serve the black people of Johannesburg Their numbers were swelling, particularly in the 'shanty towns'[2] southwest of the city. There were almost no health care facilities. These decrepit areas ballooned after the war due to a huge influx of black African people from the country, who came to seek their fortunes in 'eGoli,' or Johannesburg. The Johannesburg City Council started building houses rapidly to try and eliminate the terrible slum conditions. These new South Western Townships were being developed near the shantytowns and Orlando, the original township. The hospital's not too far away."

"It sounds as if someone was being far-sighted," Davis said.

"You're right," I replied. "In 1942, the Prime Minister, Jan Smuts, opened the hospital. He said it would be used after the war for the black people of Johannesburg."

We passed another fork in the road. "There's the road to Crown Mines, which is still producing gold," I said. "It was their dump we saw a few minutes ago. I think they offer underground tours, if you wish to go. That plantation of 'bluegum' or eucalyptus trees[3] covers their property. The trees are cut for 'mine props,' to hold up the underground workings. They are tough and do a good job. On my boyhood friend's family farm were some huge bluegums his father wanted to remove. I remember the hard time he had—he finally used dynamite to get the stems and roots out!"

I slowed the car and stopped at the side of the road. A metal hulk stood under a clump of wattle trees on the right.

"That car was abandoned a week ago. I've watched it shrink daily, piece-by-piece. First the wheels went, then the doors, seats, steering wheel, windshield, and the boot lid, the bonnet, and the engine. Even the transmission has gone. Not much left now."

"When do they do this?" Professor Davis asked.

"That puzzles me," I replied. "I never actually see anyone working on it. I suppose it's done at night. This doesn't only happen out here. Near my home, I came across a brand new hulk like this, only a block from our house. The paint was shiny and the bodywork perfect. It was stripped so far that I couldn't even determine the model of car, even though there was a notice in German in the engine compartment."

We set off again and I showed him the sign to Diepkloof Reformatory.

"That's where Allan Paton worked when he wrote 'Cry the Beloved Country.' It's a reform school for Black and, I think Colored, youths."

"What's the difference?" Professor Davis asked.

"Blacks, in our quaint South African terminology, are pure-line Bantu-speaking people, without admixture of white bloodlines. The

'Cape Coloreds' are regarded as a separate ethnic group and are comfortable being called Coloreds. They use the term themselves. They usually don't identify with the blacks, and *vice versa*, though the two groups have begun to join forces in the struggle against apartheid.

"They call themselves 'bruin mense,' Afrikaans for 'brown people', the illegitimate children of the Whites. Both statements are correct, though the wife of a white prime minister once denied this, saying she 'did not know where the colored people came from.'

"In brief, they are the blended offspring of the early white settlers in 1652 and later, the original people they met in the Cape, the San and Khoikhoi,[4] and the slaves. The indigenous people were then called Bushmen and Hottentots. They were short in stature and yellowish-brown in color. The slaves were Indians, Malays and blacks, coming from many places outside South Africa. Their descendants still have a strong Muslim influence. A separate group is called 'Cape Malays.'

"The Cape Colored people[5] are concentrated mainly in the western Cape, centered around Cape Town, where the first white settlement occurred. They are the second largest, perhaps the largest, racial group in the area. About equal to the Whites. There are fewer black African people there. Up-country, here in the Transvaal, the blacks far outnumber the whites. There are relatively few coloreds. That's the essential basis of the distinction, though the Colored race has, I'm sure, been augmented later by simple black-white miscegenation. In this mad but sunny land, these things still seem to matter."

"I loved Paton's book."

I nodded. "His son was in my class when I was teaching anatomy at Wits University, preparing to study surgery in Great Britain. I then attended a course for the Primary exam at the Royal College in Lincoln's Inn Fields and became an anatomy demonstrator there until I passed the 'Primary'. I'm sure you won't remember, but you examined me in the orals of the final F.R.C.S. exam in the Sixties."

"My goodness! I hope I was kind to you," Professor Davis smiled.

"You were indeed," I answered. I was beginning to like this quiet man. "But I must confess, that having received both Fellowships, I preferred the Edinburgh system, where we went on a 'ward visit.' The examiner conducted the candidate through his own ward, greeting the patients and presenting each one to the examinee for comment. It was just as if the consultant became the registrar, presenting cases on a morning ward round.

"One of my examiners in Edinburgh, when he heard I was going to sit for the London exam, said: 'Well, just know all about tuberculosis, syphilis and lumps and bumps. They have them by the thousands.'"

Professor Davis' laugh was open and generous. "Oh, to see ourselves as others see us."

"You certainly made me go through the hoop on a variety of 'lumps and bumps.'" I said. "But looking back, every exam I ever took was a valuable learning experience."

"I hear the kind of work you folks do at Baragwanath is unlike anything I know," Professor Davis said, changing the subject.

"That's right. As long as the Registrars get exposure on both sides of the fence, they'll become better surgeons," I answered. "There's nothing like Bara for sheer volume, hands-on surgical experience and decision-making under pressure. There's no time for 'ivory tower' contemplation on a Saturday night, when you're faced with two or three bled-out trauma victims together. You quickly get your priorities straight."

As we approached the Hospital, I pointed out Soweto across the road. There were many thousands of little gray houses with corrugated iron roofs and cinder block walls. They were all arranged in neat rows on tiny plots of land, marching up hill and down dale for 23 square miles. A smoky haze covered the area. Despite the undulating, treeless countryside, we could not see much beyond Diepkloof, which was the newest section of Soweto, just across the highway from Baragwanath Hospital.

I slowed the car and showed my guest the St. John's Eye Hospital beyond Bara and the Orlando Power Station, with Orlando Township nearby. As I drove, we had a better view of the vastness of the townships, extending into the distance, where they merged with similar monotonous African housing areas for the neighboring town of Roodepoort. I then turned the car and started back towards the Hospital.

"I have to say the houses look depressing," Davis said.

I nodded. "You get used to it. When I was in medical school, many of us did an obstetric rotation out there. We lived in a round house near the clinic in Orlando. On the inside wall were many graffiti written by medical students over the years. Lots of styles, lots of humor, lots of anger. We all spent many boring hours waiting for deliveries and reading these works of literary genius. And adding some of our own. A very bright student, who had a B.Sc. degree before he started to study medicine, wrote one of the best, most intellectual and funny poems. It occupied about a square yard of wall space. After graduation, he went straight to Britain, to join Watson and Crick in the discovery of DNA."*

"Odd that, wouldn't you say? From such rude origins to the cutting edge of science."

"We do good work, Professor, and I'm glad you're here to see it.

"The shantytowns had to be replaced as a matter of urgency, particularly when they were decimated in the Fifties by a tornado, unusual for South Africa. These townships are owned and run by the city of Johannesburg. One good feature is that only one family may live in each house, creating much more orderly and civilized living conditions, but meaning long waiting lists for housing."

As we again approached Baragwanath, I stopped the car across from the Hospital. We got out and I showed Professor Davis the huge PUTCO Bus station and the taxi stand. There were scores of buses there, parked or loading and offloading passengers. We saw dozens of 'Soweto taxis,' full of people coming and going. There were many open-air stalls, with vendors selling everything from freshly grilled corn on the cob, and buckets of animal intestines, to Coca Cola, cigarettes, herbs, animal skins or strings of beads.

A 'Sangoma'[6] or lady Witchdoctor sat outside one of the stalls. She was dressed in an elaborate traditional outfit, made of small multi-colored beads, woven into cloth. She wore many copper and bead bangles and amulets on both arms and legs. She peddled herbs and potions, and gave consultations, including the throwing of bones to solve personal problems, as alternatives to the purveyors of first world medicine across the highway. She offered us her services, which Professor Davis graciously declined.

The place was unpaved and dusty. Discarded wrapping papers and plastic bags blew around everywhere, some coming to rest in puddles left after the most recent rain. The air was vibrant with chattering and singing, the beat of Bantu and European music, and the characteristic sound of 'Kwela' and 'Penny Whistle Blues' coming from countless transistor radios and record players. At least half the people alighting from the buses and taxis started streaming across the road to the hospital, oblivious to the speeding traffic.

We returned to the car and I drove across the road, dodging the pedestrians, and turned in through the broad metal gates of Baragwanath. A guard let us pass with a cheery wave. I parked for a few minutes in front of the building and started to tell my guest about the hospital.

Patients entered through a smaller gate on the side. They walked across an asphalt courtyard to the front doors. Inside they would register and be distributed throughout the Outpatient and Casualty services, on the right of the entrance, and to areas such as X-ray or Pediatrics. This was a huge task. Each day over a thousand people came for care and hundreds were admitted to the wards from Casualty and Outpatients. The queue for admissions was always long and moved slowly.

"That's the reason the system of 'Urgent Direct' admissions was evolved," I said. "It allows the really sick people to avoid the 'normal' clerical bureaucratic process. They get a red sticker placed on their foreheads and a blank 'Bedletter' or Chart with 'Urgent Direct' stamped on it. The porter then knows he must bypass the clerks and go like hell directly to his destination, yelling 'Urgent Direct' all the way. Such patients get speedy attention when they arrive, wherever they may be going. It's primitive, but effective."

I continued to talk about Baragwanath while we drove round to the parking lot, which was near my wards and the operating theaters. It was the largest hospital in the southern hemisphere, with 2,000 beds, often holding 2,500 patients due to overcrowding.

"That's where we made our big mistake," I said. "We never turned anyone away, so they just kept crowding in. In my view, we should have told the authorities 'No more!' That might have forced them to build more facilities. Now they just think we can cope, as we always have."

Because of the large numbers, the spread-out design, and the poor education of many patients and visitors, directions were shown very simply. Painted on the concrete floors of the corridors were rows of large footprints and broad lines. These led from the entrance to the various common destinations in a variety of colors—Yellow to Pediatrics, Red to X-ray.

The layout of the Hospital was a large, diffuse series of military-style, single story, brown brick buildings, roofed with red-painted corrugated iron. There was no air conditioning,[7] and the windows were of broad louvered plate glass, designed to let in plenty of air between the slats. Long, open, concrete corridors, also covered by corrugated iron, radiated from the entrance, out and down a gentle

AERIAL VIEW OF BARAGWANATH HOSPITAL CAMPUS.
A PORTION OF DIEPKLOOF, SOWETO
CAN BE SEEN IN THE RIGHT FOREGROUND.

THE OLD GATES OF BARAGWANATH HOSPITAL.

VIEW ACROSS THE ROOFTOPS OF A NEWER SECTION
OF BARAGWANATH HOSPITAL CAMPUS.
DIEPKLOOF, SOWETO CAN BE SEEN IN THE BACKGROUND.

ANOTHER VIEW OF
BARAGWANATH HOSPITAL.

A WOMAN WITCHDOCTOR OR "SANGOMA"
IN TRADITIONAL DRESS.

slope, with several broad cross-connections, like a sector of a giant spider's web. About every seventy feet, pairs of forty-bed wards opened off the long corridors, one on each side.

I pointed out the orthopedic hospital, which had recently been built on the left of the campus, next to the maternity section. As we drove around the grounds, I had the car windows open and we could clearly hear the voice of the telephone operator over the public address system, speaking in a deliberate but staccato manner: "Would all the wards please…come to the mortuary…to fetch their blankets…as the mortuary is now full."

Professor Davis raised his eyebrows at this tragic yet somehow comic announcement.

"These guys are good but unschooled," I said. "We get some really funny ones from time to time. I'm sorry to say I've heard that one before. Often in pneumonia season, or after a big trauma weekend, the Morgue is just stuffed full of corpses."

We passed row upon row of wards, separated by lawns, with two or three trees growing in the 'Kikuyu' grass.[8] The pediatric section occupied the upper end of the corridor, with the medical wards further down. They all had long enclosed verandahs, half brick and half glass. At the end of each ward a door led down some brick steps to the outside. Several patients in pajamas had emerged and were enjoying the morning sun. In a cross-corridor, we saw many wheelchairs propelled rapidly by their occupants, using well-muscled arms.

"They're from our large colony of paraplegics," I told him. "They're almost forced to live here for socio-economic reasons. Their main problem is bedsores, which get worse if they go home. There's really no work for them. I'm a member of 'Round Table,' which is like a junior Rotary Club. I've started a project to convert an old single decker bus for paraplegic use. It'll have a chairlift, a driver, and funding to operate a service for paraplegics in Soweto. We aim to try and rehabilitate and re-integrate them into the community and the workforce. You'll see their ward and I'll tell you more later."

We were now reaching the lower end of the 173-acre campus and turned right past the occupational therapy department and the paraplegic basketball court. A few men in wheelchairs were already in action there.

Below the road, on the left, we saw the large medical staff quarters and the mess. These were also the original military style barracks buildings, with mahogany 'stable doors,' which opened onto concrete verandahs. The house doctors lived there, and there were rooms for other doctors spending the night on duty. There were also some married quarters.

I fondly pointed out the room I had occupied as a houseman many years before. A cottonseed poplar tree still shaded the verandah and the place where my VW Beetle parked.

After we passed the swimming pool and tennis court, the road again turned right. It went back uphill, between the nurses' quarters and school on the left, and the surgical wards on the right. The operating theaters, laboratory, X-ray, Outpatient and Casualty departments lay higher up along this road and on the surgical corridor.

We left the car under some shade trees and entered the back end of Ward Six, where my female patients were housed. They occupied half the ward. Each surgical unit had only 20 female beds, partly because the gynecology and obstetric wards also served women, but also because the trauma mostly involved men, and required many more beds.

I greeted some of the patients by name. We stopped by one bed and I introduced the Professor to the young woman. She had a large smooth lump on one side of her neck.

"Care to take a guess?" I asked Professor Davis.

"She looks very well. You tell me."

"It's a carotid body tumor,[9] rare as you know, but less so in our young females. We don't know why, but we can speculate on genetics and the altitude here of 6,000 feet. I could discuss this one forever, but we must move on. I'm really looking forward to doing her surgery on Wednesday, as she's about my fifth such case.

"We have a couple of patients with burns, one with Ca esophagus, a Ca Breast, a paraplegic, some leg ulcers, four traumas and several other diagnoses. Here comes Sister.

"Sister Jane, this is Professor Davis, from London, to see how we do things here."

"How do you do, sir?" she said, curtsying with a slight bob and bend of her knees.

"I'm pleased to meet you, Sister. I see you keep a very neat and tidy ward. Your patients all look happy. You must treat them well."

Sister Jane beamed, showing a perfect radiant smile. I always wondered how Africans did that without benefit of orthodontists. We walked through the rest of the ward with a few further comments.

Then I led the way across the main corridor into Ward Five, the male ward. We passed the Ward Sister's office. Next-door was the only private patient room. This was used for the occasional VIP or for strict isolation, if needed.

The morning ward round was already half done. The Ward Sister, in her distinctive wide white headgear, was walking around with the team of surgical registrar, three housemen, two students and a female interpreter and ward clerk—an impressive entourage.

We walked over and joined them. I briefly introduced Professor Davis, saying we would all meet properly over tea later. I asked the registrar to continue rounds while we looked around. The entire group stopped at each bed, talking with and briefly examining each patient. The housemen and students took the charts and wrote progress notes and orders. The Sister wrote several lines about every patient in a hardcover legal size exercise book, taking down the instructions for later reference and action. The interpreter was needed on a few occasions when more complicated concepts had to be conveyed, such as consent for surgery. She also fetched X-rays and did anything else we needed.

Ward Five had been partly renovated. It was fairly representative of the whole hospital. The old wooden floors had been replaced with concrete, covered in vinyl tiles. There were forty beds in the ward, in three rows, one along each side, facing each other, and one row on the narrow verandah. There was very little space between the beds. Naked electric light bulbs hung from the ceiling.

The beds were of black enameled steel, without any flexibility or movable parts. The blankets were of utilitarian dark gray wool and there were no bedcovers. Several patients lay with the lower ends of their beds raised on old wooden chairs or pyramid-shaped wooden blocks, to relieve swelling of the legs and promote wound healing. A few beds had similar blocks under the upper ends.

In the center of the ward were several 'extra' patients, for whom there were no beds. I explained that they would soon be seen, and hopefully sent home. Some had fractures of the jaw, others stabs in the chest. There was an assortment of other diagnoses in this group.

Professor Davis watched as the Unit worked, occasionally asking the registrar questions.

"What did you do to this man?" he asked, about a patient with a stab in the abdomen.

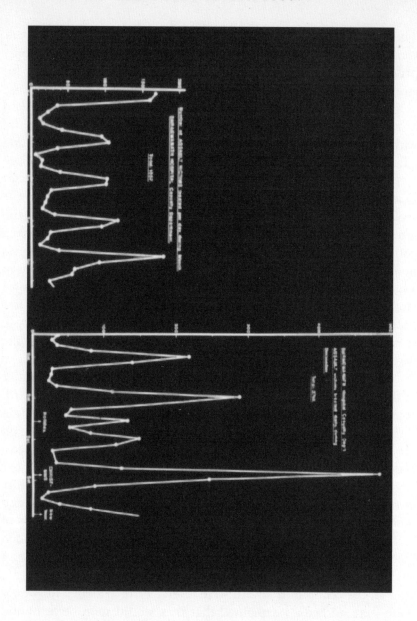

GRAPHS OF TRAUMA CASES COMING INTO BARA: MAR VS. DEC
THE PEAKS REPRESENT WEEKENDS.
MONTH-ENDS WERE HIGHER & CHRISTMAS ALONE
BROUGHT 500 CASES.

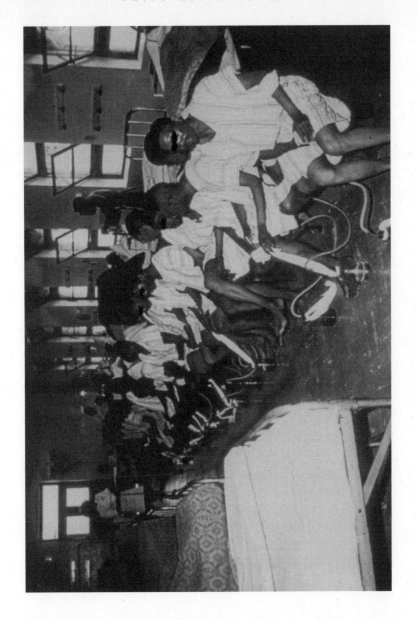

ROW OF PEOPLE STABBED IN CHEST ON ONE NIGHT.
ALL ARE CONNECTED TO CHEST-DRAINAGE BOTTLES
ON THE FLOOR.

VIEW OF WARD 5,
MALE WARD OF UNIT 5.

Peter Jones answered: "He was quite easy. I had to suture a few stabs transversely in two layers and make sure he had no other wounds in the bowel. We always count to be certain there is an even number of holes. Any single wound must have a good explanation. Otherwise we may miss one on the other side of the bowel and the patient gets peritonitis and we could go to court."

"A very good answer," said Prof. Davis. "Tell me about the next man. That looks like *parenteral nutrition*[10] in the bottle hanging there."

"You're right, sir. He has esophageal cancer and he's getting intravenous feeding to try and keep him in shape for surgery. The disease is endemic here, and we're trying to find out why. The whole country is working on it, because it's so common in the Bantu peoples. They come in too late and do very badly. This man's cancer is relatively early and Mr. Hunt is giving him chemotherapy and radiation before surgery, to go for a cure. The chemo and radiation only takes a week."

"What part will you play in the operation?"

"I'm not ready to go solo, but Mr. Hunt and I share the work. He lets me do all I can. I open and close the chest and abdomen and do more and more of the work inside."

"That sounds like good experience to me," said Davis. "How do you like the trauma?"

"We just take it as it comes," Jones answered. "There's no use in getting too upset. That's life at Bara. I've learned to think on my feet. We have to handle it correctly the first time and take care of the trauma efficiently, or we would be completely submerged. There's a huge amount of experience to be obtained. It's a great preparation for the real world."

"Sadly, I wonder if you're not already in the real world. I admire your attitude," said the visitor. "Thank you."

I led Professor Davis away from the group.

"That's a bright young man, he seems to be pretty mature," he commented.

"I'm very pleased with him," I answered. "It's just a pity they rotate through each unit so briefly and I'll lose him soon. Six months is not really long enough. But the system does protect both them and us from bad mismatches of personality or abilities. Once they've rotated through Bara, we have a very good consensus view of the Registrars. But in my opinion, they should start in the White hospitals and then come and polish their skills here, where they get the maximum opportunity for surgery. Instead, they come here first and get 'baptism by fire.' But they're certainly very competent when they leave us.

"We'd better move along to stay on schedule and get you to Professor Mason later."

I showed Professor Davis a few other patients of interest and we looked on the verandah, where most people had less acute conditions. Long-term paraplegic 'overflow' patients occupied the last five beds. These beds each had large 'cradles' over the patients, making a tunnel, to keep the bedclothes from causing pressure. This also made regular turning easier for the staff, who had to do it every four hours.

I said: "The paraplegics are all really 'lifers' in the hospital, with I believe, a drug culture of their own. Periodically, we find one of them has mysteriously died. I think that, out of boredom, some of them will drink anything that smells of alcohol, such as antiseptics in the drug cabinet."

We left the ward and visited the remaining surgical wards on the corridor, including neurosurgery and Urology/Ear, Nose and Throat. We walked into the paraplegic ward, but the neurosurgeon was not there.

"This is another forty-bed ward, purely for para- and quadri-plegics," I said. "Most of the injuries are from sharp trauma, usually purposeful rather than accidental. The perpetrators can find the spinal cord with anything sharp, such as bicycle spokes or sail needles. They do it as 'punishment' for real or imagined crimes, such as not handing over money when asked. Since the bedsore problem is bad and the socio-economic circumstances so unfavorable, these patients almost never leave, creating the overflow problem. Every surgical ward hosts about five paraplegics who cannot be accommodated here. Hence my interest in the bus project.

"How about a cup of tea and a sandwich? I see the unit has finished in Ward Five."

We walked along the communicating corridor. I showed him the laboratory and the kitchen as we passed.

"You have to be very careful here at mealtimes. An army of porters emerges from the kitchen with over fifty large metal food containers, which thunder down the corridors in a long line. Each one contains meals for over forty patients. The kitchen uses an astounding amount of food per day, like four thousand pounds of meat, for example."

We left the cross-corridor and entered the doctors' tearoom. Dozens of white-coated doctors, young and older, sat at big round tables and chatted amiably. New arrivals filed to a large open window, attended by a jovial plump Colored lady, who took care of all this. On the counter were large urns of tea and coffee, jugs of milk and bowls of sugar. She had made huge trays of small, thin, triangular, British-style sandwiches, with a variety of fillings. Everyone helped themselves and sat down, usually with their own unit.

"There are over 300 doctors here and we have a lot of students at all times, so this is quite a job for Martha," I said.

We took our tea and sandwiches and sat down with the unit. I did a proper introduction, explaining the object of the Professor's visit.

"I'm having a great time," Professor Davis said. "I'm very impressed with the setup and the kind of care you are giving, under the circumstances."

Professor Mason entered and came over to the table. A slender man of medium height, with black hair and a genial, welcoming smile, he was dressed in a long white coat over dark suit trousers, with a white shirt and regimental striped tie.

"Hullo again, David. I thought I might find you two here. How has John been treating you?"

"We've seen a lot and it's most interesting. Mr. Hunt has been a good host and guide. I don't know how you cope with all the work."

Mason got his tea and sat down to chat for a few minutes. After a decent interval I stood up and said:

"Our time is getting short, Professor Davis, as you've another visit this afternoon and you'll need time to talk with Professor Mason. Let's move along and I'll show you more *en route* to his office."

I showed my guest the pediatric corridor and the medical one, which ran nearly parallel to the surgery corridor. There was a sister medical unit for each surgical one and we did each other's consultations when necessary.

We then turned up toward the entrance and I pointed out X-ray and physical therapy, before we passed through Casualty, the 'Pit' and the Resuscitation Room, which I fully described. We looked into the large, packed Outpatient area beyond Casualty, while I continued my running commentary.

Black patients of all ages were around us on all sides as we walked. They wore old but clean European style clothes, long or short pants, and the women usually in dresses. Some wore blankets in lieu of jackets. Many women wore headscarves. Some babies were perched on their mothers' buttocks, held on tightly by blankets wrapped round the mother's waist. Footwear was often absent or shabby.

"It's busy," Professor Davis commented.

"The number of patients passing through here boggles the mind," I replied. "It is four or five times more full than this on a weekend night. We admit daily to the Surgical Admissions Ward between forty and a hundred people, depending on the day of the week. We see everything remotely surgical in the 'Pit,' which is constantly on the go. It's our surgical base from lunch until the next morning. We can easily get to Resuscitation. The housemen and students get excellent hands-on experience and very quickly learn good surgical judgment.

"That's the Casualty minor operating theater, where our housemen do five adult circumcisions every week. You might say that's how they 'cut their surgical teeth.'"

Professor Davis laughed. We continued via the direct back way to the theater suite, entered and paused to don canvas overshoes that were kept in an old zinc 'washerwoman's' bath.

"We have thirteen theaters and it's still not enough," I said. "I only get to operate once a week, for a whole day, with a morning 'septic and minor' theater, where the housemen work. We sometimes have a second theater for the registrar. At night there are three theaters going most of the time, considering other disciplines as well."

We walked up the stairs to Professor Mason's office and I took my leave.

"Jack, I've shown Professor Davis just about everything and he's talked to Peter Jones for a while. You may want to show him the ICU, if you have time. I know you have all the statistics and the University side to discuss. You're taking him to J. G. Strydom hospital this afternoon, aren't you?"

Professor Mason nodded. "I think we'll go to lunch in Town before that, but we have a good half hour left here first. John, thank you so very much for your help."

"Goodbye Professor Davis. It's been a pleasure meeting you again."

"Goodbye Mr. Hunt. I thoroughly enjoyed my visit. I even have a better understanding of South Africa's gold."

[1] Streptomycin: An early antibiotic, shortly after penicillin. It produced the first cases of cured Tuberculosis and could also be used for treatment of different germs than penicillin, so they were used in combination.

[2] Shanty Towns: These terrible areas were still present while I was a student and houseman at Bara. The 'Squatters' built their own homes, tightly packed together, on any vacant piece of land. They had no access to building materials and used cardboard boxes, corrugated iron sheets and anything else they could find. They had no doors, windows or floors. There was no running water, storm water drainage, or sewage system. There was no waterproofing, heating or electricity. Rain flowed right through the 'houses.' Sewage settled and rotted at the lowest point in the area. Illness and crime were everywhere.

[3] Eucalyptus or Bluegum trees: An Australian import. These are hardy, tough trees, with fragrant leaves and flowers, which come in different colors, depending on the subspecies. In Australia the koala bears feed only on these trees.

[4] San and Khoikhoi people: Known at the time of white settlement in the Cape as Bushmen and Hottentots. These were pale yellowish-brown people, of short stature. They were largely nomadic hunter-gatherers, though the Hottentots had cattle. They are now largely extinct as separate tribes. There are several hundred San people still living in the desert areas of Namibia or Botswana. They were wiped out in large numbers by epidemics of European diseases, such as measles, flu and smallpox. The original white colonists came in many cases without wives and families. Miscegenation was common and at one time encouraged by the Dutch East India Company, who settled the Cape.

[5] Cape Colored People: People of mixed racial descent, stemming from racial mixing of white colonists, San and Khoikhoi and black and Malay slaves. The people were separated into a racial group by the white governments over time. They live predominantly in the western Cape, round Cape Town.

[6] Sangoma or Witchdoctor: They may be male or female. Witchdoctors or traditional healers have always thrived in South Africa. Many times patients visit them in preference to European doctors and until their money is all gone, and then they come to white doctors and hospitals.

[7] Air conditioning: The climate in Johannesburg, at 6,000 feet and without humidity, made air conditioning largely unnecessary. Only a few wealthier white homes had it installed.

[8] Kikuyu grass: A rather coarse creeping grass, which takes over entirely, eliminating weeds. Used for rugby fields and can withstand the play.

[9] Carotid body tumor: A rare tumor that occurs in the neck. It comes from the carotid body, a tiny structure, smaller than a rice grain, situated at the main branching of the carotid arteries. Usually benign, some are malignant.

[10] Parenteral Nutrition: Synonymous with 'intravenous feeding.' Used when people cannot take food or liquids by mouth, as when the esophagus is blocked by cancer.

* This brilliant man recently received a share of the Nobel Prize for medicine in 2002, for work stemming from his Oxford research.

Choosing a field within medicine is seldom easy. The choice must often be made before the young person has sufficient wisdom or breadth of experience to decide on the best option. This situation is even worse in America, where medical students must select their specialty before having been exposed to every medical field, at just over three years into a four-year course of study. Most new graduates are not required to do general internship years before starting specialty training. They could easily miss the opportunity to choose a different specialty or family practice, which they might have preferred.

In most medical schools chance governs the experiences the student will have—good, bad or indifferent. The order, mix and quality of educational exposures all influence the young doctor. In South Africa, even after a six-year course, the Medical and Dental Council requires new graduates to do a year as a house doctor,[1] experiencing both medicine and surgery. They also stipulate that doctors must do two years of general practice or its equivalent before starting specialty training. By that time they should have attained sufficient maturity to select wisely.

Of course the worst motivation for a career in medicine is parental coercion. Such pressures may be brought to bear for many reasons. These include the continuation of family traditions, satisfying the frustration of parents at not having become doctors, or even trying to improve the family's social status. In my class there were two such unfortunate students, both the children of doctors, who were totally uninterested in Medicine and consequently very frustrated.

They both became alcoholics during the course. I did not know the fate of one—the person did not graduate. The other one was seen years later in London by one of my friends, lying drunk in a gutter. As another example, the son of a leading London surgeon graduated as a doctor and the next day horrified his parents by going on the stage to start his chosen acting career.

But I was certainly not immune to problems with career choice. Though I was only sixteen when I matriculated[2] from high school, I always wanted to be a doctor, thanks to the wonderful family practitioner who was my role model as a child and teenager. I had no other ambitions while at school, and never regretted my decision to pursue a career in medicine.

Once I became a medical student I was fascinated by neurology and psychology and thought I might consider psychiatry as a specialty. The study of the nervous system during the second year anatomy and physiology courses heightened my interest and I did an extra dissection of a brain. I read psychology and psychiatry books in my spare time, even though the psychiatry course would not be for another two years.

After completing the basic science studies, I began my clinical exposure to patients in fourth year. Mornings were spent in hospital work and afternoons were devoted to lectures and practical visits in psychiatry and public health. By random allocation my group did two consecutive rotations in surgery at Baragwanath hospital. Nothing I saw there in surgery attracted me to the subject.

I endured two fruitless ten-week periods in the same uninspiring surgical unit, with a surgeon who could neither teach nor operate adequately. He never completed an operation before the students took the noon Bara bus back to town. The registrar in the unit was a great person, but his surgery was also so slow that he had been likened to a snail operating under the influence of curare. He would eventually complete the case if the anesthetist[3] could keep the patient alive. At that early stage in my career the never-ending flood of trauma also seemed gross, pointless and mindless. These negative experiences dissuaded me from seeking a surgical house job at Baragwanath and left me clinging to my dreams of psychiatry, particularly as I was only halfway through the course of study.

As the days passed, however, I became progressively disenchanted with psychiatry. My initiation into this field started with a vacation job as an orderly at Tara Hospital. This was an open 'neuro-psychiatric institution,' where no one was 'lock-up crazy,' and the patients were supposed to be both 'treatable' and 'curable.' These were 'neurotics,' as opposed to 'psychotics,' who were then generally regarded as untreatable, and were institutionalized at Sterkfontein Mental Hospital. Ironically, years later, after the advent and proliferation of effective psycho-pharmaceutical drugs, the psychotic patients often turned out to be the more treatable ones. Provided they stayed on their medication, they could often return to normal lives and frequently to productive work in society.

Despite my great interest and growing knowledge of psychiatry, I soon found that I could not identify with or have empathy for many of the Tara patients. My approach to life was far too pragmatic. My first experience at the hospital was of a play being staged by a committee of both staff and patients. One of the staff members had been treated at Tara and was now supposedly 'cured.' The first rehearsal ended in serious disarray, with the cast members and staff throwing a variety of pens and other sharp objects at each other, like darts at a board. I could barely tell staff from patients by their behavior, and the supposedly cured patient exhibited the most bizarre conduct of all.

I found that many patients became dependent upon the hospital and discussed with each other their plans to return often, and certainly for Christmas each year. They also needed to stay in touch through the 'Tara Club' for ex-patients. The club idea seemed commendable, but I felt that patients who could not break away would never be cured.

One night after midnight, my four orderly colleagues and I were kept busy leaning out of second- or third-floor windows, restraining five allegedly suicidal young females by their ankles, wrists or necks. The patients were making their obligatory 'suicide gestures,' to try and show that they really were ill, without ever actually taking their own lives. Naturally, they all lived to tell the tale.

These same girls would also stage 'seizures' and fall apparently unconscious in the corridor outside the dining hall, making sure that their legs and panties were on full display. Their fluttering eyelids always gave them away. They invariably remembered the orderly who tried to rouse them with a splash of cold water. Patients with genuine seizure activity remembered nothing and would often involuntarily wet their pants and bite their tongues. Such indignities never happened to the girls who had these hysterical fits.

This was also the era of 'prefrontal leucotomy'[4] or 'lobotomy,' 'electroshock therapy,'[5] and 'insulin shock.'[6] All these treatments were either practiced at Tara, or the hospital had to care for such patients later. I worked in the wards looking after these people and was particularly repelled by the results of the leucotomies. One such patient had been an accountant and became totally irresponsible and required institutionalization. The cases of electroshock that I saw had such strong seizures that the treatment appeared to me quite barbaric. Looking after the insulin shock patients during their therapy was an awesome responsibility. I learned that the treatment was of marginal, if any, benefit and had the potential for harm to the brain. I was very grateful when my vacation job was over!

By contrast with my Tara experiences, in a strange way I enjoyed the class visits to Sterkfontein mental hospital. This was twenty miles from medical school, near the caves of the same name, where Professor Dart[7] had made some famous anthropological discoveries. I certainly learned a lot from the visits. But I thought that the incarceration of most of the patients was an appalling waste of life and a major tragedy for their families.

The most interesting person we met there was a 'moral defective' or psychopath, who was locked up for the protection of the public. This well-educated, articulate, middle-aged man put on a great show, describing graphically, with an engaging laugh, how he had barefacedly 'conned' many people out of money or possessions. His stories were tragic, but at the same time, excruciatingly funny. If they had not all been immoral, illegal and true, he would have made a great television entertainer. One of his best tales concerned taking a doctor's car from a parking lot and being stopped by the police for speeding. He waved the doctor's stethoscope out of the window, gesticulating wildly towards the hospital. The unsuspecting cops provided an escort, with sirens wailing, to help speed him on his way.

Any ambitions I still had towards psychiatry evaporated during the finals at the end of the psychiatry course. I had continued to read a lot and at exam time arguably knew more about psychology and psychiatry than anyone in my class of over 100 students.

The written examinations took place in a large hall where I had come to dances at happier times. The candidates sat in alphabetical order at school desks arranged in long rows, under the watchful eyes of several 'invigilators.' Answers were to be written in books consisting of eight legal-sized pages in manila covers. The invigilators handed out the question papers and exam books at precisely two o'clock.

The exam was scheduled to last for three hours. There were four essay-type questions, all of which seemed to me quite simple and straightforward. They were each set in a similar format, for example:

1. Write *short notes* on wills.
2. Write *short notes* on schizophrenia, etc.

I had ample knowledge to answer exactly what appeared to be required, and wrote short succinct notes on each topic, without embellishment. I finished all four questions in half the allotted time, filling one exam book. The candidates were not yet allowed to leave the room, so I reviewed my answers and made a few minor additions.

I then started looking around the hall. Nearby, in the next row, I saw a student with the initial P, who was regularly one of the top scorers in the class, but in my view, had not an ounce of practical ability. An invigilator had repeatedly brought extra exam books to 'candidate P,' and I could now count five of them on his desk. The student continued with head down to write as fast as he could. As I left the hall an hour early, I said to myself:

"One of us must be wrong. Filling five exam books doesn't sound like 'short notes.'"

The next step in the exam was the orals, a few days later. I went out to Sterkfontein Hospital, but was shown no patients. I never understood why the students and the examiners had to drive twenty miles for the privilege of meeting each other there. I met only the 'External Examiner,' who was a psychiatry professor from a university hundreds of miles away. Such examiners regularly visited other medical schools at exam time, in order to ensure uniform standards of teaching in the country.

When I entered the room, the rather chubby professor extended a clammy, tremulous hand and motioned to me to sit down. The examiner studied some papers for a while and then addressed me tentatively in a quavering voice:

"You d…didn't like the paper very m…m…much, d…did you?" he stammered.

I was startled and dismayed by this total lack of tact or feeling in any human being, let alone a prominent psychiatrist. That was clearly not the way to set a presumably nervous candidate at ease.

"As a matter of fact, sir, I enjoyed it very much!" I answered brightly.

"Oh…Ohh," was all the examiner could manage. He shuffled and stared at his papers for a long time, before finally starting the exam.

"T…tell me, Mr. Hunt, what is Schizophrenia?"

I snapped out an immediate definition, which left no doubt as to my knowledge.

"T…tell me about hysterical fits."

That was even easier, and I could elaborate on my answer, using my Tara experiences. I knew one tenet of oral examination lore: to keep talking while I knew the subject matter—there would be less time for difficult questions. I answered four more questions confidently and quickly. The examiner could not trip me up on anything. I knew I had acquitted myself well.

"D…dear me! I can't p…p…pass you all by myself. I d..don't know what to do," the professor said softly to himself, but loud enough for me to hear.

Until then I had not realized that the students did not go to two examiners, one internal and one external, as in other subjects. I began to guess that I had failed the paper and that was probably the reason I had been sent to the 'external'. But I knew there would be two examiner's meetings before the results came out, so I felt there was still hope. The Psychiatry department would probably meet and discuss the exam results with the external examiner. Their chief would then confer with the Dean and the other department heads to decide on promotions to the fifth year of study.

When all the exams were finished it took nearly a week for the results to be placed on the Medical School notice boards. Over a hundred students came crowding into the foyer of the school up on Hospital Hill, talking excitedly while we awaited the results.

Our first interest was the list of promotions and then the honors. I finally reached the front of the pack. I was relieved that I had passed the year and all my subjects except psychiatry. It did not surprise me that the 'Top First' in Psychiatry went to 'Candidate P.'

I made quite certain my name was not on the Psychiatry list. I was puzzled as to how I could have passed the whole year and yet failed one subject. I soon realized they must have considered me at the meetings and decided to pass me. The department was probably so inefficient that they had posted the original pass list without my name. I was very angry and went to the psychiatry office to ask the secretary for an explanation. My suspicions were correct. She amended the list but gave me only a half-hearted apology.

I had now had enough—my indecision was over. The die was cast. No more hankering for psychiatry! I could definitely not see myself living or working for the rest of my life with people such as those I had thus far encountered in psychiatry, be they patients, doctors or staff. At least, I now had the whole summer vacation to forget about it, clear my mind and think about another focus. I could now enjoy the last of my training for the crew of the University Eight for the Buffalo Regatta in East London on 'Dingaan's Day.'

Fifth year was a busy one, with a whole new set of experiences, including obstetrics, gynecology, pediatrics, internal medicine and many more. There was much intensive teaching and, as an experiment, the final written exams were set for the end of the year, with the sixth year to act as a 'mini-internship,' followed by the final clinical and oral exams. I was interested in everything I experienced, but developed no burning desire to pursue any one field. All were still possibilities.

The brain and its functions always fascinated me and I considered doing pure neurology, which provided a great intellectual challenge during the diagnostic process. This was a little like playing chess or completing a complex jigsaw or crossword puzzle. The end result of a skillful neurological exam would be a precise diagnosis. That appealed to me greatly. But I soon learned that there were as yet very few successful treatments for neurological diseases. So the brilliant diagnosis would be the end point—with 'check mate' being called by the disease. Since many neurological conditions were depressing and tragic, I doubted whether I could spend the rest of my life in that field.

I soon discovered that I wanted to do clinical medicine, with patient contact. This ruled out such fields as pathology and pharmacology and even radiology. I liked teaching, but would prefer to do it in a clinical field. I decided to 'go with the flow' for the present, with my first priority getting through the courses and obtaining the maximum benefit from each rotation. Time enough to decide later. The curriculum did not offer sufficient exposure to general practice—my original intention on leaving high school. In any event, I knew I would probably have to do that after my houseman year if I wanted specialist training.

As the course progressed, I decided that I could not do obstetrics or gynecology, but I loved pediatrics and dealing with children and newborns. I felt it would be good to do six months of pediatrics and get a better feel for the subject. I enjoyed medicine, both at the General hospital in white people, but even more at Baragwanath Hospital, where I saw black people of many tribal origins and levels of education and social evolution, presenting with a broad spectrum of unusual and fascinating diseases.

During my rotation in Medicine at Baragwanath I arranged a mini-internship as a *locum tenens* houseman for Dr Watson, leading on to my obtaining a house job there after I graduated. I knew that would provide a great experience and a taste of the subject.

I had a final rotation in surgery at the Johannesburg General Hospital in Ward Twenty. It was the unit of the leading private surgeon in Johannesburg, who was then senior honorary surgeon.[8] One of the assistant surgeons was a younger man who was also honorary chief of surgery at the Children's Hospital. The registrar was a young married woman, a very bright and talented surgeon.

This rotation was a whole new experience. The teaching was wonderful and great fun, no matter who did it. Everyone had a different approach, with significant knowledge to impart. The surgery was beautifully, skillfully and expeditiously done. Everyone was friendly. Working there was such a pleasure that I felt completely at home. In a few weeks I knew that was how I could spend the rest of my life, if they would only have me. I arranged a *locum tenens* house job in Ward Twenty later in my final year and brokered that into becoming a houseman in the unit after I graduated.

During my housemanship I became very impressed with the assistant surgeon and helped him on many difficult and demanding cases. Through his good graces I obtained the senior house officer position in surgery at the Children's Hospital after my housemanship. I would be working under my second role model and also getting a taste of pediatrics, while deciding if surgery was really for me.

Of small things and random chances, momentous decisions are sometimes made.

[1] Houseman year: A compulsory year of training, during which the new graduate is only provisionally registered as a medical practitioner. The graduate must do six months each of medicine and surgery in a hospital setting and under senior supervision. Permanent registration follows successful completion of the houseman year.

[2] Matriculated: The senior year in high school culminated with the Matriculation examination, held publicly throughout the country and ensuring a uniformly high standard. There was no multiple-choice element. All questions were written essay-type, with mathematical and scientific calculations expected. Most subjects were obligatory, with no simple electives. Two languages, science or biology, mathematics and history or geography and one other subject were all required for graduation. Candidates for Universities had to graduate at the highest levels. I did private classes in Latin as an extra, out of school, to qualify for Medical School.

[3] Anesthetist: Anesthesiologist (Doctor). There were no nurse anesthetists in South Africa, just as in Britain.

[4] Prefrontal leucotomy: The same as lobotomy, an operation in which needles or probes were used to undercut the frontal lobes of the brain. This took away most of the patient's inhibitions, with many disastrous results.

[5] Electroshock therapy: Also known as electro-convulsive therapy, or ECT. It involves the placement of electrodes alongside the head and the passage of an electric current, which causes a seizure. This has definite value, especially in resistant cases of depression. It is still used. Relaxant drugs and sedation now minimize seizure activity. At that time, techniques were fairly primitive and the seizures were impressive and painful, causing occasional fractures of vertebrae.

[6] Insulin Shock: Patients were deliberately sent into hypoglycemic coma or near-coma by the use of insulin. This was done on a daily basis and a ward full of comatose patients had to be woken up with intravenous or oral glucose at the predetermined time. Some patients allegedly benefited from this treatment, but it is no longer done, for fear of producing permanent brain damage.

[7] Professor Raymond Dart: One of the leading anthropologists of his era. He was Professor and head of the Department of Anatomy at Witwatersrand University, where I was studying Medicine.

[8] Honorary Surgeon: South Africa followed the British tradition of service to the public hospitals. Privately practicing surgeons or physicians donated some of their time to staff the public wards of the hospitals. In ward twenty, for example, there were five honorary surgeons sharing duties, which included patient care, teaching of trainee surgeons and students, operating room work and emergency cover. The remainder of the surgical staff were trainees—Registrars and House Surgeons— paid by the Transvaal Provincial Administration. The teaching was organized by Witwatersrand University Medical School.

As a student at Baragwanath Hospital, one of my earliest experiences was of my group standing around a bed in Ward 24, being taught by Dr. Watson, a slender, sandy-haired, dapper man with an elegant English accent. A Cambridge graduate, Watson had played ground hockey for his college. During World War Two he had been an officer in the Royal Air Force and had himself been hospitalized in the Imperial Military Hospital, Baragwanath. After the Transvaal Province took over the Hospital in 1948, Watson had become a physician there and was now the Principal Physician and headed one of the five medical units and the tuberculosis ward.

His teaching was extremely 'hands on.' Students had to know their stuff, or they would face his gentle but incisive humor. It was a great honor to be selected as one of Dr. Watson's house physicians. There was great competition for the job. All would-be candidates tried to get his attention on rounds and not to make fools of themselves.

David, one of my friends, was set the task of evaluating the heart of a nubile young woman, nude from the waist up. The privacy screens were drawn round our entire group. The patient had mitral valve stenosis, resulting from untreated strep throat,[1] which had caused rheumatic fever and cardiac damage. The findings the student sought from the damaged valve were an abnormal heart sound or murmur,[2] best heard with a stethoscope placed below the left breast, and a 'thrill,' or little rumble under the skin, felt in the same area. The patient was well educated and had probably been through this before. She waited as David started feeling around her breast for the apex beat and then placed his hand softly there, to see if he could sense the vibration.

"Do you feel a thrill?" the young woman asked innocently.

David blushed to the roots of his hair and burst out in perspiration. The entire group convulsed with laughter. Dr. Watson, in his tactful English manner, somehow managed to get the teaching back on track.

I completed one rotation in the unit without drawing undue ridicule. Later, during my senior year, the students were allowed to do '*locum tenens* houseman' jobs, filling in when an intern took a vacation. I worked for a week on Watson's ward, acting as a proper doctor, and thoroughly enjoyed the experience. My chief appreciated my keenness and I landed a half-year job for my second six months after graduation. New graduates were required by the Medical Council to do two such periods, one in Medicine and one in Surgery, before final registration as a doctor. I was glad my second one had been assured.

My co-workers were ill assorted but nonetheless became highly compatible. Among them were a young female Polish immigrant, a local Scottish farmer's son, an archdeacon's daughter, and the son of a Johannesburg business owner. The two Jewish Registrars represented the long and the short of it. One was short and dumpy and always cheerful, while the other was tall and very outspoken, with extreme leftist views. He had such a loud booming voice that I often wondered why he needed to use the telephone. We all soon settled down into a happy and cohesive team.

Our unit had charge of forty male and twenty female acute beds and the long-stay tuberculosis ward, where patients required little attention. The unit was on 'intake' duty every fifth day, and the patients admitted from Casualty or Outpatients were allocated to the five housemen in rotation. Our regular intakes of thirty to sixty patients created heavy workloads. The house doctors could return from lunch or supper and find two or more patients waiting for each of us. After midnight, there were only two house doctors on duty, making the nights especially tough. The others could be roused if need be, but it was a point of honor for those on duty not to do so.

The unit had spent the morning of our first Intake day in Outpatients, seeing new referrals from Casualty, following up our own cases, and prescribing drug refills. This activity would bring a flood of new admissions in the afternoon, so we enjoyed a meal in the mess first.

My first admission had 'mental confusion,' or more simply, 'MC,' a generic diagnosis for anyone who was confused, and one of the biggest challenges for the Medical wards. White doctors could rarely understand the complexities of Bantu psychology. The 'Witchdoctor' still had too strong a hold in their culture. Sometimes patients came in claiming to have been bewitched; something very hard for whites to deal with. There were no black psychiatrists or psychologists, certainly not at Baragwanath. The Sterkfontein mental hospital was many miles away and was also overburdened. The Bara doctors' major task was thus to be sure there was no organic medical or surgical disease causing or complicating the psychological problem before transferring the patient. In fact, some of the most interesting medical diagnoses came from the mentally confused patients who proved to have organic physical, rather than psychiatric, diseases.

I talked to the 'MC,' who was rambling and made absolutely no sense, but was not rowdy or violent. The physical exam was also relatively normal. I then asked for an LP tray[3] in order to do a spinal tap. My heart was in my boots because this would be my first solo tap. I rounded up a student nurse to help with the sterile tray and medications and two male orderlies to hold the patient, who might not wish to cooperate. Rudy Gordon, the cheerful registrar, came to help.

The orderlies placed the patient on his side, with his knees bent and his back tightly curved, in an exaggerated fetal position. I scrubbed my hands, put on sterile gloves and took the cover off the tray. I filled a syringe with local anesthetic and put it down. I then took a sponge with some Hibitane disinfecting solution and started to wipe the patient's back with the cold fluid.

"Yo! Yo-yo-yo-yo,"[4] the man yelled in horror.

The patient squirmed and straightened his back, causing the orderlies to take a firmer grip. I talked soothingly while I finished the prep and placed sterile towels over the patient and on the bed, making myself some space to work. I marked the spot I needed by feeling the bones and then said, in Zulu: "Small needle stick."

I pushed the tiny needle in and quickly delivered a small amount of the anesthetic under the skin. The patient started yelling again, pulled away from the needle and straightened his back and legs, sending the orderlies flying.

Rudy said, "John, you will have to sedate him first with some Somnifaine."[5]

The nurse ran to get the drug, while the orderlies regained control of the thrashing patient. They then presented his arm for placement of an IV needle. The nurse gave me an ampoule of fluid. I drew it up into a syringe and then quickly stuck the large needle into a vein and injected the medicine slowly and deliberately. The patient soon began to relax. The orderlies put him back in position and I started all over again with the skin preparation and draping.

"Positioning is everything, John," said Rudy. "He looks right now, so go ahead. Try and point your needle at his navel and feel your way between his spinal bones with the tip. Remember, the sensation of penetrating brown paper tells when you are entering the canal."

I started the procedure again and this time the needle was well tolerated, but I still gave more local anesthetic into the deeper tissues. I was glad I had used both the local anesthetic and the sedation. There could surely be nothing worse than to have a patient bucking with a needle deep into his spine.

I changed to the long thin spinal needle and put this through the anesthetized skin, pushing it carefully inwards, aiming towards the belly button, while trying to keep its path parallel to the floor. I felt bone once or twice and each time pulled back and changed direction slightly. Suddenly, I felt a different type of resistance and then a sort of 'pop' as the needle passed through a thick membrane. This seemed too good to be true and I watched the needle hub anxiously.

An almost clear liquid dripped out of the needle and a drop fell on the white sheet. It was not bloodstained, so the tap was good. I heaved a sigh of relief. I now collected some of the fluid in glass tubes and saw that it was slightly cloudy.[6] I put a few drops on a glass slide for our own staining and microscopic exam. I then connected the needle to a graduated glass tube and watched the fluid rise far up the tube—the CSF pressure was high.[7] The nurse pressed on the man's neck to make him strain and the liquid rose even higher, showing there was no block to flow. I pulled the needle out and placed a Band-Aid on the puncture site. The orderlies now dressed the patient in his pajamas and let him lie free in the bed. The definitive answer would be known once the fluid reached the lab.

"Good job John," Rudy said. "From the look of that fluid he's probably got some form of meningitis, which means we can probably help him."

I went to the side room and performed a Gram stain[8] on the fluid under Rudy's supervision. It showed paired bacteria, as we had expected—meningococci. The Lab soon confirmed our diagnosis of meningococcal meningitis,[9] so I started an IV drip to give large doses of penicillin and support the patient. I added a sulfonamide[10] that was known to affect this germ. The patient started to improve by the next day and was completely rational the day after, but we continued his treatment for two weeks.

My next patient was admitted 'Urgent Direct,' so I wasted no time in getting to see him. The man was barely conscious but could say he had been having terrible diarrhea for a week. His wife gave more history. Others living nearby had developed a similar disease and been admitted to hospital. One child had died. Dr. Gordon came over and listened to the story.

"What do you think he's got, John?" he asked.

"Sounds like Typhoid, Rudy. Have you heard anything from the Health Department?"

"No, but they don't always catch it early. With the neighbors ill, it's probably typhoid. If it's true, we must tell the Department and complete the forms. What must you do now?"

"Examine him fully, send stool to the lab, and take blood for blood count and Widal reaction,"[11] I answered.

As I spoke, I examined the man's abdomen, which appeared to be distended and was excruciatingly tender. The patient yelled and grimaced at the slightest touch.

"Hey Rudy," I called. "Come back and look. I think this guy's perforated his small bowel. They didn't X-ray him in Casualty, so I'll get them down here to do a portable."

Dr. Gordon came over and put a hand gently on the patient's rigid abdomen and shook his head, making clucking noises.

"Poor guy. I think you're right. I'll alert the surgical registrar while the X-ray comes. You'd better start him on some intravenous Chloramphenicol[12] now, anyway."

I asked a probationer nurse for an IV setup and a syringe for drawing blood. I inflated the blood pressure cuff on the man's arm, and found a vein with some difficulty, due to his collapsed state. I then passed a large needle on the end of a syringe into the vein, drew a few tubes of blood and then connected the IV set to the same needle and started running in fluid. I ordered the drug from the pharmacy, and told the charge nurse to give it just as soon as it arrived.

I went to the side room to check the patient list and do the lab work that Dr. Watson required of his house staff as part of the teaching process. The housemen did blood counts and urine exams on all their patients, even though the lab also did them. The side-room tests were done more quickly, often confirming diagnoses and allowing earlier treatment. The discipline also taught the young doctors self-reliance, in case they should practice in a country setting.

But on a busy night the house doctors were often tempted to hold up the urine glass to the light and take a good guess at the results. They knew the lab reports would be there in the morning and with luck they could fudge it. But heaven help anyone that Dr. Watson caught cheating his system. They would get a very cold rebuke on post-intake rounds.

The length of the admission list showed the makings of a bad day. There were already three patients for each houseman, with a wide variety of diagnoses. I counted over ten different conditions among the fifteen admissions. But this was one of my reasons for choosing this job. I planned to do surgery as a career and wanted to have the broadest possible medical training and experience beforehand. I had already done my six months of surgery at the 'Joh'burg Gen' and knew firsthand what the medical housemen there got to see and do. They would not handle one-tenth the number of cases, nor see the great variety of conditions, that we would get to treat at Bara. They would also not obtain a fraction of the 'hands-on' experience. My next six months might be hard, but the end result would be worth it.

I exchanged a few pleasantries with my colleagues, and then went across to the female ward to see my next patient. She also had diarrhea, but this time with blood in the stool and a much more chronic story than the man. I thought immediately of amebic dysentery,[13] due to a parasite in the bowel. I used a short metal proctoscope[14] to look inside the rectum and get a stool sample to examine and send to the lab. I could see the typical ulcers of amebiasis, together with the rather characteristic bloodstained mucus found in these cases. This convinced me that I had the right diagnosis, which I then confirmed in the side room and with a stool exam in the lab. Emetine[15] was the main drug in use at the time. If it failed, a newer drug, Chloroquine, could be tried. I started Emetine immediately.

The surgical registrar came from Ward Five and had a look at my patient with typhoid. The X-rays were back and there was a half-inch wide, curved black line across the top of the abdomen, indicating 'free air' under the diaphragm, which confirmed my diagnosis of perforation. The Registrar arranged for surgery a little later and said they would take over the patient after the operation and put him in their side ward for isolation and intensive care. I had not seen such a case during my surgical house job, and I arranged to be alerted so that I could watch the surgery.

I went up to the theater after supper, changed and entered the operating room. I watched as the surgeon's knife passed cleanly through the layers of the abdominal wall in turn—skin, fat and muscle sheath. Suddenly it entered the peritoneal cavity and a gush of foul-smelling gas emerged, followed by a flood of opaque green fluid and old food particles. The houseman suctioned furiously to try and get the field clean, while the surgeon pulled loops of bright red, highly inflamed small intestine out onto the drapes. The bowel was partly covered in a thick greenish-gray membrane, which he started to pull and rub off with a laparotomy sponge.

"My God, I wish these people would not wait so long to come in," the surgical registrar exclaimed. "How in the world can we do anything with this mess? I guess that's the hand we're dealt. It goes with the territory—working at Bara."

The registrar now found the source of the fluid leak to be a hole near the lower end of the small intestine. He gently applied a small instrument to mark the spot.

"Only twenty more feet to look at," he said.

Using his right hand, the registrar then carefully pulled the entire small bowel through between the fingers of his left hand and flipped the loops back and forth, looking for more holes, but he found none. He then progressively milked the liquid contents along the bowel towards the existing hole, while the houseman repeatedly pushed the sucker tube inside the bowel to help drain the fluid. The entire length of the small intestine gradually collapsed as they worked.

"Emptying the bowel really helps you to close the belly at the end," the registrar said. "I'm sure it also helps their recovery."

The surgeon now started to trim the edges of the hole with fine curved scissors, and then he sewed it together with two layers of sutures, and tied a piece of omentum (fat)[16] over the sutures. He now addressed the housemen and students:

"We always suture bowel crosswise so as not to narrow it. If you have a piece of fat, always tie it on for added safety. The omentum is great, because it would close the hole in nature anyway. It does a wonderful job. Fortunately, he perforated only one of his Peyer's patches.[17] Let's hope the Chloramphenicol does the trick and prevents more trouble."

The surgeon then carefully washed out the peritoneum with saline, put in two drains and started to close with 'tension sutures.'[18] I thanked him and left, having gained some valuable surgical insights.

Back in Ward 24 I found two more patients under my name. The first one had uncomplicated pneumonia, requiring only a quick work-up and intravenous penicillin. Since the housemen had to do all our own IVs and blood drawing at this time, I still had work to do— I spent fifteen minutes there before I could get to the next patient.

The second case was decidedly more complex. The patient gave a history of chronic diarrhea, but had recently become much more ill, with abdominal pain and swelling and shortness of breath. Physical examination showed a large liver, with a big swelling along its lower edge, extending down into the center of the abdomen. His X-rays showed only diffuse grayness in the liver area and perhaps some cardiac enlargement. I thought I knew the answer, but called Rudy Gordon to help. I told the story and showed him the X-rays, then said: "I'm sure he must have a liver abscess from amebiasis,[19] given his chronic diarrhea. I think we should stick a needle into it, or at least, *you* should, Rudy."

"Thanks a lot, John."

Gordon examined the patient and then called for an aspiration tray.[20] He made me scrub with him and we worked together. He injected local anesthetic into the skin and then put a thick, three-inch long needle through the same spot on the abdominal wall and into the large lump we could feel. Gordon drew back on the plunger and out came thick, reddish-gray fluid. This was the so-called 'anchovy sauce pus,'[21] characteristic of amebic liver abscess. That meant our diagnosis was right, and there was hope that the patient could be successfully treated.

"Now it's your turn for glory, John," Gordon said.

He handed the syringe to me and I had to continue the laborious process of emptying the large fluid collection. After I had filled the 20 cc syringe a couple more times, I got smart and changed to one of 50 cc capacity. I drew off another 600 cc of the fluid, (over a pint) before it stopped flowing readily. I felt sure I had most of it. The abdominal swelling was much smaller and the patient said he felt a bit better. The lab now called and confirmed that the patient's stool showed amebae, so I felt good about starting the treatment.

I had three more cases before midnight, when I was scheduled to be off 'early.' One was a re-admission of a chronic heart failure patient with very swollen legs. She had run out of medicine and not taken any for a week. Such cases were not unique to Bara. In hospitals worldwide, patients with CCF[22] who do not take their drugs are among the commonest repeat admissions. I gave her a brief lecture on the subject, and prescribed her treatment. She would spend a few days in hospital, while diuretics drew off the excess fluid and helped to bring her out of failure.

My next case was a skinny old alcoholic with pellagra,[23] a form of severe malnutrition, due to Niacin (vitamin B) deficiency. It was easy to tell, because he had all of the 'Three Ds'—Dementia, Dermatitis and Diarrhea. The characteristic dark peeling rash of sun sensitivity was obvious on his cheeks and in the V of his neckline. A bit of good food, some vitamin B complex and a few days of abstinence would soon have him 'right' (and ready to start drinking again, I suspected).

My last case before bed was also not hard to handle. The man had a chronic cough and weight loss, but his chest X-ray was not definitive and we would need Dr Watson's input on post-intake rounds. The patient would then undergo the work-up we decided on.

I felt bad leaving my two friends to work after midnight, but I would be on duty the next night and needed some sleep. Once my cases were tidied away, I walked the half-mile down to my room, went to bed and started reading about typhoid. I fell asleep with the textbook open on my chest.

Work started early the next morning, with the house doctors and Registrars all there at seven. We were gathering lab reports and seeing all our patients, to be able to talk sense to Dr. Watson on the ward round. I made time to see my typhoid patient in the surgery ward. He was doing remarkably well.

Promptly at 8 a.m. Dr. Watson left his office and came to start the ward rounds. He would methodically see every patient in his wards, with breaks for teatime and an X-ray session before lunch. The house physician who had worked up the patient would present the case to the best of his ability. Questions followed if he or she hesitated or was in doubt. Interesting cases invited more discussion and teaching. My obscure lung case was fully discussed. Dr. Watson's view was that TB was our most common diagnosis and therefore the most likely.

"If in doubt, call it TB and treat it as such," was one of his favorite sayings.

"What about sarcoid?"[24] boomed Hal Sender, the other registrar.

"Of course we must think of that," Watson answered. "Would you like to get the surgeons to do a scalene node[25] biopsy?"

I wrote out a consultation card to be given to the surgical unit at teatime. Rounds continued, with a wide variety of cases having been admitted, things that doctors in other places could only read about. The list included ascites,[26] scurvy,[27] beri beri,[28] schistosomiasis[29] and neuropathic foot.[30] There were several diabetics who had been admitted in coma and had given their housemen and the registrars a load of trouble. There was one patient with a hypertensive stroke and several others with congestive heart failure and many with pneumonia. All of them were discussed as being of equal merit and interest.

I proudly showed my patient with amebic liver abscess and Dr. Watson was suitably impressed. The man said he felt slightly better, but he was still plainly breathless. When I had finished talking, Dr. Watson stayed at the foot of the man's bed for a long time, just looking at him. He finally spoke: "Dr. Hunt, look at his neck veins."

"They're up sir," I answered in a few seconds.

"How big is his heart?"

I could not find the apex beat[31] so I 'percussed out'[32] the heart outline, by placing my left middle finger on the chest and tapping it repeatedly with my right long finger. I moved my finger slowly to the left, repeating the tapping each time. A change in the sounds located the heart border. The area with a dull 'percussion note' was far bigger than usual—the heart was much enlarged. I marked the border with a pen for all to see.

"Now apply a blood pressure cuff, inflate it, make him breathe, and tell me what you find," Watson said.

I inflated the cuff three times and deflated it slowly each time, making the patient take some deep breaths. The first time I felt the pulse at the wrist while the cuff deflated. The second time I placed a stethoscope over the brachial artery at the elbow and listened carefully. Then I checked my findings.

"The blood pressure varies with his breathing," I said. "It's ten points lower when he breathes in. That must be 'pulsus paradoxus'[33]— I've never seen it before."

"Give me your new diagnosis."

"He has a pericardial effusion, sir."

"Yes, I agree. He has all the classic signs, as you have so ably demonstrated. But *why* does he have the effusion?"

"Aren't those we see mostly due to TB?" I replied.

"True, but this one isn't. Try and think of only one disease at a time. There's no need to invoke TB, though I know that people often do have two or more diseases together. I'm sure that liver abscess you and Dr. Gordon drained yesterday probably also burst upwards through his diaphragm, into his pericardium. That's why he is still so breathless and ill, his veins are up and his pulse is alternating. I am sure that after tea, Dr. Gordon would like to show us all how to drain an amebic abscess of the pericardium. He may even like to write it up in a journal later. These cases are fairly rare, even at Baragwanath.

"You see Dr. Hunt, Medicine is really quite logical and sensible. You just have to be aware of the possibilities and use the senses that God gave you," Dr. Watson said, not unkindly.

The legendary depth of my chief's clinical abilities always astonished me.

We broke for tea and trooped up the corridor together, chatting animatedly. In the large break room were many round tables with white linen tablecloths. Different groups of doctors and students were already sitting at each one. Dr. Watson led our group to the large open counter window and we helped ourselves to tea and plates full of small English-style 'tea' sandwiches, which we took back to an empty table. Dr. Watson took his usual number of sandwiches. He was a severe 'brittle' diabetic. Keeping his blood sugar under tight control required that he ate correctly and at defined times. He was very careful to do this, consuming his exact quota of sandwiches at the same time every day.

Our unit got to know each other a little better after the hard work of the day before. Hal Sender, an extremely bright, academically oriented doctor, got into a fairly heated discussion with Dr. Watson on some esoteric subject and had to be quieted by Rudy. The house doctors exchanged a few consultation cards with other units. Sender started a new discussion on the need for 'one man one vote.' He had decidedly leftist views for South Africa at that time. Before the conversation could get too heated, Dr. Watson called the team back to the ward.

Our first duty and pleasure was to watch Dr. Gordon very carefully stick a needle into the pericardial sac[34] of our patient. This he did from the abdominal side, below the rib cage. He pointed his needle upwards to get into the sac from below, aiming to miss the heart in the process. He hit the right spot, and the familiar grayish red fluid came into the syringe. This time he kept hold of the syringe himself and carefully went on with multiple exchanges until he had withdrawn eighty cc of fluid and the flow slowed down appreciably. He withdrew the needle and placed a Band-Aid on the puncture site.

"He should get a whole lot better with that out of there," said Dr. Gordon. "We can always come back later if he needs it. In any event, the drug should take care of it in a few days."

"Good show, Rudy," Dr. Watson said.

We finished the ward round in the same way as before and split into two groups to do the female ward. Then it was the X-ray session to discuss the unit's cases before lunch. Sitting in the dark with the pictures on the screen, the droning voice of the radiologist sent several of us to sleep, a not unknown situation with overworked house staff anywhere. This lasted until Dr. Watson directed a question at one of the offenders, who promptly started paying more attention.

After about thirty minutes, however, Watson started to mumble and lose his concentration. He shook himself, reached in his pocket, found his supply of sugar tablets and chewed two of them. The registrars carried on with discussion of the X-rays until their chief's blood sugar returned to normal. Dr. Watson apologized to us and soon ended the session.

After lunch in the mess, the afternoon presented the opportunity to tidy up and do the chores resulting from the night and the ward round. The other housemen all passed on details of their sick patients to me before quietly escaping to bed, or at least to home.

I did complete rounds with the charge nurses in both wards, telling them of any major problems, and then went down to my room for a nap before supper. It was midwinter, with early sunset, so there was no time or inclination for sport in the afternoon. After supper in the mess I gossiped for a while with the other on-duty housemen, then returned to my room to read up on the more interesting cases of the day. Suddenly the phone rang.

"Doctor Hunt, Gabriel is in trouble again—he can't breathe and he's coughing up blood."

I had heard from the departing housemen that no night was complete without seeing Gabriel. They had shared the treatments that had worked best for his attacks. I was prepared.

"I'm coming, Staff Nurse. Please have the four blood pressure cuffs available now."

I threw on my shoes and white coat and ran out of the room. To save time I took my car for the short distance. I rushed into the ward and found the patient.

Gabriel was indeed purple and panting for breath and plainly scared out of his wits. Frothy pink-stained foam was coming from his mouth. It was a truly impressive sight. I listened to his chest with a stethoscope and heard the characteristic loud crackling and bubbling sounds of fluid-filled lungs. I could not hear the loud cardiac valve murmurs the man was known to have. Gabriel was in the throes of a severe attack of pulmonary edema—fluid backing up in the lungs.

"Cuffs please, Staff Nurse," I asked. "And get me some Somni-faine and Lasix."

She sent a junior nurse for the drugs, while she and I applied the cuffs to the tops of all four limbs. We inflated them to above the venous pressure, but below the arterial level and then clamped off the tubes so that the air did not leak out. These measures would have the effect of trapping blood in the limbs for a while and giving the heart and lungs a chance to 'catch up.'

The nurse returned with syringes and the medication. The staff nurse and I drew up the medicines into syringes. I took the one with Lasix and placed the needle easily into a vein. I made sure it was securely in place and then let down the cuff above it while I injected the drug. I gave the Somnifaine rather slowly through the same needle.

Gabriel was settling down a bit by this stage, no longer frothing at the mouth. I listened to his chest and found it was a little better. I took out the needle and placed a tight dressing to stop the bleeding. I let the staff nurse deflate another cuff while I inflated the one where I had been working. We went on alternately deflating and inflating cuffs until Gabriel settled down entirely. We then slowly let the cuffs down, one by one. The patient stayed out of trouble and was clearly far less anxious. He gave me a weak smile.

I knew the patient had severe rheumatic heart disease affecting several valves, but even Dr. Watson could not explain why he did this just about every night. He had expressed the hope that the new facilities for cardiac surgery might offer Gabriel relief from some of his problems. The attacks were so severe that the only way they could be controlled was by using the cuffs to temporarily keep some fluid away from the struggling central lung circulation. There was clearly an emotional element to this. I had gone through all the motions as prescribed and was delighted and surprised to see the patient's rapid response.

I then did another brief survey of the ward, answered a few questions and returned to my room. This time I would try and get some sleep, as I had heard bad tales about the night shift, who would come on at eleven p.m. I soon dropped off and slept for a few hours, until about one a.m., when the phone rang. It was a new voice to me.

"Doctor, the patient in bed 32 on the verandah has changed condition."

"How has he changed, Staff Nurse?" I asked sleepily.

"Doctor, he seems not to be breathing right."

"I'm coming, Nurse."

It was bitterly cold on a bright moonlit highveld winter's night. I slung my raincoat over my white coat and pajamas and flew up to the ward. I followed the nurse to the bed on the verandah. There lay one of our old chronic patients, motionless, cold and stiff with rigor mortis. He must have been dead for a couple of hours at least.

"He is *dead*, Nurse. Did you not know that? Anyway, just bring me the death certificate." I did not see any point in getting mad or chastising her, as I knew she could make my life miserable with repeated calls. I signed the form and left, vowing not to be caught again into rushing over to save a corpse.

The next time I was on duty, a similar phone call came after midnight.

"In what way has the patient changed condition, Nurse?" I asked.

"He is not breathing, Doctor."

"That's bad. Is his heart beating, Nurse?"

"No Doctor, that seems to be the problem."

"Then, Nurse, I think he is dead."

"Hau Doctor! Don't say that!"

"Yes, Nurse, he is dead. Call your nursing supervisor and ask her advice. I will come if she says so. Otherwise I will sign the certificate in the morning."

I went back to sleep, pleased to have learned another Bara trick.

Each of the House Physicians had to spend about a month looking after the TB ward. Dr. Watson did his own rounds there daily. The pace of progress was slow, the patients often being kept in to make sure they took their drugs. Once a month every patient had an ESR test done by the doctors personally. Blood was set up in calibrated ESR tubes, and the rate at which the red cells sank to the bottom was measured. This was the Erythrocyte Sedimentation Rate. It correlated well with disease progress, falling as the patients improved. The test remains valid to this day for some diseases and as a non-specific indicator of 'sick' versus 'non-sick.'

Tuberculosis causes cavities to form in the lungs. These contain bacteria and cause the patients to be infectious to others by coughing up infected sputum. Dr. Watson used 'collapse therapy' to control this. Patients with cavities in one lung had the lung collapsed by the injection of air into the pleural space, similar to the effect of a stab wound. The doctor in charge of the unit had to refill their pneumothoraces[35] whenever the amount of air decreased too much on X-ray. This involved sticking in a needle attached to a special machine to inject the right amount of air.

By a combination of double or triple drug therapy, Streptomycin, PAS and Isoniazid, many patients were declared cured after many months. They were finally discharged on PAS and Isoniazid as outpatients. Collapse of the lung helped cure many others. Complete failure to eradicate cavities or large 'tuberculomas'[36] sometimes led to surgery to remove the disease.

Dr. Watson loved his TB patients and was quite dedicated to their care.

I thoroughly enjoyed my six months in Dr Watson's unit at Baragwanath hospital, regarding it as the best possible foundation for my career. Seven years later, I returned to Baragwanath as a fully trained specialist surgeon, and as luck would have it, I came to work in Unit Five, with Dr. Watson's unit as my medical opposite number.

[1] Strep throat: A sore throat due to the streptococcus organism. Before the advent of penicillin and adequate antibiotic treatment, this condition caused a host of serious consequences. These included rheumatic fever, with severe heart valve damage, 'St. Vitus' Dance' (chorea,) glomerulonephritis (severe kidney disease), puerperal sepsis ('Childbed Fever'), and several others. Scarlet fever is an allergic type of reaction to the same germ. All have become preventable by the timely use of penicillin or other suitable antibiotics. The conquest of this organism is one of the more important and dramatic changes in health care caused by antibiotics.

[2] Murmur and thrill: Rheumatic heart disease produced severe damage to one or more heart valves, causing either narrowing (stenosis), or widening (incompetence) of the opening. The heart then labored at a disadvantage, trying to maintain adequate blood flow. Flow through the damaged valves became 'turbulent,' causing a loud noise that could be heard with a stethoscope, and a 'thrill,' which could be felt with the hand. Much teaching time was devoted to the diagnosis of these conditions by finding these physical signs.

[3] LP Tray: Lumbar puncture = 'spinal tap.' The equipment for this examination was packed on a tray, sterile and under a green cloth cover. Sterilization was done in a central hospital unit and the wards fetched them as needed. The unit of intake kept several such trays on hand.

[4] Yo: An expression of shock and pain. Pronounced as in your.

[5] Somnifaine: A strong intravenous sedative drug. A proprietary drug, precursor to Valium, made by the same company.

[6] Cloudy spinal fluid: CSF (see below, #s 7&9) should be clear like water, and have no blood. Cloudiness suggests infection of some kind. The fluid is sent to the lab for cell counts, stains for bacteria and a variety of other tests. In Dr. Watson's unit housemen did their own staining in the side ward for immediate results.

[7] CSF pressure: Cerebrospinal fluid pressure. This is measured very carefully, together with the Queckenstedt test for a block to flow between the brain and the needle lower down. This is all important diagnostic data.

[8] Gram stain: A basic way of differentiating between germs. Two stains are used, a red and a blue one. The germs either stain red or blue—Gram negative or Gram positive. The stain also shows the shapes of the bacteria and how they relate to each other—in clumps, pairs or chains, for example. So this first test gives a huge amount of data—enough to start 'presumptive treatment.'

[9] Meningococcal meningitis: A frequently fatal disease, spread rapidly by close contact, as under dormitory living conditions. It is a bacterial infection of the softer membranes surrounding the brain and the spinal cord.

[10] Sulfonamide drug: This class of drugs preceded the true antibiotics, such as penicillin. They were, and still are, effective against a number of bacterial infections, but antibiotics have largely displaced them. It has been said that if they had been introduced after antibiotics they would have been considered a greater advance!

[11] Widal reaction: A serological blood test for typhoid infection.

[12] Chloramphenicol: One of the first antibiotics, with a broader spectrum of use than penicillin. The only successful drug against typhoid at that time. Has some specific dangers, so should not be used for long periods or for trivial reasons.

[13] Dysentery: Bloody diarrhea. Broadly divided into that caused by parasites, such as the ameba, and those caused by bacteria. See # 19 below.

[14] Proctoscope: A short metal tube with a light, used to look inside the rectum. A longer one is called a sigmoidoscope and could also have been used.

[15] Emetine and Chloroquine: Two drugs effective against parasites, but not in the same class as antibiotics. Chloroquine is also used for malaria, which is also due to a parasite in the blood stream.

[16] Omental fat: Fat from the omentum, a sheet of tissue that hangs down like an apron inside the abdomen and actually wanders round looking for trouble. It sticks to any spots where there are problems, such as perforations of bowel, and seals them. It is very useful to surgeons for reinforcing and sealing things in the abdomen. It has many other uses in modern reconstructive surgery.

[17] Peyer's patches: Small patches of lymphoid tissue in the small bowel, where typhoid bacteria collect. The patches tend to perforate when infected by typhoid.

[18] Tension sutures: Very strong sutures used in infected wounds to act as a second layer of defense in the closure of the wound. 'Suspenders and a belt.'

[19] Amebiasis: An infection with *entamoeba histolytica*, a parasite, which infects the bowel, but may go elsewhere in the body. See Dysentery, above #13.

[20] Aspiration tray: Like an LP tray, pre-sterilized and packed to have all that was needed to remove a lot of fluid from some part of the body.

[21] Anchovy sauce pus: A colloquial medical term derived from the reddish-gray color of the pus. Typical for amebic liver abscess.

[22] CCF: Congestive cardiac failure (British terminology) = CHF or congestive heart failure in the USA.

[23] Pellagra: A severe form of malnutrition due to lack of niacin, a B group vitamin. Worse in alcoholics who can't afford both drink and food.

[24] Sarcoidosis: A chronic granulomatous disease of unknown cause, resembling and often confused with Tuberculosis. In the lungs it may produce tiny little nodules, like the miliary form of TB.

[25] Scalene node biopsy: The scalene lymph nodes lie low in the neck, very close to the lung. A biopsy of one of these nodes could often give the correct diagnosis in lung diseases like sarcoid or cancer.

[26] Ascites: Fluid in the abdomen, usually due to severe liver disease. Often present in huge amounts, rendering the patient almost incapable of moving around.

[27] Scurvy: Vitamin C deficiency, due to lack of fresh fruit and vegetables. Interestingly, this disease is the reason that the Dutch first settled at the Cape of Good Hope. Mortality from scurvy on Dutch ships going to the East was up to fifty percent of crewmembers per trip. Fresh fruit and vegetables from the Cape completely changed the outlook.

28 Beri-Beri: Severe vitamin deficiency of thiamine—VitaminB1. Causes severe swelling of the legs and heart problems.

29 Schistosomiasis: Also known as Bilharzia, after Dr. Bilharz. Due to a parasite with a complex life cycle, from water to snails to man. Causes urinary bleeding and a unique cirrhosis of the liver.

30 Neuropathic foot: Otherwise known colloquially at Bara as 'vrot voet'—Afrikaans for 'rotten foot' (due to the terrible appearance and evil smell.) Usually associated with chronic alcohol abuse, causing severe degeneration of the nerves to the feet. Patients could not feel damage to their feet and severe infection followed.

31 Apex beat: The maximum cardiac impulse. Can usually be felt between the ribs at a certain point on the chest wall. Finding it will give an idea of heart size.

32 Percussion note, dullness and resonance: A basic physical sign. One finger is placed over the area in question. Percussing it with another finger gives a sound—dull for liquid or solid, resonant for air. Hence used for finding the heart outline. It can confirm fluid at the base of the lung, or in the belly, and has many more uses.

33 Pulsus paradoxus: Found with a pericardial effusion or collection of fluid round the heart. The cardiac output decreases temporarily during inspiration. Significant if there is over 10 mm. of difference between blood pressures taken during inspiration and expiration.

34 Pericardial sac: The membrane that surrounds the heart, allowing it to beat freely inside. In this case the liver abscess had burst from just below the diaphragm into this sac, which lay just above it. The fluid was now compressing and embarrassing the heart.

35 Pneumothorax: Air in the pleural space. Plural is pneumothoraces.

36 Tuberculoma: A large collection of infectious tuberculous material or 'caseation.' This was soft cheese-like material, hence the name.

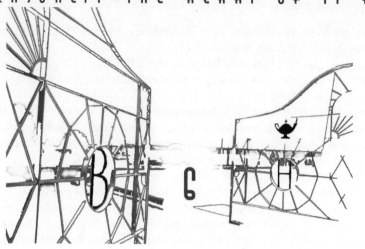

The Casualty Department or Emergency Room (E.R.) is the heart and soul of a good hospital. It never dies. The beat goes on, day and night, slowing at times and speeding up to bursting at others. Always it sends the fruits of its labor to nourish the rest of the hospital. Good Casualty officers and nurses are worth more than their weight in gold. They help the public and also protect the hospital and its reputation. Bad ones quickly ruin the place; they create chaos in the wards and areas like X-ray. Because of the arduous work, 'burn-out' in Casualty personnel is rapid, causing high staff turnover and scarcity of good people.

To help solve these problems the Transvaal Provincial Administration created part-time positions for Casualty officers to 'moonlight' in all its hospitals. Any registered doctor who needed extra money could fill these posts. Since provincial hospital salaries were far from princely, full-timers from other departments or hospitals often did such 'Casualty sessions' in their spare time. Many private practitioners and other doctors became involved. Such part-timers were an indispensable source of Casualty Department staffing.

I did more than my share of work in various Casualty departments around Johannesburg. This started 18 months after graduation, while I was teaching anatomy at the medical school, and preparing to go to Britain for surgical training. This work fulfilled my requirements for 'Casualty time,' needed to write the London F.R.C.S. exam.

After my return from the U.K. and throughout my life at Bara, whenever some new family need arose, such as money for a new car or private school fees, I added a few more 'sessions' to my busy schedule. I could thus keep faith with myself in my desire to serve the people of Baragwanath and Soweto and also to remain in the academic sphere, where I loved the teaching and research. I would have greatly missed these activities if I had gone into the busy private practice of surgery. I continued with this 'moonlighting' during my entire career in South Africa as a full-time surgeon. After doing many years of 'sessions,' my memories of the various Casualty departments became inextricably interwoven with those of my surgical work in the 'Pit' and 'Resuscitation Room.'

My Casualty experiences in fact started before I was registered as a doctor, in the December of my houseman year, while working for Dr. Watson. All Baragwanath house doctors at that time had to spend a month of their six-month term working in Casualty. This was due to the ever-increasing patient load at Bara coupled with an acute shortage of Casualty officers. The 'session' solution to the staffing problem had not yet been devised.

The housemen allocated to Casualty were fairly happy with this arrangement because we could double up our shifts and by shrewd planning and cooperation we could rewrite the duty roster. We each wangled extra time off during the December holiday season. I arranged a whole week away, but the other three weeks were hell. I could make good use of the week, since I had just met Ann, the young woman who was to become my wife.

On my first day in Casualty I saw a sea of patients, all sitting in rows facing my small examination room. I had to go on working as long as anyone was there. Since the people kept on filling up from the back, I couldn't imagine an end to the task. I saw one of my surgical houseman colleagues working close by and realized there might be some hope. I was delighted to find that there was even more help near at hand. Registrars from medicine, surgery and gynecology had also been seconded to Casualty in order to offer immediate specialized advice and help to both Casualty officers and housemen. They also prevented unnecessary admissions to the overfull wards. Specialty support and consultation for unusual cases was thus quick, easy and informal. A brief note on the Casualty card was enough. The interpreters and nurses directed the patients to the right physicians.

Our group of young doctors dealt with the bulk of the 1,000 and more patients a day that came to Bara for treatment. We did the triage,[1] made full diagnoses, prescribed treatment, made referrals and generally got the patients started on their way to healing. We rarely saw the patients a second time, so it was important to be as accurate as possible. If our admission criteria were too stringent, patients could become worse or die. But doctors who were too lenient could create havoc in the wards with unnecessary admissions.

My chief ally was Mary, the interpreter assigned to my room. She was a multi-talented person with years of Casualty experience. Mary had been a domestic servant in white households and had learned to speak several of the eleven languages used in South Africa, enabling her to get this job. She spoke fluent English and Afrikaans, together with her native Xhosa, Zulu and Swazi. She had a working knowledge of Sotho and its variants. Her pay at Baragwanath was far better than she had received as a servant and it allowed her to live with her family in a proper home in Soweto. She could also educate her children and keep them in school—a major aim of most black people with whom I worked. With her sharp mind and long experience, Mary could diagnose many common conditions herself. She did this just by seeing the patient walk in and asking a few questions.

But my first case baffled her. This was a young, slender woman with an almost black skin, characteristic of her tribe—she was a Shangaan from the far northern Transvaal. None of the Casualty interpreters or nurses could understand the Shangaan language and the patient did not speak any other. So Mary found another solution. She went to fetch help, leaving a student nurse to assist me. I dealt with the next patient while she was gone.

Mary returned with a huge, dark-skinned, boiler room attendant in blue overalls, with greasy cotton waste stuffed in his pockets. A friendly man, he spoke both Shangaan and Zulu, so he could work with Mary. I asked a question and Mary asked the man in Zulu and made sure he understood. He then addressed the patient in their language and she replied. The attendant gave the answer in Zulu to Mary, who translated it to English for me. We repeated this cumbersome process until I could make a diagnosis.

Through this four-way conversation, we managed to extract from the shy and unsophisticated country girl that she had a gynecological complaint. She was having irregular menstruation, with continued severe vaginal bleeding for a few weeks. Her menses had previously been quite regular. This sounded to me as if she had undergone an incomplete abortion. Rather than putting the patient through two pelvic examinations, I sent her straight to the gynecology registrar, with her big personal interpreter in tow. Mary told me later that my diagnosis had been correct. The patient was admitted for a D. & C.[2]

The more 'normal' cases then started coming in—heart failure, chronic cough, swollen abdomen, malnutrition; each one apparently at a more advanced stage of disease than the one before. I could treat most patients myself, with referrals to one of the Outpatient clinics for follow-up. I referred others to the registrars for consultation or admission.

The registrars were also overloaded, often trying to shunt cases that were not clearly in their specialties to other departments. On one occasion the 'surgical registrar,' who was an orthopedic surgery trainee, sent a case to his medical colleague as 'Pain in the shoulder.' Some hours later, after an X-ray, the very sharp medical registrar was pleased to return the patient with just as brief a note—*Medical Registrar's opinion*: Fracture dislocation of the shoulder. See X-rays. The medicine department crowed about that case for days.

A few years later the same quiet, unassuming medical registrar scored a world first. He and his medical chief described the hitherto unknown complication of diabetes called 'Hyperosmolar coma.'[3] This was one of the many fine contributions made by Baragwanath Hospital doctors to the international medical literature.

Our next patient was a young man.

"What's the matter?" I asked.

"Where do you hurt?" Mary asked in Zulu.

"I didn't say that, Mary," I said. "Not everyone has pain."

"I know, Doctor, but if I say that he will tell me. There are no words to say it better." But she asked again in a slightly different way.

"Drop," the man replied.

"Show me," I asked.

The patient unbuttoned his pants and with no hesitation or embarrassment he squeezed his penis, producing a creamy white 'drop' of pus.

I knew the most likely diagnosis was gonorrhea,[4] with syphilis[5] as a probable 'fellow traveler.' The most medically effective and cost-efficient treatment was to use enough penicillin to cure both diseases together. Then I need not waste money on tests for the diagnosis. It would be wrong to give only sufficient penicillin to treat the gonorrhea, which required far less of the antibiotic. If the 'drop' went away after a small dose of the drug, this could hide the underlying syphilis, which was a much more silent, sneaky and dangerous disease. So I ordered a large shot of long-acting penicillin into each buttock. Mary told the patient to return for follow up. With that treatment, it didn't really matter if he failed to come back—both diseases would be cured—until next time.

One day I saw a sixteen-year-old girl with an obviously bulging abdomen.

"Pregnant?" I asked.

"No, doctor," she said, in English. "That's what they told me last year, but there has been no baby. I can't be pregnant because I have not been with a man. They wouldn't believe me last time, so I went away. My stomach is now *much bigger* than before."

"Does it hurt you?" I asked.

"No, Doctor, it's just *too big*. I can nearly not walk."

Mary helped her get onto the couch and exposed her abdomen. I saw a huge bulge, far larger than a full-term pregnancy. It was firm, smooth and perfectly round, filling her whole belly, from pelvis to ribs. It was even expanding her rib cage. As she was rather slim and small, the swelling made her look grotesque. She couldn't lie flat on her back because the lump flopped over to one side or the other, pulling her small body with it.

I made Mary put her own open hand on edge along the middle of the patient's abdomen. I put my left hand flat against the left side of the swelling and used my right middle finger to flick the right side of the lump a few times. Each time I felt a marked 'fluid thrill'[6] with my left hand. We could actually see the waves travel across her belly.

My diagnosis was *giant ovarian cyst*. The patient seemed too healthy to have *ascites* (free fluid) in the abdomen, the only other possible diagnosis. Because of her youth and small size, I did not do a pelvic exam. It would probably add nothing. The uterus would be normal and perhaps only displaced up or down by the cyst. So I took the patient to the gynecology registrar and watched him examine her and confirm the diagnosis. I later learned that at surgery the cyst held six liters (1½ gallons) of fluid and was quite benign. I decided to visit the patient in the gynecology ward before discharge. Her abdomen was really flat; in fact it was quite hollow. She was overjoyed with the result.

"You are a clever doctor," she said.

I met my future wife, Ann, during the month I was doing my Casualty stint. She came through Casualty one day to meet me and go for lunch in the mess. Her youth, slender figure, red hair and ready smile got many admiring glances. She was in advertising and had no medical background, so this was a new experience. It was Saturday and the place was busy so I could not leave immediately.

Ann sat nearby, quietly watching the proceedings. The patients moved slowly and patiently sideways along the benches until it was their turn to see a doctor. She watched and wondered about a man who seemed to have a humpback or some other deformity, because the back of his shirt was bulging. He finally reached the head of the line.

"What's your problem?" I asked.

The patient turned round and flipped up the back of his shirt, to reveal a huge carving knife stuck in his chest, next to the spine. Only a short length of the blade near the handle was still showing outside his chest.

"Only at Baragwanath," I said. "I wonder why he's still alive."

I took the patient to show the surgical registrar and get an X-ray. It was a sight neither of us would easily forget and one Ann often mentioned in future years. I have always felt very fortunate that she was so understanding and supportive of me and my profession. She would certainly spend a lot of time alone, bringing up the children virtually on her own—the fate of many doctors' wives. Without a happy home, life would have been intolerable.

At lunch we met a number of other doctors and the duty radiographer, Cathy, who was dating one of my colleagues and was soon to be married. There was the usual chitchat going on. Suddenly we heard a new switchboard operator talking over the P.A. system. He spoke clearly but his pronunciation made him a little hard to understand.

"The radiograapher has lorst a leetle yellow bed. Would anyone having seen such bed please report to the radiograapher," he said.

"Cathy, what's up? How did you lose your bed? Why is it yellow?" everyone hooted.

"It's my canary! That's the little yellow bird. He escaped and we can't find him."

Everyone had a good laugh and wished her well in the search.

The doctors started to talk about medical topics, forgetting Ann's presence, something she soon learned about the medical profession. But she was interested and didn't seem to mind too much. A staff nurse in one of the wards had died of a penicillin allergy the night before.

"That must be terribly rare," one of the housemen said. "Think how many millions of penicillin injections we dish out in Casualty and the wards."

"Well, this one was for real," answered another. "This was a senior staff nurse, who said to a probationer nurse "I'm allergic to penicillin. I wonder what will happen if I take a tablet instead of an injection?" Well, she went ahead and took it. She dropped dead in the ward, on duty and in front of her terrified junior, who told us the story."

That account raised a stir, and then I said: "Allergy is not a funny subject. Cathy, I know you're very allergic to shellfish. I'm personally allergic to both procaine[7] and bee stings. I nearly died once after a bee sting at my mother's home in Vereeniging, when my airway started to close off. The family took me to the small local hospital. They had to call in the Casualty doctor from his home. Before he arrived the charge nurse went to supper and said to the untrained orderly: "'If he can't breathe, give him some oxygen.'

"I don't know how she thought it would get through my laryngeal edema. I kept having visions of that doctor in Welkom who died of bee stings. Fortunately, the Casualty doctor soon arrived and gave me an intravenous steroid shot, which quickly opened my airway. But that was a shaky time."

Ann had the option of going to my room and waiting several hours for my shift to finish or going to the pool. With a quick goodbye, she chose instead to return home and meet up with me in the evening.

Back in Casualty a far bigger crowd was waiting. The doctors were fully occupied and the trauma victims were starting to arrive. I went to a patient on a stretcher, since they were usually the worst cases. The man was drinking in a Shebeen the week before and woke up next day on the ground outside. He got home by taxi, but felt bad and stayed in bed next day, unable to go to work. Day by day he felt worse, with increasing abdominal pain and swelling. He stopped passing urine, became alarmed and came to hospital.

He was dehydrated, with low blood pressure and a racing pulse. His belly was very distended and tender. I diagnosed a 'ruptured viscus'[8] (a general term for any organ burst open). I sent the man straight to the surgical registrar, who agreed with my opinion, even though the X-rays did not show the 'free gas'[9] often expected with that diagnosis.

The patient went immediately to the theater for exploration. He was found to have a rupture at the lower end of the bladder, with a belly full of urine. This explained the unusual presentation, and the lack of gas on X-ray, since the bladder contains no gas. The tear must have come from a kick or some other injury inflicted in his drunken state, probably with an overfull bladder. The alcohol prevented him from remembering the event.

The admitting clerk typed his own original version of my generic diagnosis on the addressograph. But he was more specific. He typed 'fractured piscus'. A colleague later kidded me about the diagnosis and gave me one of the stickers, saying: "John, the clerk is smarter than you are. He got it right without seeing the patient."

"Thanks for the news," I replied. "I'll keep the sticker among my treasures."

I became aware of a foul smell, becoming ever stronger. It was midway between a public toilet and a sewage disposal works. I turned to the interpreter and asked: "What *is* that dreadful smell?"

"It's that man over there, doctor—he is a Baca."[10]

"How in the world do you know his tribe, you haven't even spoken to him. What's the matter with him anyway? Why does he smell so bad?"

"I know his tribe, doctor, because of the smell and his long rubber boots. It is said that years ago the Chief of the Bacas went to

Queen Victoria and asked her for an easy job for his people. She granted them the task of working with the 'night soil' or sewage. Since then the Bacas have done that job, and they do it to this day. At one time they had to empty the pails from open toilets or help to empty tanks of sewage. There are still many open toilets in outhouses in Soweto. They also empty the dustbins, clean the public toilets and work on the sewage farms. So the Bacas always wear these rubber boots. And they stink!"

I went over and dealt with the man at arm's length. Happily, he had a rather mundane problem, which could be handled with a simple order written on the Casualty card. The Casualty staff and the other patients were delighted to see him finally on his way.

My next patient was sitting quietly in a wheelchair, but having some difficulty breathing. His legs were markedly swollen. The sun-exposed skin on his face and limbs was an unhealthy dark granular black color, not glossy at all. He told the interpreter he was weak and breathless and could barely walk a few yards. This had been getting worse for quite a while. On direct questioning, he confessed to some years of heavy drinking. He had been to a witchdoctor and other white doctors, with no real improvement.

During my examination I found the man had swollen veins in the neck, excess fluid in the belly and a big liver. His heartbeat was rapid and his lung bases sounded wet. As I examined the heart, I found that the witchdoctor had already been there and had correctly marked the 'apex beat.'[11] It was well to the left of normal, indicating a very large heart.

These 'witchdoctor marks' were small straight scratches, with tiny scabs already formed, arranged in a radiating rosette formation around the spot where the tip of the heart could be seen pulsating between the ribs. The witchdoctor also found the abdominal fluid and placed a similar row of marks around the swollen abdomen. All the scratches appeared healthy.

But I became worried and made the man remove his shoes. I found that the witchdoctor had been active there as well. There were scratch marks over the worst of the swelling, extending right round both ankles. But these were oozing and infected. I thought that might present a definite problem. I would admit the patient for his heart failure, so the infected scratches could at least be treated in the ward at that time.

Based on the classical physical signs, I made a diagnosis of congestive cardiac failure.[12] I thought it was due to 'alcoholic cardiomyopathy,'[13] because of the man's alcohol history, dark complexion and lack of heart valve murmurs or hypertension. The blackened skin came from his drinking, since traditional Bantu beer was often brewed in tin-coated iron containers. The acid brew removed the tin coating and the exposed iron rusted and leached into the beer.

Heavy drinkers thus took in much more iron than their bodies could handle and built up iron deposits or 'siderosis,' especially in the skin and liver. This often produced severe liver damage. The condition of 'hemosiderosis' was the subject of much research in Johannesburg. Since I had just finished doing five months of medicine, I was confident enough in my diagnosis to justify admitting the patient directly to a medical ward. But out of courtesy I sent the man first to the medical registrar via the X-ray department.

As I went to the break room that day, I thought about the witchdoctor, who had found the site of the man's problems, but was unable to do anything meaningful about them. In the last century, an English doctor named Southey had tried to drain fluid from the swollen legs of patients with edema,[14] using small rubber tubes inserted under the skin. I felt the witchdoctor was not far off the mark with his cuts, which plainly drained some fluid. But I knew that both alcohol abuse and cardiomyopathy were notoriously difficult to treat. I wondered if Bara could do much better than the witchdoctor.

In the tearoom at the back of Casualty all kinds of ideas and topics were always being discussed. Much cross-fertilization of minds occurred, since the part-timers were from a variety of medical disciplines and of many ethnic groups. I got to know some of the regulars pretty well. The roster was made up in advance and people only gave up the 'good,' or less busy, sessions with reluctance. There were always many takers. As I grew more senior in the service I managed to get some reasonable sessions, but others were still at peak drinking times or at late hours.

Once a week I worked with an older diabetic Asian doctor who had a practice near Soweto. We had many a long talk during slack periods over the front desk or in the tearoom. One quiet night this doctor asked me for a favor: "John, they told me that if I was circumcised my sex life would be better. Well, I had it done and let it heal. But it's a lot worse now. Can you put it back for me the way it was?"

I thought quietly for a few moments before answering, trying to hide my amusement at the poor man's plight.

"I'm really sorry, Ishmael, there's just no way to do that," I replied. "The skin has gone, together with the nerve endings, which gave you sexual sensation. You now have much less skin, so much less sexual feeling. No one can put it back. It's really unfortunate. Maybe you should see a urologist or a diabetes specialist. The urology people handle such problems all the time."

Soon after that, my unit was on intake and I went over to help out in Casualty at a particularly busy time. A man brought in his teenage son, who had been up in a thorn tree and slipped, sliding down the trunk. His crotch got caught on a thorny branch that tore the skin covering off his penis. The piece of skin was left in the tree. The father retrieved it and now opened a small paper bag, displaying the dirty and ragged piece of tissue.

"Can Doctor fix it?" he asked.

I examined the boy, who was writhing in pain, and ordered him some sedation. His penis had been stripped bare and showed a bloody white shaft, in stark contrast to his brown skin and scanty black pubic hair. Since I was the surgeon on intake, I had to find a way to repair the damage.

"I will do what I can," I replied. "The skin is too dirty to put back. I might have to do a skin graft and take some skin from his leg to patch it up. Do you know what that is?"

The man said he did not. I explained it to him through the nurses and the interpreter. He then agreed to the procedure for his son.

In the operating room I took the dirty piece of skin and scrubbed it thoroughly with various solutions, but it was bruised and mangled and looked terrible. I thought it would be better to prepare the thighs for a skin graft, so I scrubbed them really well after scrubbing the penis. I then draped the entire area.

While scrubbing the penis I had an idea and told the houseman: "The boy has not been circumcised. The inside layer of his foreskin may still be there. We should see if we can use it in the repair."

There was indeed a fairly long piece of skin present, the tear having occurred right at the fold. I now pulled the remaining 'inside skin' backwards over the shaft and scrubbed it well. It was a bit of a stretch, but I was able to pull the tissue back far enough to meet the normal skin at the base of the penis and scrotum. I placed two delicate 'skin hooks' in each side and gave all four to the houseman to hold so that the skin edges were held next to each other. I then carefully stitched them together. After the repair, tension was not too great and the boy again had a skin-covered penis. It now had about an inch of hairy skin that came from his scrotum and pubic area. This had stretched nicely up onto the shaft, where it was joined to the former inner lining of the foreskin.

"Not perfect, but fully functional. It will be a bit like a 'bottle brush,'" I chuckled. "He'll grow into it. You guys do all those circumcisions on Fridays," I said to the houseman. "I'll bet you've never heard of a 'reverse circumcision.' Neither have I. Well, there's one for you."

One busy evening our regular Casualty crew had been having a hard time and had at last managed to get our area cleared out. We went for 11 o'clock tea and a sandwich and sat around telling stories. The talk turned to bad experiences in Casualty and we each had a good tale to tell. It was finally my turn to tell a story: "I had been qualified for only 18 months when I started doing Casualty sessions, some at the Gen. and some here. It was a Saturday at the Gen. and a young railway patient came in with a head cut, bleeding a lot. The railway surgeon was supposed to deal with him and he made good money, so I didn't worry. The surgeon, who had never even met me, phoned from the country club. He asked me to do him a favor and put in a couple of big stitches, 'just to stop the bleeding' until he could finish his golf game and come in to see the patient.

"Since I was young and innocent and Casualty wasn't too busy, I agreed. I took the man into the small procedure room, where I started to prep his head and asked the Sister to prepare the suture set. I talked to the man and he seemed a fairly educated person, clearly in a white-collar job. When I looked at the wound it seemed pointless to just place the big sutures. I decided to do a neat job and finish it properly. I got some Procaine local anesthetic from the Sister and gave this into the wound edges as I talked to the patient.

"'What are you doing at the railways? What's your job?' I asked.

"There was no answer, and for a moment I thought it was because I was hurting him. I finished injecting then I asked him again. Still no answer.

"'Sister, feel his pulse and see if he's OK,' I asked.

"'*It's gone! He's dead!*' she shrieked, and ran out of the room, not to be seen again.

"I checked his carotid pulse myself and she was right.

"'Andy, Sister, Nurse, Anybody! *Help!*' I shouted, while I turned him onto his back. I started pounding on his chest with my two clenched fists, like wielding a sledgehammer. The other sister and my friend Andrew came running in to help. I asked them to raise the foot end of the couch to try and get some blood to his brain. Meanwhile I continued to thump on his chest. I asked the sister for a knife to open his chest and do internal cardiac massage, since that was all I had ever seen. We did not yet have defibrillators or monitors. I'm not sure they had yet been invented. External cardiac massage and mouth-to-mouth breathing had certainly not been developed. Guys called Kouwenhoven and Jude described the technique a few years later, if I remember rightly.

"The Sister handed me the knife. As I took it the patient started to speak again. I nearly fainted with relief. I finished stitching him up and we continued to talk. I told him what had happened. He didn't believe me. I warned him about procaine and sent him to the Railway ward, noting in big red letters on his chart that he was *allergic to procaine*.

"I thought very thankfully that I had so far escaped harm from my own allergy to procaine, which is a long story for another night. I have only realized in the last few years that I had probably performed the first successful external cardiac massage, or at the very least, what we now call a 'precordial thump.' It's not an experience I would care to repeat."

---

[1] Triage: From French, sifting or sorting. Essentially a military term, meaning the prioritizing of casualties at the front according to their likelihood of survival. In hospital emergency rooms it means much the same—someone decides where the patients will best be treated and directs them accordingly. The most urgent cases get immediate treatment.

2 <u>D & C</u>: Dilatation and curettage. Done the same way as procuring an abortion. The patient is anesthetized or at the least, heavily sedated, and the cervix is gently dilated and then a special long spoon or curette is passed through it and the inside of the uterus is scraped out until all products of conception are gone. Also done for diagnostic purposes.

3 <u>Hyperosmolar coma</u>: In diabetes the cause of coma is frequently a high blood sugar, with excess production of acetone. Less often coma is due to an excessively low blood sugar, caused by inappropriate use of insulin, without eating enough to 'cover' the dose. Hyperosmolar coma is neither of these, but results from dehydration and an excessive level of sodium and other solutes in the blood. It requires different treatment and it is important to recognize the differences.

4 <u>Gonorrhea</u>: One of the commoner sexually transmitted diseases (STDs). It causes severe itching and irritation in both sexual partners and can cause scarring in the penis, with obstructed urination. In women it can get into the uterine tubes, causing severe infection and infertility or ectopic pregnancy.

5 <u>Syphilis</u>: The major STD at that time (before the advent of AIDS). Apart from a local sore on the genitalia, it was a sneaky, silent disease. If untreated, it caused many severe consequences, including brain damage and dementia.

6 <u>Fluid thrill</u>: Feeling the waves in the fluid transmitted across the abdomen. In those days, before ultrasound machines, CAT scans and MRIs, doctors had to rely on good basic physical diagnostic skills.

7 <u>Procaine</u>: A local anesthetic used before the advent of Xylocaine, which is much less dangerous. It was also used in long-acting penicillin to make the injections less painful. Many penicillin allergies may in fact have been procaine allergies. This is how I found out about my own procaine allergy (fortunately mild).

8 <u>Ruptured viscus</u>: The hollow organs in the belly, if ruptured or perforated, let out irritating and usually infected contents which make the patient very ill. Usually gas leaks out at the same time, visible on X-Ray as 'free gas.' Bleeding from a ruptured spleen or liver, or indeed urine from a torn bladder, does not produce gas.

9 <u>Free gas</u>: Gas in the belly that is outside its normal place (within the bowel). See explanation, # 8, above.

10 <u>Baca</u>: A member of the Baca tribe, from the Eastern Cape. Part of the larger group of Xhosas.

11 <u>Apex beat</u>: This is the point of the heart and is often clearly felt between two ribs. It is also called 'maximal cardiac impulse'. Doctors look for it and use the position to tell the size of the heart.

12 <u>Congestive heart failure</u>: The commonest cause of medical readmissions to hospital. The heart cannot pump out all the blood with which it is presented, so fluid backs up in the lungs and sinks to the lowest parts of the body—the ankles.

13 <u>Alcoholic cardiomyopathy</u>: The chronic alcohol use poisons the muscles of the heart and they become unable to pump properly, causing heart failure. Initially this responds to some drugs, but eventually the heart fails entirely and the patient dies. (Modern heart transplants, of course, have a place here.)

14 <u>Edema</u>: Swelling of a part due to fluid collecting in the tissues. This happens in cardiac failure, as in this man, and in kidney failure.

"Two all."

I was playing singles with Michael Jonas, the gynecology consultant on duty. The court was on the lower half of the hospital campus, near the doctors' quarters and the mess. The surface was made of red clay, derived from anthills,[1] two or three-foot high red domes, common in the South African veld. This surface was almost as hard as concrete. But it became dusty after a few games, giving a light red coating to tennis shoes and socks.

Though it was Saturday, I was able to take some time off in the afternoon. I had the luxury of having an assistant surgeon, and was taking full advantage of it. David Levine, newly returned from London with his F.R.C.S.[2] diploma, was looking after the 'Pit.' Things were temporarily under control. We planned to switch later if it wasn't too busy.

The clouds were piling high in the west, ominously dark below, and with billowing white thunderheads. A soft rumble told me the usual highveld afternoon thunderstorm was not far away. I wondered if we could finish the game. Suddenly the loudspeaker, mounted high on a pole above the court, answered my unspoken question.

"Mister Hunt, please call Casualty."

"This sounds like work," I said.

We left the court together and I walked to the phone and dialed.

"Hang on a mo, Mike, while I see what this is," I said.

David Levine answered: "There's a guy up here with his leg cut off by a train and he won't give it up. He told the ambulance crew that someone at the hospital would put it back for him. He's lying here with the leg under his arm. Fat hope he has!"

"Maybe he's right," I replied. "Just keep it cold, on ice, and I'll be there."

Turning to my tennis partner, I said: "Excuse me, Mike, they have a man with his leg chopped off by a train. I must go. Thanks for the game—I'll have to beat you up another time. I'll see you later."

I jumped into my car for the half-mile trip to Casualty.

Lying on the stretcher was a slender Zulu man, with a wide, almost toothless smile. He proudly clutched the amputated leg under his arm, the raw end in front for all to see.

"I told them, Boss, that someone at the hospital would fix my leg and put it back. They wanted to take it, but I said NO! Aikona.[3] I am going to keep it."

I smiled at him and looked at the leg. A ragged-looking stump of thigh was still present above the knee, with the round bone in the center, showing a fairly clean break. I lifted the sheet and saw the matching upper end, pulled to a vertical position by the strong thigh muscles, without the counterweight of the rest of the leg. I looked into the ragged stump. The muscles, nerves and blood vessels were all present and partly covered in blood clot. Someone had put an artery forceps[4] on the main artery to stop the bleeding.

My mind was working overtime. I had just read in a newspaper of the first case of an arm re-attachment in America, and had seen pictures of the boy. So I knew it was possible. The article said a leg had never been done. Now this patient was begging to be the first one. I knew that technically I could do it.

"What's your name?" I asked.

"Zephania—Zephania Ndlazi."

"What happened to you?"

"The Tsotsis[5] push me off the train," the man answered.

"We get a lot of these cases," I told the students.

"Either the bad guys push the good guys off the train, or the good guys take revenge on the bad guys. The other people who lose limbs under trains are the 'Staff Riders.' Do you know who they are?" I asked. There was no reply.

"They're foolhardy youngsters who try and avoid paying the fare. They imitate what they see the conductors do on these packed trains. They grab hold on the outside of the carriage at the last minute.

They try to ride there all the way from Joh'burg to Soweto. That may be an hour. If they lose their grip, they may lose an arm or a leg as well."

I turned back to the patient and said: "Zephania, we can try and join your leg back on, but you must know that the leg will be very short and it might not work properly. If it doesn't work, we might still have to take it off later. There's never been an operation like this in the whole world. In America, across the sea, far away, they have put back only one boy's arm and it doesn't work very well. It's still hanging on though."

I wondered how much of that had really got through to the patient.

"Sister, you must explain all of that to him in his own language," I said.

The sister spoke at length to the patient in Zulu. Zephania answered that he still wanted to try and keep his leg. I completed and signed an operative consent form and gave it to the sister to go over with the patient.

"Sister, please explain it carefully to him, step by step, and let him sign the form."

I now picked up the phone and dialed the operating theaters.

"Sister, we are going to do something special and I'll need a lot of help," I said. "We're going to try and put back a man's leg that was cut off by a train."

"Hau Doctor! How can you do that?" came the answer.

"Not easily. Tell Sister Maria that I want a Kuntscher nail setup, a vascular set and a side table for the leg. We want another team for that table. Get a bucket with lots of ice, from the refrigerator or the kitchen, not sterile. She must do it now because we're coming."

I made sure the consent form was completed, the IVs were running and blood had been typed. Then we all set off for theater. Zephania was sent 'Urgent Direct,' with a red sticker on his forehead and a chart with Urgent Direct stamped on it in red. I led the way with some students and housemen, who were babbling and bubbling with excitement.

We all put on shoe covers and green cover-up gowns and went to Theater Three. I slipped on a cap and was tying my mask when I started giving orders in rapid fire.

"Sister Maria, I want a bucket of ice…"

Before I could finish, she handed me a bucket, already filled with ice.

"Maria, you're too good! Now let's have a bath towel or a green towel and a big plastic bag, like a garbage bag, or a sheet of plastic."

I wrapped the leg in the towel and then in the plastic bag and slid it into the ice.

"That's to stop it getting frostbite," I said.

The nurses had already draped a table for me to work. I placed the bucket and leg on the green towels.

"Now Jane, get me an IV set with a big blunt needle or cannula,[6] to tie into the artery. Put an amp[7] of bicarb in the bottle of Ringer's lactate[8] and put some more bottles on ice. Make sure the IV set has a blood pump."

The porter now arrived with the patient. I took charge of the limb but sent the patient around the corner to the recovery room.

"Get the anesthetist to go to recovery—I think Dr. Brobeck is on," I told a nurse. "Ask him to come and see me here first.

"Put one mega-unit[9] of ordinary penicillin in the bottle. Ask them in recovery to give penicillin to the patient, together with a gram of streptomycin."

I started working on the exposed end of the leg, flooding it with Betadine solution and saline and letting it all overflow on the floor. The nurses threw down a constant supply of dry towels to soak up the mess. I located the artery and vein and identified the other structures we would need for a successful repair. A staff nurse handed me the end of an IV set, which I grasped with a gauze sponge soaked in Betadine. I liberally wiped the tube with the brown solution.

"It's the best I can do," I commented. "These sets are not sterile on the outside."

I then tied the cannula into the artery and the nurse started running in the fluid.

"Now Joe, start working the blood pump," I told one of the students.

This was simply a matter of repeatedly squeezing an inch-thick plastic tube, containing a filter and a white one-way ball valve. We could see the pump was working because after each squeeze clear fluid poured into the chamber above the ball. In a minute or two, murky dark bloodstained fluid poured out of the vein and onto the wound. It finally cascaded onto the table and fell in a steady stream on the floor. I simply let it go.

"That's great!" I said. "Sorry for the mess, sisters, but it's just what I want. For starters, it shows the circulation is intact. We're also washing out 'bad blood' from the leg. The muscles have no blood supply and hence no oxygen.[10] They've been pouring out lactic acid, potassium, and many other bad things we know nothing about, into the tissues of the leg. If they get back in his circulation, any or all of these could kill the patient, or make him ill. So, instead, as we perfuse the leg with fluid, the poisons are going on the floor instead.

"To save some mess, Sister, if you give me another big cannula and some IV tubing, I'll tie it into the main vein and let that fluid drain into a basin."

Jules Brobeck now poked his head into the room, while I placed the cannulas.

"I've heard the bad news. *Where do you find these cases?* Perhaps I shouldn't ask—you might tell me. To be serious, you know me; I guess you want hypotensive anesthesia?"

"Jules, you know best. I know that's your favorite anesthetic. Who knows? It might even do him some good. Just keep him peeing. That's all I want. Would you look after him in Recovery? Bring him back when he's stable. I'm about ready here. I'm going for some food while the leg cools down and the junk is washed out. This could be a long night."

I could now see almost clear fluid coming out of the leg through the cannula.

"You can stop pumping now, Joe," I told the student. "Just set it for rapid gravity flow. That should be OK. Sisters, when you change the bottles, use the cold ones and put in the bicarb. When I come back we'll start the real operation."

I popped into recovery on my way to supper and saw my friend Jules hard at work, ordering blood, giving the penicillin, and generally preparing the case for surgery.

"I'll see you in a few minutes," I said and went to my car.

As I drove rapidly down to the doctors' mess, I realized that I had no idea how this should be done. But then, only one other team in the world knew, and they were 10,000 miles away. They must have found out the same way I was, by doing it. I was making it up as I went along, using what tools I had, and relying on logic, science, my own research into shock and acidosis and some good South African common sense.

I thought immediately of the old Afrikaans farmer's remedy: ' 'n Boer en 'n stuk draad kan alles regmaak.' (A farmer and a piece of wire can fix anything.)

As I sat down at table, David Levine said, with an edge to his voice: "I'm coming to watch this *attempted replantation.*"

"Be my guest," I replied. I practically inhaled my supper, gobbled the dessert and took my coffee in the car. I was on my way back to the theater in about ten minutes.

I stuck my head into Theater Three before going to change my clothes. The patient was now in the room.

"Are you all ready here?" I asked.

"He's ready and he'll be asleep when you've changed and scrubbed," Jules answered.

I changed into green scrubs and returned to the sink outside the theater. Roger Douglas, my registrar at the time, joined me there. While we were washing, I answered a few last minute questions from the nurses. I asked for a separate sterile side table. We then entered the room and gowned up.

"Roger, will you clean up and prep the 'patient' end of this operation? Pour Betadine and saline through the wound first. Use the Water Pik[11] if you like, so that we get it really clean. Then drape so that we can also get at his hip for the top end of the rod."

"Sister Jane, you and I will clean up the leg end. I'll scrub again after that."

Roger Douglas got the Water Pik and started spraying the wound copiously, accompanied by a loud yammering sound from the compressed air running the machine.

I pulled the leg out of the ice, took off its coverings, and put it down.

"Nice and cool," I commented. "Its metabolism must be near zero by now."

Sister Jane and I now washed and scrubbed the leg, from cut end to toes, with Betadine soap and solution. When we were done, we placed it on the sterile table.

"Now Sister Jane, do that all over again, while I go and re-scrub."

I saw that clear fluid flowed quite rapidly from the vein, so I had them slow the drip some more, while I left the room. The sister repeated the entire process and placed the leg on the sterile table. After scrubbing, I returned and re-gowned before joining Roger at the operating table.

"OK, Roger, we must do the top end first."

The patient was now covered in green towels and drape sheets and all we could see was the lacerated end of the thigh, showing all too clearly in the glare of the operating room light. We cut off the more obviously shredded bits of flesh and trimmed the skin edges carefully all round. I taught Roger how to test any doubtful muscle with the cautery[12] current to see if it was alive. If it twitched poorly or not at all, we 'fried it off' with the cautery machine.

"It should be pink and bleed, and twitch when we touch it with cautery, or we don't want it," I said.

"Saw please, Sister."

She handed me a shiny version of a workshop 'Tenon Saw.' I used it to trim off half an inch of bone, making a clean cut, and we noted with joy that the end bled freely.

"Let's see your K-Nails,[13] Sister."

She handed me a couple of shiny metal rods about two feet long. I chose a likely one and tried it in the hollow end of the bone for fit. It looked snug, but about right. I pushed it up in the bone and it slid in quite nicely. I then started tapping it in gently and deliberately with a special hammer, pausing after each blow, in case it should get jammed. I measured it repeatedly against one of the others to see progress.

"Not much to go now. This is about the easiest K-Nail I've ever done. I'll have to tell the Orthopods about the new approach—first cut off the leg!" I chuckled.

I hammered once more and said:

"Roger, go up to the hip and feel for the rod coming up. Cut down on it if it comes through, though we may not need to go all the way. It looks about right already."

I then went to the side table and fetched the leg, with its IV still running. I placed it in line with the thigh on the operating table, and measured the length of thighbone attached to the knee to see how it matched the exposed piece of rod.

"The rod's too long. We'll need to whack it through. Here it comes, Roger," I said.

I hammered on the free end, fairly strongly now, until the registrar motioned me to stop. Roger felt for the end of the rod and then cut down and exposed the protruding steel at the top of the hip. He wrapped the end in a green towel and came back to join me.

We now started on the lower end, trimming the muscle, skin and bone, just as before. Since there was no bleeding or proper color to help us, we used logic and common sense as our guide. Once I was

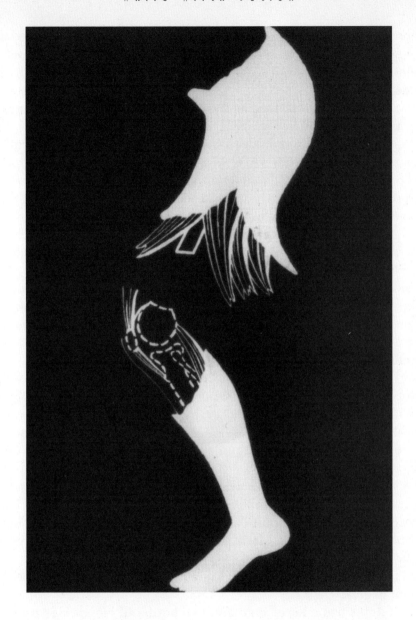

SKETCH OF ZEPHANIA'S LEG AS AMPUTATED BY TRAIN.
SHOWS SKIN & BONE LOSS.

satisfied, I put the amputated leg in place over the rod and pushed it upwards, with the rod going down into the marrow cavity. It would not go in all the way, leaving a two-inch gap in the bone, with bare metal showing.

"Roger, hold the leg and give counter-pressure on the knee, while I tap the rod in."

I moved up to the side of the patient above the hip and gently hammered on the rod, while Roger pushed the leg up from below. The gap in the bone closed appreciably with each hammer blow. I was satisfied when the two bones made firm contact. Roger bent the knee back and forth to check that the rod had not gone too far down.

"I know this won't stop the bones rotating around the K-nail," I said. "But it will hold the leg straight, stabilize the fracture and allow us to get on with the vascular repairs quickly. That's what matters. We couldn't have waited for a long fancy orthopedic repair. Roger, come up here and stitch the skin, while I find the blood vessels for suture."

We swapped places and I now located the ends of the artery and the vein and started to free them up. Their normal elasticity had pulled them back in amongst the muscles.

"You see," I said to the students. "When I pull on these vessels, there is enough length, partly because the leg is much shorter. A piece was squashed on the track, and we cut off some of the bone. If we're really short of artery, we can always steal a little piece of the saphenous vein[14] for a graft. I'm going to tie that vein off anyway, so he can spare it."

Roger returned to the field and we began the repair. I took the temporary clamp off and milked a plug of clot out of the end of the artery. This caused a spurt of bright red blood. I shut it off rapidly with my fingers, while Maria passed me a flat-bladed clamp to stop the bleeding.

"That's wonderful flow!" I said happily. "Jules, you must have him in great shape."

"He's had a lot of fluid and two bottles of blood. He's peeing like a racehorse," Jules answered. "I'm very satisfied at this end. Warn me before you join the vein so that I can give more bicarb and maybe some calcium, to prevent his BP from falling off the clock."

"He should be OK," I said. "We're nowhere near doing the vein yet. We've been washing out the leg with buffered Ringer lactate and cooled it fairly well, so its metabolism must be pretty low. There can't be much potassium or lactic acid left in it. But I'll be sure and tell you, anyway."

I now removed the cannulas from the lower end of the leg.

"Roger, I'm trimming both ends of the artery obliquely, to make a longer suture line. Now, watch my next trick."

I inserted a medium size artery forceps into each end of the artery in turn, and slowly opened the jaws a little. The artery visibly stretched and widened.

"Those two maneuvers can make the ends nearly twice their size, and eliminate any spasm.[15] It makes sewing far easier, and prevents bad scarring and narrowing later—he'll have only one artery to rely on."

"Why are you doing the artery first?" one of the students asked. "Won't you have a big mess from the vein when you connect up?"

"Logically, you're right," I answered, "but I'll welcome the mess. As I keep saying, the leg is likely full of poisons from prolonged anoxia, and I want to restore its perfusion with well-oxygenated blood for a few minutes before we connect the vein. I'll waste the first blood that comes out, and only then re-connect. Even so, we might have to divert venous flow again if he deteriorates when we complete the circulation. In fact, I won't hesitate to amputate the leg permanently if he doesn't do well. As one of my chiefs used to say: 'Better a living problem than a dead certainty.'"

I started to sew the pencil-sized artery together with one continuous suture of fine purple Prolene.[16] I first did the front, with tiny over-and-over stitches, and then rotated the vessel completely over to do the back in the same manner. I was satisfied with the stitching and took off the clamps, first the lower one then the upper. There was only a slight leak of blood between two sutures. I covered my handiwork with a gauze sponge and held it gently but firmly in my hand, to prevent leakage, while the life-giving fluid pulsated into the leg.

"Arterial clamps off," I called to Jules. "His blood pressure may fall a bit—we're going to bleed him into his leg for a while. I'm sure you and the blood bank can handle it!"

"Thanks a lot," the anesthetist answered.

For what seemed like minutes, nothing came back from the vein despite the inflow. I was beginning to worry. Suddenly, the whole ragged lower end of the leg seemed to come alive—blood started leaking from everywhere. There were large streams of blood from big veins and little streams from smaller ones. The whole wound started to ooze at once. Even a few small arteries began to pulsate and spew out tiny jets of blood.

So the student's prophecy and my wish for a mess were both fulfilled.

"Hooray!" I said. "Jules, you'll need to give him a couple of bottles of blood rapidly, to replace what's gone to fill the leg and what we're shedding on purpose. I guess the leg itself contains at least a pint."

Roger started to touch many of the smaller bleeders with the cautery and tie off some of the bigger ones, except for the main veins.

"How is he, Jules?" I asked.

"Just fine and stable. *John, why don't you just get on with it now* and close up the vein, so that we can get done?" Brobeck said, irritably.

"I actually agree with you for a change," I replied. "We're about ready for that."

Roger and I placed a temporary flat clamp across the artery to limit inflow. I put similar clamps[17] on the vein, above and below the intended join. Roger injected some heparin anticoagulant solution into the arterial side through a small needle, to try and stop clotting in the vessels while they were closed off. We then repaired the femoral vein, using exactly the same technique as before, except for a slightly thinner suture.

"Watch out Jules, we're ready to open the vein. Give him your bicarb," I said. "We'll open flow when you tell us."

In a few minutes, Jules gave us the OK. I took the clamp off the artery first and saw that it was pulsating well into the leg and no longer bleeding. I then opened the vein to flow, and again saw only a minor leak, with a nice, full, fat vein, both below and above the suture line. The circulation to the leg was now completely restored and I couldn't have asked for a better result.

"Bombs away!" I called. "How's he at your end?"

The EKG stayed regular, and Jules waited a few moments before replying: "Keep your fingers crossed. Everything's just dandy at the moment. I'll give him some Lasix and watch his pee like a hawk. *Now can we get finished?*"

"I'll try, but we still have a little way to go," I replied. "You'll be pleased to know I don't plan to do his nerves tonight. We've all had enough. He's short of skin to close the wound and it's potentially infected. We'll cobble his muscles together to cover the blood vessels, and put on a big greasy dressing. If it's clean and pink tomorrow, we'll do a skin graft in a few days and then consider the nerve repair.

"Roger, use some big 0 Vicryl or catgut[18] sutures to hold the muscles together. We'll get some *Tulle Gras*[19] to cover it all and put a great big wet dressing on top.

"Sister Jane, please have them bring up an orthopedic bed with a Balkan beam.[20] We can set him up in theater, with his leg in a Thomas' splint[21] to take the weight off, and keep the limb from twisting at the fracture site. He has no sensation and it won't return for many months, so we must guard his leg from pressure."

I turned round: "Well David, what did you think?"

"Not bad! I must admit, I didn't think you could do it. Congratulations. I suppose I'd better get back to the real world of Bara Saturday night."

[1] <u>Anthills</u>: Termites or grass-eating ants build extensive structures, both above and below ground. In much of the country, the soil is red and these domed red structures stand up to four feet above the ground. Africans have long used the hard clay material in home construction and it was used for the surface of tennis courts, before the advent of asphalt or concrete for that purpose.

[2] <u>F.R.C.S.</u>: Fellow of the Royal College of Surgeons, in this case, of London. There are also colleges in Edinburgh, Glasgow and Ireland. These exams are roughly equivalent to the American Boards in Surgery. I held the diplomas from both London and Edinburgh.

[3] <u>Aikona</u>: No.

[4] <u>Artery forceps</u>: British word for the American 'hemostat.' An instrument with rings like scissors, and serrated jaws. It is used to clamp blood vessels and stop bleeding.

[5] <u>Tsotsis</u>: Essentially unemployed gangsters or thugs.

[6] <u>Cannula</u>: A blunt-tipped fat needle, used so as not to damage the inside of the structure it is put into. Often made of plastic.

[7] <u>Amp</u>: Short for ampoule. Used in medical and nursing speech all the time.

[8] Ringer's lactate: A balanced multiple electrolyte solution, roughly resembling the make-up of human plasma, without the protein. Used commonly as an intravenous solution for resuscitation, and in this case for irrigation and perfusion.

[9] Mega-unit: A million units. Quite a high dose.

[10] No oxygen supply: When tissues of the body, particularly the muscles, are deprived of oxygen, they try and live without it. Their metabolism becomes anaerobic and they pour out lactic acid and potassium, amongst other harmful substances. The same thing occurs in shock and cardiac arrest. In this case the limb behaves as if it is severely shocked.

[11] Water Pik: A giant derivative of the dental machine. A strong jet of sterile water is used to clean out dirty wounds, remove gravel and dirt. A shield and goggles protect the surgeon from splashing.

[12] Cautery: An electronic machine, delivering a modified electric current through an electrode. This enables surgeons to cut and seal tissues or to coagulate medium-size bleeders and stop bleeding without using ties.

[13] K-Nails: Kuntscher nails. Long hollow rods of various sizes, with one side open. Made of very strong metal. They are driven down the marrow cavity of fractured bones to splint them in position from the inside. Usually permanent.

[14] Saphenous vein: The second largest vein draining the leg. Universally used for artery or vein grafting since it can be spared. Has long been used for coronary bypass procedures.

[15] Spasm: When arteries are cut or damaged, the muscle in the wall contracts and helps close off the vessel to prevent blood loss—nature's survival mechanism. It is hard to eliminate the spasm and such vessels can easily block again, if sewn up. This causes failure of the operation. Hence the use of this trick.

[16] Prolene: A proprietary name for polypropylene, a very strong suture material, used particularly in vascular surgery. It is very smooth and glides well through the tissues, without any 'drag.'

[17] Vascular clamps: Special instruments with ring handles for finger and thumb. The jaws are gentle, to avoid damage to the vessels, and have a wide variety of patterns, sometimes narrow, sometimes wide and flat. They are used to close the vessels temporarily while surgery is done.

[18] 0 Vicryl or catgut sutures: Thick absorbable sutures. Taken up by the body and need not be removed later.

[19] Tulle Gras: From French. Basically greasy gauze. May be medicated.

[20] Balkan Beam: A large overhead frame on a bed, used mainly in Orthopedics.

[21] Thomas' splint: A classic orthopedic appliance, consisting of a large padded ring that goes around the thigh at the groin and a long metal hoop, longer than the leg, attached to the ring. The whole device is suspended in the Balkan frame to take weight off the limb. Usually used if the fracture has not been fixed by a metal rod or appliance.

On Monday morning the story broke. The local and national newspapers and radio played it large. There were many favorable comments, pictures of Zephania and write-ups on Baragwanath Hospital. This was great publicity for them, since events in Soweto or Baragwanath usually received little attention. There was a buzz all over Bara. I received many congratulations and had to tell the story over and over. The medical superintendent and the chief of surgery both offered their full support.

South Africa did not yet have television, as the government was too concerned that the minds of the people might be polluted by outside influences. Nonetheless, the story was soon on the newswires, and several overseas TV networks came calling.

Despite the general goodwill, some orthopedic surgeons were disenchanted that they had not done the case. A few snide remarks were passed. At that time, the general surgeons handled the acute fractures. The orthopedists did only 'cold' or elective orthopedics. They rarely came out at night or on weekends, so I didn't feel too sorry for them.

On the whole, however, people were kind, congratulatory and helpful. Out of interest or curiosity, most of the medical and nursing staff came to see the patient and his leg.

I obtained very useful consultations from the neurosurgeons and the plastic surgeons. I also consulted the rehabilitation department and they started to work on keeping the patient's leg and his mind in shape. The physiotherapists did passive movements and gave Zephania thigh-strengthening exercises. The occupational therapists brought him a small weaving frame, for both diversion and to assess his abilities, and to start training him for a new occupation. They had a whole host of other ideas and facilities available in their workshop, including leatherwork, if weaving did not work out.

Zephania loved all the publicity, and reigned like a king in the side ward of Unit Five. He graciously granted interviews, and posed for photographs and TV. Thanks to the overseas media, 450 million people in 40 countries saw his face and the now famous leg, and heard him talk about the experience. He often said, "Doctor Hunt is a white witchdoctor." This tickled me greatly. I thought it was a great compliment; something I would never forget.

On Tuesday morning, when I arrived at work, I was surprised to find that the orthopedic surgeons were in their operating theater, about to provide a live demonstration of a Kuntscher Nail operation for an overseas television team. I bumped into one of the photographers before the operation started and chatted for a while, then wished him well and promised to come back later. I went to Ward Five, checked on Zephania, and did the normal administrative chores and ward rounds with the unit for a couple of hours before returning. I thought the operation should be nearly finished by then.

As I entered the operating room suite and started up the stairs to the tearoom and change rooms, I encountered the same photographer. Now, however, he was pale, sweating profusely and in a state of near collapse.

"Crikey, Doc! You should just *see* what's going on in there," he panted.

"What on earth is the matter?" I asked.

"They've got that damned rod stuck in the bone and it won't move," the photographer blurted out. "They can't drive it in any further, and it won't come out either. There's blood everywhere and a big pool of clot on the table, like thick red jelly. It's dripping down onto the floor in a huge puddle. The surgeons are slipping on it. The anesthetist is pumping in bottles of blood. I just couldn't stand it in there any longer."

I helped the man upstairs, found him a seat and poured us both some tea. We sat down and talked quietly for a few minutes. Then I went to change clothes and see what was going on downstairs.

In the orthopedic operating theater the rest of the camera crew, dressed in green cover-up gowns, stood quietly on one side. They were warily watching the procedure, but not doing any filming. Their hot lights still shone brightly on the operative field and the surgical team. The operating table, the drape sheets and the floor were all bathed in red jelly. The orthopedic registrar doing the surgery was obviously rattled. Cursing softly and sweating profusely, he was trying everything he knew to get the rod to move. He was using a large metal hammer to try and drive the nail upwards, but to no avail.

The consultant orthopedic surgeon was already scrubbing to help. They now used a K-nail remover, a strange-looking metal 'hammer-in-reverse.' There was a hook on one end, which passed through a hole in the tip of the nail. A large metal weight on a central rod was then hurled repeatedly downwards against a strong platform on the other end of the tool, producing heavy distracting blows. It yielded precious little movement of the nail.

I asked cheerily, "Hi folks, how's it going? You know, it's a lot easier if you cut off the leg first."

Receiving black looks, but hearing no answer, I waved to the camera crew and left the room. I never knew how the 'orthopods' solved their problem. I didn't see the film, nor did I know if it was ever shown. The orthopedists never again raised the topic in my hearing.

The next weekend, my son, David, aged four, wanted to see Zephania and the leg. I took him out to make rounds on the Sunday. Zephania was very sweet to David and the boy really enjoyed his morning. He was impressed with the leg. We met up with Staff Nurse Maria, from Botswana, who was second in command of Ward Five and was in charge that Sunday. She and David formed a mutual admiration society. For many years thereafter, she never failed to ask me about David and his mother and siblings.

The medical superintendent invited me to his office a few days after the surgery. He said that a white architect from the state capital, Pretoria, had offered to pay all expenses for Zephania. He would also replace Zephania's lost income and look after his wife and children in Zululand while he was off work. Needless to say, we gratefully accepted this generous offer on behalf of the patient and his family. Social services made the appropriate arrangements.

Zephania was delighted. Some days later, the architect visited him to cement the deal and see firsthand what he was undertaking. He and Zephania became firm friends. He continued his generous support during the entire hospitalization, and for many more months.

I arrived home early one day, to find my mother-in-law working in the flower garden, agog with excitement. She met me at the front gate and blurted out: "They'll be back in a little while!"

"Who'll be back? What are you talking about, Ouma?"[1] I asked.

"The television people from London. They want to take pictures of your hands."

"Really? How should I hold them? Praying, cutting with a knife, supporting my chin, or relaxed in my lap?" I asked, miming to accompany the words. "Sorry, Ouma, I'm not here, and I won't be back for a while. I'll give a regular interview, but no dramatics. I'll call them tonight if they still want me."

Ouma remained standing at the gate, dismayed and disappointed.

I got back in the car and drove around for a while. I called home to find that the T.V. team had returned and were still talking to my family. I came back and talked to them and set up an appointment for an interview. It took place without any drama at the hospital the next day. I introduced the team to Zephania and arranged for them to take suitable pictures of the patient and the hospital.

On Saturday mornings, the Wits University Medical School's Department of Surgery held teaching conferences at the Johannesburg General Hospital. All the University teaching hospital units could present interesting cases or give talks. The surgeons from these hospitals

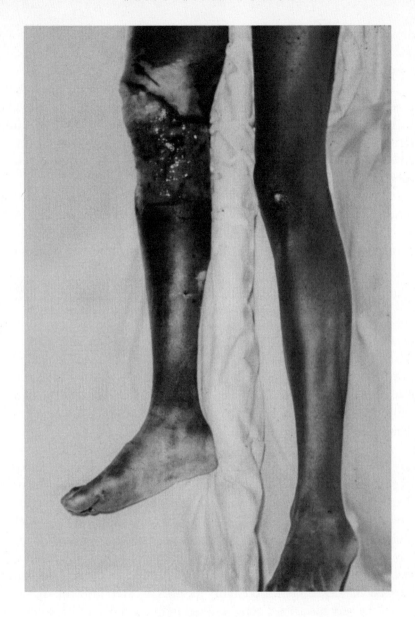

ZEPHANIA'S LEG ABOUT 1 WEEK AFTER REIMPLANTATION.
AREA OF MUSCLE EXPOSED BY LOSS OF SKIN CAN BE SEEN.
IT IS RED, SHINY & READY FOR SKIN GRAFT.
LEG IS CLEARLY SHORTER DUE TO LOSS OF BONE.

attended as part of their morning routine. Attendance by the registrars was obligatory. The meeting was open to all interested doctors and medical students.

Two weeks after the surgery I presented the case at one of these meetings, using color slides and hand-drawn illustrations that Ann had prepared for me. She was there to watch. I received a standing ovation and there was animated discussion among the younger doctors about the details of the operation and its possible future place in surgery.

This was tempered by skepticism from Professor Du Toit, the head of the department, about the long-term prognosis for the limb. This was fair criticism and was not unexpected. He was an authoritarian, dominant personality, so there was no room for further discussion.

Zephania's subsequent surgical care was straightforward, but drawn out. The open wound, with exposed muscles, was pink and healthy from the outset. Repeated Eusol[2] dressings made it ready for skin grafting in a few days. The grafts took well on the exposed muscle, as I had expected. The neurosurgeons thought that the nerves should not be joined until the skin was healed. This surgery was delayed for another week.

Though the physical therapists were working with the leg every day, it was felt that the severed nerves would probably prevent a return to complete function. The entire length of nerve beyond the cut would first have to degenerate. Then new nerve fibers coming from above would need to grow down in the old channels. The rate at which a repaired nerve was known to grow was only one to two millimeters a day (1.2 to 2.4 inches a month). Since Zephania's foot was about two feet from the join, even under ideal circumstances the nerve fibers would have taken between ten and twenty months to extend the full distance.

The very specialized nerve endings in the skin that served sensation in the foot were furthest away from the repair. These complex, delicate structures would probably have atrophied[3] or died before the nerve fibers could reach them. The foot and leg would thus most likely remain permanently without adequate protective feelings.

The nerves to the large muscles of the calf came from much closer to the join. Though these muscles would also undergo some atrophy, they would be the first to regain any nerve supply and get partial return of function. Even that innervation[4] would be several months away and probably far less than perfect. The neurosurgeons and I felt that in the light of then current knowledge, the best that could be achieved would only be some return of crude large muscle function. They speculated that very little or probably nothing would be restored in terms of sensation or feeling or small muscle function in the foot.

I explained this to Zephania as well and as kindly as I could, but the concepts were too sophisticated for him to fully understand, especially so soon after the accident and surgery. The patient was certain that the leg looked good and was going to be fine. He insisted that he wanted us to go ahead and try to suture the nerves. This we did, with some difficulty, but with complete restoration of normal anatomy. I knew that this nice-looking suturing did not necessarily ensure long-term functional success.

The bone healed well. X-rays taken at one month showed good callus,[5] or new bone formation around the fracture. Zephania was soon able to get out of the cumbersome Thomas' splint and sleep in a normal bed. Despite all our precautions, teaching and demonstrations of the needed protection for the leg, he developed several small pressure sores[6] on the outside of the calf and the foot, where the leg lay in contact with the mattress. These sores proved exceedingly difficult and slow to heal.

The physical therapists worked assiduously with Zephania and had him walking with crutches as soon as I would allow it. The therapists loved it, because the work was right up their street. None of them had seen anything like this before. Their patient worked hard and did very well, taking the weight on his good leg, while he swung the other one through and tried to flex the knee. He constantly exercised to build up muscle strength in his quads and hamstrings.[7] But as he walked, the foot of the reimplanted leg was over five inches off the ground, due to the loss of that much of the thighbone. This also meant that his knees were at very different levels. His shoe would need to be raised to the extent of the shortening, or some sort of prosthetic appliance[8] would have to be built for the purpose.

Meanwhile, Zephania gained insight into both his abilities and severe limitations. He realized he had only one good leg. His re-attached leg was very short and had no power or feeling and kept on developing sores. While he was at physical therapy, he saw amputees being rehabilitated, walking well on their artificial legs. He also talked to several of the paraplegics, who had both legs paralyzed. They told him about their bedsore problems.

The deeper significance of his own bad leg gradually dawned on him. He now understood that he would have to protect it for the rest of his life. He realized that without feeling, it was as much or as little a part of him as an artificial leg might be. He could also see that amputation, unattractive as it might seem, was a viable alternative.

Zephania continued his rehabilitation for a further month before seeking counsel from his architect friend. After a long talk, they decided he might be better off without the leg.

After much research and many consultations and medical discussions I was grudgingly reaching the same conclusion. Though the leg was anatomically intact and the procedure appeared successful up to that point, I realized that the long-term outlook was probably unfavorable. The downside far outweighed the positive psychological effect of the reimplantation. Zephania would probably be better off without the leg. That meant I would have to undo my own handiwork.

With the benefit of 20/20 hindsight, I now doubted if there would ever be a place for limb reimplantation at such a high level, unless scientific research could produce something that would hasten nerve growth. Replacing fingers and toes and perhaps hands or feet might be reasonable, but not whole limbs. The slow pace of nerve regeneration[9] was the limiting factor that had bedeviled us all and would prevent success with limb reimplantation for the foreseeable future. If that hurdle could one day be overcome, both reimplantation and the replacement of limbs by transplantation from cadaver donors would become possible. During the same year, Dr. Tom Starzl from the USA had demonstrated the first kidney transplants in South Africa in Johannesburg, so transplantation had a long way to go.

Despite this dawning insight, I agonized about the situation for a while longer. Once I had made up my mind, I took the ward sister along to have a discussion with Zephania, so that she could explain the gravity of the decision. I need not have worried.

"Zephania, you know we have tried very hard to save your leg and you too have worked hard to help it get better," I began.

"Yebo Dokitela.[10] I understand. I see from your face that you want to tell me that the leg must come off."

"Zephania, you are a wise man. You can read what's in my mind. Your leg won't work like a man's leg. It will always be short and have sores. It won't be strong. You can't do a man's job with a leg like that. You'll have to look after the leg—it won't look after you. We can watch and wait for years and hope, but it'll only get a little better. While we wait you won't work. These other big doctors who have seen you, they all say the same thing. They don't think it will ever be strong. You'll be better with an artificial leg. You'll get out of hospital quicker, to go home and be able to work and look after your family."

"Dokitela, I have seen men at P.T. with one leg. They walk very well on their new tin legs. I can learn to do that. My white friend also says yes. What will be, will be."

"Thank you, Zephania. This is right for you. I know it makes you very sad. It makes me sad also. We will do it on Wednesday. We will see that you get a new leg quickly."

"Ngiyabonga Dokitela."[11]

I ordered tests to document progress before we did the amputation. X-rays showed the femur had good union, with strong bone in the callus. An angiogram X-ray done with dye in the tied-off saphenous vein showed good flow. The blind upper end of the vein had grown small branches or collaterals,[12] which looked like the roots of a plant. They went up to connect the closed end of the vein with the upper part of his thigh. I thought this was an amazing example of the body's repair mechanisms and held definite hope for the future of limb reimplantation, or even transplantation, once nerve growth problems were solved.

The following Wednesday, my usual operating day, I reamputated Zephania's leg, at a slightly higher point, and above the level of the skin grafts. I made sure the skin cover of the stump had no scarring or skin graft and would be healthy and durable enough to tolerate a prosthesis[13] as soon as possible. I had anticipated problems with the Küntscher nail, but once the bone was cut I was easily able to remove it.

I had to see this operation as a scientific exercise, since my emotional attachment to the leg was so great. My worst moment came when I placed the severed leg in a plastic bag for delivery to the pathologists. The emotion resembled what I had felt at age 17 during my father's funeral, when the coffin was lowered into the grave and a handful of dirt was thrown on top of it. I wondered if others in the room had noticed my tears. I tried to divert attention by keeping up a constant stream of banter with Sister Caroline, my usual and favorite scrubnurse. I was certain she knew. She was kind enough to make no comment.

From the outset Zephania was highly motivated toward recovery. He worked hard with the physiotherapists to get his remaining thigh in good shape for fitting his new leg. He was back on crutches almost from day one. He knew that the muscles had to be strong and he exercised constantly. The therapists also had to shrink the stump before fitting the new limb. He tolerated twice daily bandaging with crepe bandages[14] without complaint. This was followed by the application of a tight elasticized 'stump shrinker,'[15] which he wore for 24 hours a day. He was prepared to undergo any discomfort to speed the process.

Zephania had no local home, as he lived in the Jabulani hostel[16] for migrant laborers. He was no longer a worker, so he needed to stay in the hospital while he waited for his new leg. We transferred him to a convalescent ward near the gym and Occupational Therapy. He enjoyed getting up on his crutches and walking across for both exercise therapy and work sessions. He tried his hand at every type of handwork available. He walked down on his crutches to watch the paraplegics play basketball on the court near the workshops.

Once the stump was in good condition, his permanent prosthesis was fitted. At the same time, a second plaster-of-paris cast was made of the stump, with thin padding. The lower portion of a wooden crutch was built into the end, and a broad webbing strap with a buckle was added at the top, to go over his shoulder and hold the cast in place. Using this temporary leg enabled him to regain his balance and start his proper walking rehabilitation.

From then on, with his high level of motivation, he needed crutches for a very short while until he started walking independently on his temporary leg, using a walking cane. His permanent prosthesis soon arrived. It fitted well and he was able to transition to stiff-legged walking in the new leg. He soon learned to walk with a flexible knee joint.

During his entire recovery period, the social service people had been working on his eventual discharge from hospital. He wanted to go back to his family in Zululand.[17] They gave him a train ticket, some cash and the means to keep contact. Unfortunately, given the socio-economic circumstances for black people in both their home areas and Johannesburg, and considering his disability, chances for his employment were cloudy at best. It was hoped that some of the skills he had learned in occupational therapy would provide the basis for a new line of work. Perhaps also, his architect friend would have a few ideas.

When I said good-bye to Zephania after four months of daily meeting, I felt a great sense of loss. I felt my eyes brimming, as I tucked away a bittersweet memory of a surgical odyssey that started out with such high hopes, but had to be deemed a 'failure' for reasons beyond my control.

My patient left with a handshake and a big smile.

"*Ngiyabonga Hahulu*[18], Doctor Hunt, white *Sangoma*.[19]"

"*Hamba kahle*,[20] Zephania," I said.

"*Sala kahle, Inkosi*,"[21] Zephania replied.

---

[1] <u>Ouma</u>: Afrikaans for grandmother. Our children's pet name for Ann's mother.

[2] <u>Eusol</u>: Sodium hypochlorite. A sterilizing and bleaching agent. Much used for wound dressings at Bara.

[3] <u>Atrophied</u>: Wasted away with passage of time. Muscles atrophy from lack of use or lack of nerve supply

[4] <u>Innervation</u>: Provision of a nerve supply.

[5] <u>Callus</u>: as fractures heal, fibrous tissue and calcium, called 'callus,' replaces the clot around the bone ends. This goes on to form bone, leading on to firm union when the gap is firmly bridged.

[6] <u>Pressure sores</u>: The same as bedsores or decubitus ulcers. In this case, they resulted from the loss of protective sensation or any feeling in his leg. The leg would lie on the bed at night particularly, with no sensation to tell him when to move it, so these sores developed in the skin over 'pressure points,' where there was something hard pressing on the bed, e.g. his heel bone, or the side of his knee or ankle.

7 Quads and hamstring muscles: The big muscles of the front and back of the thigh. Quads=quadriceps.

8 Prosthetic appliance: He would need a boot with a high built-up platform of some kind, built by a prosthetist.

9 Nerve regeneration: The growth of new nerve fibers down old channels, to re-connect with nerve endings in muscles, skin, or elsewhere.

10 Yebo Dokitela: Yes Doctor.

11 Ngiyabonga Dokitela: 'Thank you, Doctor.' Pronounced Nyabonga.

12 Collaterals: Small blood vessels that form around a blockage in a blood vessel, to undo the effects of the block, and continue to carry blood beyond it. This is a natural process to bypass the block.

13 Prosthesis: Artificial leg, in this case.

14 Crepe bandages: Strong elasticized bandages. 'Ace Wraps' in America.

15 Stump shrinker: A strong short elasticized sock for the stump, to shrink it and prepare it for limb fitting.

16 Jabulani Hostel: There were many of these single sex dwelling areas for migrant laborers from the distant countryside. They were named for the township in which they were situated. There were several hundred workers in each one. I believe Jabulani means 'Happiness.'

17 Zululand: The homeland of the Zulus, the largest ethnic group in South Africa. Situated in Natal province, about four hundred miles from Johannesburg.

18 Hahulu: Big or very much. 'Thank you very much.'

19 Sangoma: A Witchdoctor, male or female. Training period said to be 25 years. The other traditional healer is an Inyanga or herbalist, literally 'Man of the trees.' There are currently many times more traditional healers in South Africa than Western style doctors. Attempts are being made to integrate them into modern medicine and to benefit from their methods and to study their drugs and potions for possible use in pharmacology.

20 Hamba kahle: Go well.

21 Sala kahle, Inkosi: Stay well, Chief.

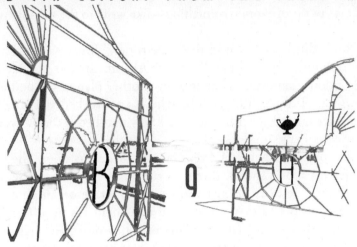

I had just finished operating and was sitting in the downstairs break room. This bare and utilitarian area was on a corner of the corridors next to the recovery room and the operating theaters. It was open on two sides. The other two had continuous rows of chrome-plated armchairs with hardwood arms and unyielding maroon vinyl upholstery, not made for comfort. In the corner stood a black rotary dial telephone. I was writing up my last operation of the day. Michael Jonas, my colleague from gynecology, joined me. He was also in green scrubs, waiting to do a case, and obviously anxious to talk.

"John, did you hear about Eve and the M.R.C.O.G.[1] exam?" Jonas asked.

"No, Mike."

"Well, she presented her book of fifty cases for the exam, as we've all had to do. The examiner looked at it and found she had included a dozen ruptured uteri occurring during labor, and was forced to do several cesarean hysterectomies. He jumped on her for that, so she tried to explain how late our patients come in at Bara, with the uterus often already ruptured. He failed her anyway for 'bad prenatal care.' So much for her expensive trip to Britain."

"That's terrible! Eve is really good, isn't she? What will she do now?"

"Eve must either stay over there and study or get a job, or come back here and try again next time. She hasn't made up her mind. Darned expensive, any way she does it."

"Can't your professor do something—like write to the examiners?" I asked.

"I don't think that would really help her," Jonas said. "They won't take too much notice of us. We South Africans are too 'provincial' for the London examiners. They live on another planet. Or perhaps we live on one. I don't think anyone who hasn't worked at Bara can understand what we deal with here. You know that better than anyone else, John.

"Take tonight. I have a 17 year-old girl at death's door. She has peritonitis and septic shock, due to a ruptured 'pus tube.' (Septic uterine tube.) The boss doesn't want us to operate on these cases 'because they all die.' But with medical treatment it's no different. The patients still die. It just takes longer. They don't see such bad stuff at the 'Ivory Towers' of the Queen Vic or the Gen, let alone in London. This is real Third World gynecology."

"What are you going to do for this one?" I asked.

"I'm senior enough now so that he lets me alone to do more or less what I want, even if he disagrees. He can't say too much because of my recent promotion to full specialist status. So I'm going to open her belly and see what I can do. Do you want to come and see what we're up against, John? You're into bad bellies."

"Sure, I'm finished, so I have time. There must be a way to help these young people. Congrats on your promotion, Mike—I didn't know. Are you now in charge of a unit?"

"Yes, I've quit being an Indian—I'm now one of you chiefs. We're splitting Ob-Gyn into a couple of sections and I'll have charge of one."

We walked to Jonas' operating room and scrubbed. Inside, Jules Brobeck, our anesthetist friend, had the patient asleep and the scrub nurse was cleaning her abdomen.

"She's a sick girlie," Brobeck commented.

"You bet! That pus from the tubes is really toxic," Jonas said. "While it's contained in the tubes it doesn't seem to do much harm, except for pain during intercourse. But once those bags of pus[2] rupture, all hell breaks loose. John came to tell me what to do about it."

"I can just show you what we're trying to do for our bad bellies," I answered.

As we approached the table, the patient's abdomen was already draped and ready.

"Mike, are you going to do one of your cosmetic low incisions?" I asked.

"No, I think we need better access, so I'll go vertical midline."

With that, Jonas made an incision from navel to pubic bone. He progressively deepened it through the fat and muscles, while I stopped the bleeding points with the cautery. I had the suction ready as his knife reached the last layer and entered the peritoneal cavity. A huge stream of foul-smelling creamy-green pus came pouring out, cascading all over the abdomen and the drapes. Despite my strenuous efforts with the suction and Jonas' mopping with towels, the pus started to run onto the floor and Jonas started jiggling around uncomfortably.

"Suck John, suck!" Jonas called. "It's getting in my shoes. I'll have to pitch them."

"Yuk! I'm sorry, Mike," I said. "Charge them to the hospital administration. But you must be right—it can't be good to leave that nasty stuff in there. What is it they say about surgeons? 'The best thing they do is to drain pus.' Well, there's a grain of truth in that. Remember, in previous generations it used to be called 'laudable pus.' I'm not sure exactly what's 'laudable' about this, except maybe we'll be 'laudable' for getting it out! Anyway, let's do that, stick in some drains and get out of Dodge."

We cleaned up, suctioned and washed out the pus as best we could. Once we could see well enough, Jonas showed me the ruptured left fallopian tube.[3] He clamped it and firmly stitched the stump at its base on the uterus. He suture-ligated several feeding arteries.

He then demonstrated the unruptured right tube. It was like a tense fat sausage, ten inches long and two or three inches thick. He removed it in the same way as before, taking great care not to rupture the thin-walled bag of pus in the process.

"The normal Fallopian tube is a floppy little pink thing," Jonas said. "It's about two inches long and under a quarter of an inch thick. It's amazing how it can expand. Of course, both ends must first close off due to previous infection and then the fun begins. The pus that's continually formed now has no way out and the tube just goes on expanding. The bacteria continue to multiply and the body pushes out more white blood cells[4] and chemicals to try and kill them. That's what makes up the witches' brew we're dealing with.

"But it's really the release of the bacteria and their exo- or endo-toxins[5] into the peritoneum[6] that causes the harm. The peritoneal membrane has a huge absorptive surface, bigger than the body's skin area. It's only one cell thick and absorbs things like toxins rapidly into the blood stream, rather like an IV. This causes the 'endotoxic shock.'[7]

"Now the poor girl is sterile, in addition to her other problems. At least she can't get 'pus tubes' again—if she lives to tell the tale."

"Do you ever drain the subphrenic[8] spaces, Mike?" I asked.

"No, should I?"

"That could be part of the problem," I replied. "Let's look."

I managed with some difficulty to get my hand and much of my forearm through the incision up towards the diaphragm, first on the left and then the right. A further flood of pus came down from each space, oozing down around my arm. Jonas extended the incision upwards by several inches, nearly to the ribs, to give better access to the subphrenic spaces—between the diaphragm and the liver on the right and above the spleen and stomach on the left. We carefully washed out both spaces and suctioned them clear.

"Broad corrugated drains[9] please, Sister," I asked. "I roll these up to try and get better drainage. I think it keeps the hole in the belly wall open. Those floppy Penrose drains[10] some people use just can't cope. They block up with fibrin in a few hours."

I took a sheet of red corrugated rubber from the sister and rolled it lengthwise. I then made a cut in the abdominal wall just below the left ribs and pulled the rolled-up drain into the subphrenic space, leaving an inch sticking out. I repeated the process on the right and put two similar drains into the pelvis, through cuts in the lower abdomen. I placed a thin red rubber catheter through a tiny hole, leaving the end free in the abdominal cavity. We then sutured the drains and the catheter in place.

"We'll run in neomycin[11] through that tube, to get it to the source of the pus," I said. "Anyway, Mike, for what it's worth, that's what I'm doing for my bad cases right now."

"Thanks for your help and new ideas, John. We'll give it a go and see if she does better than the girls only getting antibiotics. Please come and see her in the ward."

I followed that patient, only to see her die. I operated on several more with Jonas. Though patients lived longer, they still died of infection, with kidney failure and severe weight loss. Another surgeon did a similar case with Jonas, with the same depressing result. When we could get autopsies on these cases, there was residual infection in the subphrenic spaces and pelvis, despite our drainage. Even with the rolled drains, the holes were blocked with fibrin[12]—part of the body's defense system for closing off infection.

Jonas and I continued working on these cases together. We had countless discussions and did extensive research on the subject of peritonitis.[13] General surgery cases with the most severe abdominal infections were also dying. Their peritonitis arose mostly from injuries of the intestines, so the organisms[14] and problems were somewhat different.

We studied the gynecology deaths for a year and found that cancer caused two thirds, and sepsis the remaining third. Of the 27 deaths due to sepsis, two thirds were from induced abortions,[15] with accidental perforation of the uterus or vagina, resulting in peritonitis. The remaining third died from infected uterine tubes with peritonitis. Either way, it was a tragic loss of life for too many young women, who often left young children at home.

I learned a great deal about the sad effects of the laws that made performing an abortion into a criminal offence. No doctors or hospitals dared to do abortions for fear of the law. The 'back-street' abortionists in Soweto and elsewhere were very busy. They were not medically qualified. To induce an abortion, he or she, and often even the unfortunate pregnant woman herself, used any available sharp object to do the job. These makeshift instruments ranged from knitting needles to straightened coat hangers or pieces of wire. The abortionist repeatedly pushed this tool up inside the vagina, hoping it would pass through the cervix or 'mouth' of the uterus and dislodge the pregnancy. These procedures usually caused vaginal bleeding, causing the patients to legitimately seek hospital care.

Sometimes such attempts caused a 'simple' septic incomplete abortion, with infection confined to the uterus. These cases could be safely handled in hospital by uterine curettage to empty the uterus, under cover of intravenous antibiotics. (Spontaneous miscarriages were generally *not* infected. Thus the term 'septic' abortion really meant 'induced' or 'criminal').

But more often the case became much more complicated, as the instrument frequently missed the cervix and did not enter the uterine

# BARAGWANATH GYNAECOLOGY UNIT

## Discharges, first 8 months 1974.

| | |
|---|---|
| Total | 1995 |
| Abortion | 613 |
| Pelvic infection | 380 |

STATISTICS FROM THE GYNECOLOGY UNIT IN 1974

cavity, or it passed through the muscle wall. Instead of dislodging the fetus it would repeatedly perforate the vagina or the uterus, piercing the pelvic floor or the abdominal cavity, and introducing infection. In passing, it could also tear the rectum, bladder or small bowel, further compounding the disaster.

This amateur meddling and instrumentation with primitive, unsterile, and infected tools often caused very severe infections of the whole uterus, the surrounding pelvic tissues and the peritoneal cavity. Such patients were much more ill even than those with peritonitis from ruptured tubes. The germs introduced during the procedure were different. They were more dangerous, often including tetanus or gas gangrene. Attempts at cure dictated the removal of the entire uterus and tubes, in addition to the surgery needed for peritonitis.

During our research Jonas and I found an experimental study showing that the only way to properly drain the peritoneum was by the use of tubes attached to a closed irrigation and drainage system. We also found some successful animal studies, describing thorough washout of the abdominal cavity with anti-bacterial solutions[16] at the time of surgery and for the post-operative period. A number of different tubes, drainage systems, antibiotics and antiseptic agents were used in these studies.

Since nothing could be worse than our present results, we were ready for change. Our new approach combined knowledge of the patients' problems, the reasons for our prior failures and ideas gleaned from our research. We made a list of tubes, instruments, peritoneal dialysis fluid[17] and antibiotics that were available, and obtained supplies for the theaters. We discussed our plans with the operating theater staff.

We would do the usual operation, with a more meticulous washout during surgery, and add a closed irrigation and drainage system. This would use three flexible nasogastric tubes,[18] with multiple side holes near their tips. About ten inches of each tube, including the holes, would be buried in the three potential trouble spots—the pelvis and both subphrenic spaces—to wash them clean continuously and remove the bacteria and their toxic products.

The tubes would be connected to bottles of peritoneal dialysis fluid containing an antibiotic, in order to fill the abdomen with washout solution. The fluid would be pumped in rapidly, using a plastic blood pump. After thoroughly washing the peritoneal cavity, the tubes would be detached and connected to urine drainage bags in order to empty the abdomen. This cycle would be repeated every three hours for several days.

The fluid would actively wash out the three places with the greatest potential for further infection. The antibiotic would be at a higher concentration in these spaces than could be safely used when given intravenously. This should be at a supra-lethal level,[19] enough to kill most of the bacteria we expected. We chose the fairly new antibiotic Gentamicin[20] to put into the fluid, while giving penicillin or a new cephalosporin drug by vein. We wanted the blood levels of Gentamicin to be low, as too high a level could cause deafness or kidney failure, particularly with the poor kidney function in our very ill patients.

Our first case was a patient with a septic abortion and peritonitis, who was already in septic shock[21] and early renal failure. She had been admitted two days earlier and was receiving maximal medical therapy. A medical unit had been called in for consultation to help manage the renal failure, and the medical registrars were seeing the patient frequently. Jonas and I wrote down our plans in the patient's chart and obtained informed consent as best we could from the very ill patient and her father. We planned surgery for the afternoon. Mike and I had lunch together, and then went to the theater.

I was browsing through the chart outside theater three, while the nurses asked me some last minute questions. I suddenly stiffened and called out: "Hey Mike, come and see what this ass-hole has written here!"

Jonas came and saw, written in black felt pen, and signed by a medical registrar: *There is absolutely nothing that can be washed out of this patient's belly!*

"We'll see about that!"

We had requested Jules Brobeck for the anesthesia. While he got the patient ready, we went to change and then scrubbed together in the small anteroom. The scrub-nurse prepared the patient's skin with Betadine solution, and then she and Jonas draped the abdomen with green towels, exposing the entire front of her trunk, from below the breasts to the pubis.

"Wish me luck," said Jonas.

"I certainly do! This has got to be right. We'll give it our best shot."

"Doctors, what will you do with all those things in the corner?" the sister asked.

"We'll show you, Sister. We call it 'peritoneal lavage.'[22] That's French for 'washing out.' as in 'lavatory,'" I said.

The sister and the other nurses in the room laughed at this analogy. Many of them had their very first experience with a flushing toilet when they started in nursing school at Bara.

The case went very well, with the usual flood of evil pus that we expected. The perforated and infected uterus was swollen, soggy and rotten, oozing foul smelling pus.

"That's so gross!" I said. "My kids wouldn't believe what I do for a living."

Jonas performed a very rapid and skillful hysterectomy with my assistance. We then carefully scrubbed out the peritoneum from top to bottom with gauze sponges, using many liters of warm saline solution. We paused when the irrigating fluid began to come back clear, and added an antibiotic called Ancef[23] to the last wash. We then placed our three tubes as planned and sutured them firmly in place. To avoid leakage we made sure the entry holes were tight around the tubes.

At last we were satisfied. I was pleased to see that the surgery had taken only ten or twenty minutes longer than our usual ones. Jonas now closed the abdomen securely, while I broke scrub and started writing the detailed instructions for care. Since Bara had no intensive care unit at the time the best plan would be to use a side ward, with a 'Special Nurse' to take care of the patient. Though the orders looked complex, I thought they would be quite easy for the 'Special' to follow once I had shown her the technique.

"She's somewhat better already," Jules Brobeck said. "Her B.P. is more stable. She's also beginning to pee a little. She was quite dry when you guys started."

Jonas and I applied the dressings and then walked out, all the while congratulating each other about the case. We showered and changed clothes. By the time we had dressed and were back downstairs, the patient was in the recovery room. I instructed the nurses there on the new system. They used warmed Ringer's lactate for irrigation until the patient reached the ward. The blood pump delivered the fluid rapidly. The inflow and outflow cycles worked perfectly.

So far our *peritoneal lavage* was a success!

The two of us spent the rest of the day, into the evening, taking turns watching the patient every half hour and making sure the technique worked flawlessly. The 'Special' was a bright senior student, about to graduate from nursing school. She had no difficulty in mastering the process and took great pains to do it all correctly. She realized she was helping us break new ground. Whenever we praised her abilities she positively glowed and gave us a happy smile.

The patient continued to improve throughout the evening, though the fluid in the bags stayed bloody and dirty. I helped the nurse hand over to the next 'Special' at 11 pm. She did an excellent job of explaining the process to her colleague. After answering a few questions from the night nurse I felt comfortable about leaving her in charge.

Mike Jonas and I both arrived early the next morning to check on the patient and help with the handover to the day nurse. There had been further steady improvement overnight. The patient was quite sane and rational, able to talk and to thank us. Her blood pressure had risen to normal and her pulse was down from over 120 to about 80 beats per minute, just above normal. Her fever was markedly lower. The previously high white blood cell count (indicating infection) was also near normal. She had little urinary output, but the chemical signs of kidney failure in her blood analysis were dramatically better.

"I guess that's due partly to the dialysis we get as a bonus from our *lavage* system," I commented. "She won't need much renal function while the tubes are in place—she has her own 'artificial kidney.'"

Michael Jonas grabbed my hand and pumped it enthusiastically up and down and gave me a bear hug. (South African equivalents of a 'High Five.')

"Well, John, I think we've done it!" he said. "I guess time will tell. How long do you think we'll need to leave those tubes in?"

"We certainly don't know that yet," I said. "The fluid in those bags is still quite bloody and cloudy, with a few stringy bits of fibrin in it. Let's just say 'until the fluid is clear'. We'll take them out then if her general condition goes on improving like this, and she shows no more signs of infection. I'm afraid to leave the tubes in contact with the bowel for too long, in case they make a hole and cause further grief."

"That sounds good to me—and logical," Jonas said. "You're the boss of the tubes."

"Mike, when you consider that fluid is still so dirty, you can see why we failed with the old procedures," I said. "There's just too much infected junk to be easily cleared out. Simple drainage plainly didn't get it all. The fibrin also did a job on us by blocking the drain holes. So the process started all over again, forming new abscesses. As for what your boss used to do with antibiotics alone—that was clearly doomed to failure."

The patient continued to improve so that even the medical registrar was impressed. He admitted he had been wrong in his assessment. He wrote and signed an apology in the chart. I removed the tube from her nose and she could take liquids by mouth. Bowel function returned even while the lavage continued. Her kidneys also started to function normally. There were no more signs of infection. The lavage fluid grew clearer every day. With no guidelines and being scared of a return of infection, I left the tubes in for five days, perhaps a day or two longer than strictly necessary.

The patient's wound healed perfectly and she was soon up and about. She left the hospital on the tenth day, with not the slightest sign of infection. Even the head of Ob-Gyn was impressed, but remained highly skeptical.

It was not long before we got a second case to do, and a few weeks later I had a bad surgical case. The patients all did well. Soon we had treated seven cases of severe generalized[24] peritonitis in the new way. All survived to go home.

This was unprecedented in our experience, so we arranged to show these results at a Saturday morning surgical Grand Rounds at the Johannesburg General Hospital. My wife, Ann, prepared diagrams for slides and we showed color photos of the surgery.

The presentation went well and we received considerable applause. But no one who had not experienced the problems of these cases could really appreciate how much we had achieved. Professor Du Toit was his usual skeptical self. He wanted us to do an equal number of 'control' cases in the old way.

"But sir, we have been doing a prospective study[25] for nearly a year, so we've really done that," I said. "All our previous patients were dying, whether we used antibiotics alone or added very adequate surgical drainage of all the areas with abscesses. We obtained autopsies and studied the causes of failure. There was residual sepsis in the subphrenic spaces and the pelvis and the drainage holes had all closed. We developed our technique based on those findings, together with experimental data from the literature. Now, for the first time, all the patients are living. I think that shows we have done something right."

"Well, Hunt, I might believe you," said Prof Du Toit. "But unless you have 'control' patients, your work will have no scientific validity and no one will accept it."

"I'm sorry, sir, but we're treating people, not laboratory rats," I replied.

Du Toit frowned, shook his head, raised his eyebrows and went on to the next case.

As we walked out together, Jonas said, "Can you credit that? The old bastard."

"I warned you not to expect much different," I replied.

The two of us stuck to our beliefs. We decided to continue our present course for the good of the patients, and would go on cooperating and carefully collecting cases and data. We would write them up only when we had an adequate series and were secure with the safety and efficacy of the technique.

We learned a few more lessons as we pursued our studies. We still had occasional deaths, largely in patients who were moribund[26] on admission and who failed to respond even to our resuscitation efforts. I had one who started his stay with a cardiac arrest in Casualty. He never recovered completely from the arrest and soon died.

As we learned more, the deaths became less frequent and there were unbroken runs of first ten, and then twenty consecutive patient survivals. One patient developed a leak from the small bowel, which I felt could have been related to leaving the tube in too long, so we found the softest tubes we could and removed them just as soon as the fluid was clear. The time was reduced to an average of three days.

I had other problems in the surgical cases. They did not have 'pure' peritonitis like the gynecology patients. Most of them were due to bowel damage, with escape of infected stool or small bowel content causing the peritonitis. Any repair of the bowel could easily break down again and leak, due to the infection and impaired healing. I found it was safer to bring the damaged ends of the bowel out through the abdominal wall. They could then not leak to contaminate the peritoneum. When I did that no patients died.

One of my patients had perforated *mucormycosis*[27] of the stomach, a very rare and generally fatal fungal disease. The fungus was not sensitive to antibiotics, so death was inevitable, despite lavage or any form of surgery.

One day my registrar swapped duties with his colleague from Unit Four, who thus worked with me and learned the technique of peritoneal lavage. A few nights later that registrar used his new knowledge on a patient in Unit Four. His chief did rounds the next day and was distressed to see the tubes in place. He pulled them out in anger. I secretly followed up on the patient. The man soon developed a subphrenic abscess, as I suspected might happen. The space was no longer adequately drained since the tube was in for only a few hours overnight. I felt this helped validate the lavage approach.

Jonas also had a bad experience, with a sad object lesson. He had a pregnant sixteen-year-old patient with severe peritonitis, which proved not to be gynecological but due to a ruptured appendix. Unfortunately, I was not available and they had to call the duty surgeon. Mike Jonas saw the seriousness of the peritonitis and suggested politely and diffidently, as was his nature, that this would be a good case for peritoneal lavage.

"I don't believe in that fancy stuff," the older surgeon said.

He closed the belly without adequate drainage. The young patient deteriorated in the familiar manner—and died.

A further year of this work convinced us that we were really on the right track. We published our first report on over thirty cases in the South African Medical Journal. This was followed over the years by several papers in surgical, obstetrical and gynecological journals. I presented the work at an intensive care congress in Rio de Janeiro. The paper was well received. Someone from Giessen, Germany heard the presentation and invited me to speak at a congress there. I did so and followed with a paper written in German with the help of a young visiting German surgeon. The work was very well accepted.

By the end of our collaboration we had done a total of 147 cases, with minimal mortality or morbidity. We compared them to a series of comparable patients treated in more 'standard' ways. We obtained details of these from the record room. The cases included our own earlier patients and those of other doctors. We showed a vast, statistically significant difference in survival between the two groups of cases.

We found two papers in the literature in which people had used operative and lavage techniques reasonably similar to ours, and had used simultaneous control cases. These series also showed great superiority for the lavage principle. We felt this obviated the need for us to do a 'control' series of our own.

Though the technique was simple to do and to teach, very few people adopted it. Many claimed it was 'too much trouble.' I was called in after the event in a few cases in other public and private hospitals. I invariably found that the wrong tubes had been used, often in the wrong places. I could frequently not help the patients at that stage.

Whenever I got into discussions about the technique, I liked to quote Dr. De Bakey, who visited the Johannesburg General and demonstrated repair of an aortic aneurysm in one-third the time usually taken by the local vascular surgeons he was teaching that day.

"If you do what I do, you will get the results that I get," the great surgeon said.

[1] M.R.C.O.G. examination: The British higher exam in Obstetrics and Gynecology. 'Member of the Royal College of O & G.' As with the F.R.C.S., candidates had to go to Britain to write the exam and fulfill certain requirements before doing so. One of these was a 'book' of 50 cases handled personally. The exam formed part of the basis for becoming a specialist in the field. It was equivalent to Board Certification in America.

[2] Pus: The body makes pus in an attempt to control infection. It is composed of the bacteria, white blood cells sent to combat them, and other chemical agents the body manufactures to assist in the process. It also contains poisons or toxins put out by the bacteria and body cells killed by the germs. It is often closed in a membrane, made from body tissues, chiefly fibrin. In these cases it is contained in the blocked uterine tube until it bursts.

[3] Fallopian tube: Scientific name for the uterine tubes, one on each side, entering the upper end of the uterus.

[4] White blood cells: The body's primary defense mechanism. They are involved in fighting bacteria. Their numbers in the blood increase dramatically in an infection. See Pus, # 2 above.

[5] Exo- or endo-toxins: Bacteria produce some or all their bad effects by creating poisons, which are either inside the bacteria—endotoxins, or outside—exotoxins. 'Endotoxic shock' is very dangerous and often fatal.

[6] Peritoneum: The thin lining of the abdominal cavity. It also covers the entire surface of the small and large bowel, the liver, the spleen and the stomach. It is a huge area, one and a half times the body surface area.

[7] Endotoxic shock: A serious and often fatal condition caused by the release of bacterial endotoxins into the circulation. See # 5 above.

[8] Subphrenic spaces: Spaces under the diaphragm on each side, between it and the liver on the right , and between the diaphragm and the spleen and stomach on the left.

[9] Corrugated drain: Pieces of sterile corrugated rubber, cut into strips and pulled through holes in the abdominal wall in an attempt to let fluids escape readily. Drains can be of many shapes, sizes or materials. Plastic and silicone rubber are the commonest. There is much controversy over when or whether to use drains and which ones to use.

[10] Penrose drains: Very soft drains made of condom-type rubber. They are popular because they are so soft.

[11] Neomycin: An antibiotic effective against some of the bacteria found in these cases. Not used much otherwise, because of toxicity. It was being used elsewhere in the world for the same purpose.

[12] Fibrin: As part of its defense mechanism the body produces a tough fibrous substance, which tries to glue things together and close holes. It also wraps around abscesses. Sometimes it harms while trying to help.

[13] Peritonitis: Infection of the peritoneum, as described here. See # 6 above.

[14] Organisms: Another word for bacteria. Nonspecific.

15 <u>Induced abortions</u>: Abortions produced by unqualified operators, since abortions were illegal and could lead to heavy penalties for doctors doing them. Since conditions were not sterile, or even clean, many women and girls became infected or 'septic' from the procedure.

16 <u>Anti-bacterial solutions</u>: Researchers tried many drugs, as long as they would not harm the patient. Certain ones, which were not antibiotics, had a vogue, but were found of no value.

17 <u>Peritoneal dialysis solution</u>: A balanced electrolyte solution with much the same makeup as blood plasma, without the protein. It is used to cycle through the peritoneal cavity to act as an 'artificial kidney.' Now becoming a commonly used method to treat chronic renal failure.

18 <u>Nasogastric tubes</u>: Plastic tubes over three feet long, with multiple side holes near the tip. Soft and flexible, they are usually passed through the nose and used to drain the stomach after surgery.

19 <u>Supra-lethal level</u>: The level of an antibiotic required to kill an organism is known as the 'minimal inhibitory concentration,' or MIC. This differs with the organism and the antibiotic. Calculations showed that the antibiotic Gentamicin, which they used in the dialysis fluid, was at three times the MIC required to kill many of the organisms they encountered.

20 <u>Gentamicin</u>: An antibiotic of the aminoglycoside class. It was very effective against many organisms, but had potential toxicity at high or prolonged levels, causing renal damage or deafness. Putting it in the fluid gave high local levels in the abdomen with low levels in the blood.

21 <u>Septic shock</u>: The same as endotoxic shock. See #s 5 & 7, above.

22 <u>Peritoneal lavage</u>: Thorough washing out of the peritoneal cavity.

23 <u>Ancef</u>: Proprietary name for a Cephalosporin type broad-spectrum antibiotic—Cefazolin.

24 <u>Generalized peritonitis</u>: The infection had to involve the entire abdomen, from pelvis to subphrenic spaces. They did not do the lavage if the peritonitis was only in or around the pelvis or in a single area of peritoneum.

25 <u>Prospective study</u>: One of the aspects of a good scientific study. The other key elements are that the patients should be randomized to the two groups of treatment to be compared. The researchers should have no part in the selection process. These elements are hard to justify when the end-point is death or survival and one treatment is known to work, while the other does not.

26 <u>Moribund</u>: In the process of dying.

27 <u>Mucormycosis</u>: A very rare but serious fungus infection, possibly contracted by eating moldy bread.

After completing another of our combined cases one afternoon, Mike Jonas and I went upstairs for a cup of tea, joining a group of surgeons and anesthetists in the lounge. This was a sparsely furnished cafeteria-style room. It had cream painted walls, with no pictures, bare vinyl tile floors, chrome and plastic chairs and Formica tabletops. A large stainless steel urn of once-hot tea stood on a table in front of the window, surrounded by dozens of heavy utilitarian white cups and saucers. A large jug of milk and a bowl of sugar were nearby. The steel-framed, uncurtained windows looked out across the highway to the bus stops and Soweto beyond.

"I'll buy today," I said, pouring us each a cup before sitting down.

"Cheapskate, why don't you take me somewhere decent? I don't think they change this urn once a week."

"It's the 'wishee washee' surgeons again!" said Jules Brobeck. "How was your case?"

"Just fine," Jonas answered. "We missed you—where were you?"

"I was doing boring stuff, keeping a patient quiet while the carpenters screwed some bones together. I must admit though, that I like it when they operate under a bloodless field. There's no mess and the theater smells a lot better than when you two guys work."

"Come on, Jules!" I responded. "You know you really prefer working with us because you like a challenge."

"Some days I can just manage to get by without one," Brobeck answered. "Thanks anyway for your kind thoughts."

"Thinking of challenges," I said. "Does anyone remember that strange Obstetrics registrar called Sinkovitz, or something like that? He was the world's worst chain smoker. He was at the Queen Vic when I was a student, some time ago, I must admit. I don't know where he is now."

"He's long gone to the East Rand,"[1] Jonas said.

"Well, when I was doing my rotation at the Vic, he used to terrorize us," I continued. "Whenever he pressed the buzzer, which was frequent, we all had to rush out of our rooms and be on parade to watch the master at work, even for the most trivial things. We also had to endure his heavy-handed sarcasm. I heard he even had a surgical mask with a hole in it, so that he could smoke while doing a pelvic exam.

"One night at two a.m. he pushed the button yet again. I shook myself awake and splashed my face. Four sleepy students hastily made it to the labor room in our scrub suit 'pajamas' and slippers. We soon woke up when we saw the charade that was being enacted.

"An enormous middle-aged woman lay on the delivery bed. She was already up in obstetric stirrups, lying flat on her back, with her abdomen bulging, her huge legs flexed and her extensive perineum exposed. A 'Playboy' model she was not. Sinkovitz was gowned and gloved, standing between the stirrups, conducting the labor and cajoling the patient in his guttural voice and thick eastern European accent. The room was full of people. A houseman, three staff midwives, four medical students and two student nurses were all gathered round, intently watching.

"'Puush!' said Sinkovitz.

"'But I'm not pregnant!' the patient responded, in an accent as thick as his. They could have come from the same village.

"'I don't care, puush!! voman.'

"'But Doctor, I'm *not pregnant*,' she replied again.

"'Mrs. Goldberg, you remember you had a pain in the belly. You went to Casualty at the Gen. Well, they found you were pregnant and sent you here for us to deliver the baby.'

"'Yes Doctor, I remember, but they are wrong. I'm *not* pregnant.'

"'Are you telling me they don't know their business? Well, let's find out.'

"He promptly did a pelvic exam and reported that the baby's head was presenting high in the vagina, with the cervix fully dilated and stretched around it. The patient should have been able to deliver the baby in a couple of minutes, if only she would help herself.

"'There *is* a baby in there, Mrs. Goldberg, *whether you like it or not*. It's ready to be born right now,' he said. 'Come on, Mrs. Goldberg!! Pleeease! Puush, puush, puush.'

"Again nothing happened. They repeated this fruitless dialogue once or twice until the doctor tired of it.

"'Get me the forceps,[2] staff nurse,' Sinkovitz said. 'If you won't help yourself, Mrs. Goldberg, I have to use some big metal tongs to pull the baby out. I hope you understand.'

"'I know vot you're saying, Doctor. Truly, I'm not pregnant. You gotta believe me.'"

"'Well Ma'am, *you are pregnant and you gotta believe me!*' He was getting angry.

"'You leave me no choice. I must use the forceps. This may hurt you a bit, but I must get the baby out now or it's going to die.'"

"'Oi Vey,' she responded.

"He put on new gloves and took the forceps from the nurse midwife. He inserted the two pieces one by one through the vagina, carefully placed them around the baby's head and locked the handles together. I had to admire his skill. In a few minutes he had delivered the head, followed by the shoulders. Then the whole baby slithered out, kicking actively.

"He handed the squirming child to the midwife, who held up the big, beautiful, baby boy for Mrs. Goldberg to see.

"'Oi!' she said. 'My husband vill be surprised. He t'ought I had de change of life. T'ank you Doctor. A fine healt'y boy. Really a vonderful gift from God.'"

"That's a really great story, John," Jonas said. "I ran into Sinkovitz only once. He was a little before my time. But he certainly was a character."

"I had the opposite experience once, when I was still young and cocksure," Jonas continued. "I was doing Mission work in the Transkei, before I decided on a career in gynecology. I was called to this Chief's place in the deep country, because a baby just wouldn't come. I drove perhaps ten miles on terrible dirt roads to get there. There was a huge *middelmannetjie*[3] between the tire tracks, so high that I feared for the oil sump on my car.

"When I entered the round, dark, windowless hut, I could barely see the chief's youngest wife, lying on a rush mat on the floor. All the old crones, who act as midwives, were sitting in a circle round the teenage girl. I uncovered her belly and saw it was very blown up. I knelt down and examined the distended abdomen. There were witchdoctor marks in a circle all around. It was soft and smooth. I could feel no uterus and no fetal parts. The *percussion*[4] note sounded like beating on a drum, so she was clearly full of gas. I then did a pelvic exam right there, on the floor, with some difficulty. This confirmed that she was definitely not pregnant. She had a *pseudo-cyesis*[5] or false pregnancy.

"I told them she wasn't pregnant, but no one believed me. Only the chief spoke any English. Detailed explanations of pseudocyesis were thus impossible. So Doctor Smarty decided to show them. I took a bottle of ether from my bag and slapped an open drop ether mask over her face. She was soon asleep. Her belly relaxed and the swelling disappeared.

"'You see Chief, I told you so,' I said, proud as a peacock.

"'Where is my baby?' he demanded. 'What have you done to him, white magician?'

"He looked very threatening and I saw other men gathering round the door. I chickened out and hastily stopped the ether. The patient woke up rather quickly, because it had been such a short anesthetic and she was not deeply asleep. Fortunately for me the swelling soon reappeared. I happily patted her swollen belly.

"There's your baby, Chief," I said, with a big smile. "He is just not ready to come out.'

"I grabbed my bag, hastily got in the car and made my getaway as fast as I could down the same rough tracks. I was never going to return to that *kraal*.[6]

"The psychology behind pseudocyesis must be pretty powerful. It's not only country girls who get it. We periodically see them at Bara. In this society the ability of women to have babies is fundamental to their well-being. I suppose that's what pushes them into it."

I spotted Eve Parsons in the group. She had recently returned from England with her new M.R.C.O.G.[7] diploma.

"Congratulations, Eve! How did you manage it?" I asked.

"Thanks, Mr. Hunt," she smiled. "I had several strokes of good luck. I saw an advert for a *locum tenens* registrar job in a journal. It was at the 'country branch' of St Thomas' Hospital in Surrey. A few of Tommy's consultants[8] and registrars also worked there. I applied, with my fingers crossed, and got the job. As you know, St. Thomas' is the most snooty and prestigious of the London teaching hospitals. I was amazed they would even consider a woman, let alone one from South Africa. The second piece of luck (for me anyway) came when the registrar whom I replaced could not return due to illness, and they kept me on. That job was a great help to me.

"I told the chiefs about my problems with the exam and my book. After I'd worked and talked with them for a while and shown them a few of my clinical and sociology slides, they began to understand how things are at Bara. One of the consultants helped me rework the book. I substituted a few cases that I did with them for some of my ruptured uteri. I suspect that they probably also discussed the situation at high level in the College.

"When I took the exam again, after a year's work in Britain, I started out with far more confidence. I'm sure I did well in the written papers. The orals were easy enough. When it came to my book, I had a very rational discussion with the examiner and he passed me.

"So here I am! Eve Parsons, M.R.C.O.G. I can even be a specialist soon, as I've done all my registrar time. Maybe I've also done some good for future Bara candidates."

"Congratulations again, Eve," I said. "I heard about your earlier exam problems from Mike when we started working together. Thinking of that exam, what are you folks doing now about the android pelvis[9] causing prolonged labors in the Bantu women? I know someone here even tried symphysiotomy[10] in these very young girls, with a long reproductive career ahead, as they once did in Ireland."

"It's still a serious problem," Eve answered. "I'm particularly sensitive to it, as you can imagine, Mr. Hunt. A 'symph' does make the pelvis pretty unstable. That weakness lasts for life as far as we know. We certainly don't do them. That means we must do 'trials of labor' in everybody and, of course, Cesars on those who can't deliver after a trial.

"You may wonder what happens about repeat pregnancies after an early Cesarean. We know that the uterus can rupture through the scar, even during normal vaginal deliveries. But it doesn't have to happen. It's far less frequent with modern 'lower segment'[11] Cesars anyway. We just have to watch like a hawk during pregnancy and labor. The old saying 'once a Cesar, always a Cesar,' no longer applies.

"It all depends on improving antenatal care, as my earlier examiner implied. I'm now on a crusade to obtain better help for pregnant women in the townships. We'll no longer accept bad care as inevitable. We're pepping up the staff and facilities at the clinics in Soweto, so that all patients can get free pre-natal care close to home. They can come in earlier, before something bad happens, such as a dead baby, a ruptured uterus or a V.V.F., (vesico-vaginal fistula)[12] from days of 'pushing' against a small pelvis.

"We'll certainly have to do some Cesars because of the small pelvis, but far less hysts for ruptured uteri. As you know, our boss is a world authority on repair of V.V.F.s. We might put him out of business! But we can't do much good outside our area, so he'll still get referrals from elsewhere."

"Speaking of tribal obstetrics," I said. "I also had my 'baptism by fire.' When I was newly qualified, I took a *locum tenens*[13] job in Zeerust for the district surgeon. I had to go out in the tribal areas near Botswana to see patients, just as Mike did in the Transkei. Ann, my brand new young wife, often came out on these calls, to support me and see the countryside. On one such call I also went to a mud hut with a straw thatch roof to deliver a baby. I must say that my obstetric knowledge stopped growing after I left Dr. Sinkovitz at the Vic. It was just enough to get me through the final M.B., B.Ch.[14] exam.

"In the hut, lying on a rug on the smooth cow dung floor[15] was a well-built nineteen-year-old black woman. She looked exhausted from five days of pushing to try and get her baby out. A quick listen to her belly told me the fetus was probably dead. Fortunately for me, the days of strong labor had compressed and squashed the fetal head, which was already in the vagina. I thought I could deliver the baby pretty easily. Meanwhile Ann was bustling round, trying to get clean towels and hot water, both non-existent in that hut.

"Then the rains came. The roof started leaking a stream of cold rainwater onto the patient. Ann stood, holding a small basin over the young woman, trying to catch the water while I worked, kneeling on the floor. I finally pulled out a big and beautiful, but dead, baby. The baby's size probably helped to prolong her labor.

"Ann held the patient's hand and tried to comfort the sobbing young woman. They were not far apart in age so there was a great degree of empathy. Neither of them had dreamed that this kind of thing could even happen. Ann's big eyes filled with tears for both mother and baby, while the girl sobbed inconsolably.

"I finished up and gave the patient *ergotrate* to contract the uterus and stop the bleeding. I also gave long-acting penicillin. I could offer little else, since the new Zeerust hospital was not yet open. I told her to start eating and drinking as soon as possible and I gave her a note to a clinic for a diabetes test because of her big baby. If I understand you, Eve, she would probably have developed a V.V.F. in a few weeks."

Eve Parsons nodded her head and was about to speak when Jonas chimed in.

"You did well, John. I didn't think you had it in you. Eve, we'll have to stop teaching him so much gynecology or he'll put us out of business."

"Enough of obstetrics!" Jacob van Eck chimed in. "Since nobody seems to want to go home or to do any work, I'll quickly tell you my latest urology stories.

"John's unit just sent me this sweet old guy of 79 years. On the tip of his penis he has a huge, smelly 'cauliflower' type of cancer, almost as big as a tennis ball. He says it's been growing for a couple of years. We did a work-up and cleaned things up a bit and then I scheduled him for surgery. I plainly had to get consent for partial amputation of his penis. I asked him during the ward-round, after explaining to him the implications of cancer."

"'Aikona Doctor! No—I've still got a lot of playing to do,' he responded.

"'But it will kill you,' I said.

"'I don't care,' he replied. 'You are not going to cut it off. I need it.'"

"He finally agreed to at least take radiation therapy, and he stayed in hospital. That will give him an auto-amputation anyway—if it works."

"Thanks for the follow up," I said. "I wonder who would still be prepared to 'play' with him?"

"I can't imagine. I'd rather not think about it," van Eck said. "Now for my second story. You also know this one, John, because you were an actor here. Maybe I'm stealing your thunder. You'll soon remember this case you recently sent us. This guy was seen in Casualty several times with 'Drop,'[16] and received 3cc of Crysticillin each time."

I recognized the case immediately and smiled broadly.

"He never came for anything else," van Eck continued. "So his card carried only a vertical row of cryptic one-word notes for the date of each visit: 'Drop.' 3cc Crysticillin. 'Drop.' 3cc Crysticillin. And so it went on for many months. He never seemed to be cured, until the casualty officer got tired or suspicious and sent him to the surgical registrar, probably without undressing him. You saw him there and probably examined him for the first time ever. You concluded the series by writing 'Dropped off. Admit for urologists.'"

"Yes, I'm afraid that was 'gallows humor,'" I said. "The poor guy had lost over two inches of his penis to cancer, with a large eroding malignant ulcer chewing it up. It had also spread to lymph glands in both groins, with cancer fungating[17] through the skin. It's too advanced for any hope of cure. It's a sad object lesson in the dangers of not properly examining patients at every visit and also the perils of accepting the patient's self-diagnosis.

"On a lighter note, tell me something, Jake," I continued. "As a urologist, I'm sure you must know what the Swazi men wear under their kilts."

"I can't say that I do," van Eck replied. "You tell us. I didn't know they wore kilts."

"Well, I had another fascinating working vacation, this time in Swaziland, where I'd thought of joining a private clinic. Our hotel was just outside town at the head of the Ezulwini Valley, where you could see forever to the East, between hundreds of hills. There was often low cloud or valley fog, like a gray veil, suspended at eye level over the valley. We could often see over it and sometimes under—like coming through the cloud ceiling in an airliner. The whole setting was incredibly beautiful and ethereal, like a dream world or a fairytale. I used to imagine 'Brigadoon' appearing out of the mist.

"Anyway, I got to see a wide variety of new places and people I couldn't imagine even existed. Though Swaziland[18] had been a British protectorate and was not part of South Africa, the social structure and conditions were in some ways similar. The elite few were wealthy but most of the people rather poor. There's no industrial or mining base to provide employment, so many Swazi men had to find work on the South African gold mines to provide some family income. There are no real cities, except Mbabane, the capital, which is so small it hardly qualifies for the title. It was a monarchy and I had the privilege of treating members of the royal family, both while I was there and later at Bara.

"I saw many local men wearing straight wrap-around skirts or kilts, usually of sober colored patterned cotton material, unpleated, quite unlike Scotsmen's kilts. This was their traditional tribal garb. I examined one of the men medically one day. After he undressed I saw that he wore no underwear, but he had a small, round, brown gourd about two inches across, fitted snugly over the tip of his penis. I encountered one or two more while I was there and my interpreter told me the gourds were regular men's wear—for 'protection'—I never found out what the danger was. I guess they're the Swazi fashion equivalent of our 'Jockey shorts.'

"We bought a few craft items at the local open-air markets. One of our favorites is an enormous carved wooden bowl that was handmade from a single piece of their local black and white wood. It is about two feet in diameter and stands six inches high, on three stubby legs. We still use it for salads when we have a party. It really holds a lot of food."

"And now for a change of pace," van Eck said. "Why don't I tell you about the penalty for being caught in adultery? This man had marks around his big toes and his wrists, where he had been tied down with thin ropes. The wronged husband then cut off his penis at the root and threw it away. All we could do for him was to create a skin-level opening in the front of his scrotum for him to pass urine. I don't think he could do it standing up after that, though maybe he learned. I'm sure losing a penis and sitting down to pee would be severe indignities for a man in any society."

"I wonder if you've all noticed the male dominance and yet matriarchal society these people have," I started again. "Many Africans have told me that the men must have the potential to conceive a child every time they have intercourse, 'otherwise they will go crazy.' So they are not interested in contraception. They 'don't like to', and simply will not, wear condoms. The women have to take care of the task, as they do with so much else in their home and family life.

"For example, our well-educated, very smart, house servant already had two children. She wanted a break, and to provide better for them. She went to a clinic for help. Her husband had good job skills and a reasonable income. But he beat her up unmercifully whenever he found she was using any form of contraception. Often on a Friday or Saturday night, when he'd been paid and had been drinking, she came running to us for protection, with her face pulped and purple from his assault. I don't know how she stuck with him."

"We get to deal with it all the time," Mike Jonas commented. "We're constantly handling contraception requests and we put in a lot of I.U.D.s.[19] Unfortunately, they're not foolproof and can be dangerous. We tie tubes when it's appropriate and if they'll allow us."

"We took advantage of one of their more bizarre sexual beliefs at our house," I said. "Over the years we have had several bulldogs as pets, and once we had a pair together. They are big and lovable, but very stupid animals, and probably would never hurt anyone. They even have to be helped to mate and to deliver. The servants told us that many Africans believe a bulldog bite will make a man sterile or maybe impotent. So Ann painted small notices for our back and front gates, showing our two animals, over the words 'Beware Bulldogs.' We've been pretty much free of petty thefts and crime since those signs were posted. They may even be better than having a burglar alarm sign outside one's house.

"Which reminds me," I added, "our one neighbor had no alarm, but posted a fake burglar alarm sign with an unknown name—'Failsafe Alarms.' Soon after the sign appeared they were away for the weekend and their house was totally cleaned out by burglars. None of the neighbors heard or saw anything or knew about it until the owners returned."

"Thanks John, I often wondered whether it was the sign or the alarm," Brobeck said.

"Jake, have you seen many 'love bites'?" I asked.

"I can't think of any," van Eck replied. "What about you?"

"Well, I've seen them in both men and women. The males often come in with their consorts in tow, both parties looking very shamefaced and taciturn. The men usually have an extensive laceration of the scrotum, with one or both testicles hanging in the breeze. Their partner eventually owns up to being the cause. I don't send them to urology because they are really quite easy to fix. We simply scrub up the injured area and then return the 'Ozark Oysters' to their home in the scrotum and suture the skin fairly lightly to allow drainage. If there is any skin missing, the scrotum is very forgiving, and stretches to cover the gap. If the scrotum is all missing, usually from a different type of trauma, we will bury the family jewels in the thighs instead. That also works pretty well."

"Mr. Hunt, where in the world did you get the term 'Ozark Oysters,' for goodness sake?" Eve Parsons asked. "'Family jewels,' I know."

"It was when Prof. Mason and his wife were in the States," I answered. "They were traveling in or near the Ozarks and saw the item 'Grilled Ozark Oysters' on the menu. She was adventurous and ordered some. They tasted good and she wondered what they were. To her horror, the waiter told her they were calves' testicles. She was too embarrassed to tell us how she reacted to that piece of news."

"Well, I guess we eat kidneys, livers and hearts. Some people even eat brains—why not testicles?" van Eck asked. "With all that DNA they probably taste very good."

"You urologists are *so* disgusting!" Eve Parsons answered.

"To each his own," chuckled van Eck happily.

"To get back to 'love bites,' I continued. "The injuries in the women are quite different. The patients usually seem to come in alone, wearing a headscarf or *doek*,[20] like an old-fashioned movie bandit does, covering the mouth. No one else wears them that way. The *doek* hides the ghastly deformity caused by a big bite of the lip.

"When she removes her scarf, the patient shows a horrifying bloody grimace, exposing the full length and spread of almost all the teeth, framed by bloody muscle and skin. The laceration allows the circular muscle round the mouth to pull the edges of the hole far round, showing most of the teeth. It's usually the lower lip that's been bitten, or even torn right off.

"Sometimes these injuries are not the result of sexual passion, but of assault by another woman. In such cases noses, ears, fingers or other body parts can also suffer."

"What on earth do you do for these poor souls?" Eve Parsons asked.

"What I've learned to do is very simple," I replied. "It's natural to think first of putting in a horizontal whipstitch to tidy up and stop the bleeding. If you do so, you will perpetuate the defect and have to refer them to Plastic Surgery. Instead, the key is to undo the sideways retraction of the *orbicularis oris*[21] muscle. I put large skin hooks or even bone hooks into the vermilion part of the lip on each side and pull the flaps towards each other and the midline. This needs quite a stretch, but the lips again cover the teeth, even if the tissues are tight. I stitch the two sides firmly together, making a vertical scar. It gives the patient a 'rosebud mouth' for a time, but it's far better than before. It's very functional and the lip soon stretches as it heals. The plastic surgeons seldom need to change things."

"John, do you remember that girl who had the root stuck through her vagina?" Jonas asked. "I called you to theater to see her and we spent the whole night tidying the mess. The root had perforated a whole lot of small bowel loops and even tore her liver."

"Only too well!" I answered. "They never caught the guy who did it. The girl went crazy and landed in Sterkfontein. I can't blame her. It was really tragic. Injuries through the vagina are not that common, though I suppose you folks see more than I do. But I've had a couple of other interesting ones."

"Such as?" said Eve.

"You may remember, Mike, when I called one of your predecessors to theater. This woman was trying to get away from her 'boyfriend for the night.' She was climbing through a small window, when he took a potshot at her behind with a pistol to say 'Good-bye.' She developed an acute abdomen and I operated on her. We never found an entrance wound before surgery, but on opening her belly and exploring, we found the bullet had gone right up her vagina and out of the lateral fornix[22] into the belly, where it perforated a few other things, just like that stick did. I guess you could say he hit the 'Bull's Eye'!"

"Very funny, John," Jonas said.

"I had a tragic case like this when I was in Britain," I started again. "A lady from a geriatric home came in with an acute abdomen. She was demented, so could give no history. The home knew nothing, except that she used to wander around outdoors. Surgery showed that something had perforated the top of her uterus and also pierced some small bowel. We had to take the uterus out, but microscopic exam in the lab yielded no cause. We never found out what happened or who had done this to her.

"Her husband told me that she had been a wonderful artist, but as she sank rapidly into dementia, her paintings lost their color and became progressively blacker. He started to realize she was going off mentally when she drove the car into the closed garage door, saying it was open. When she was finally put in a home, he found over a hundred unworn outfits of clothes in her closet, together with many new shoes and twenty-four new cameras. He had been giving her cash from his business, 'under the counter,' to avoid taxes. This explained where his latest ten thousand pounds had gone!"

"That served him right!" Eve commented. "But that's a really sad story."

"One more male story and I'll have to go back to my ever-loving spouse and the boys," I said. "I know it's rather rare, and I've had only one case. Jake probably sees more than I do. A few years ago I had a man with persistent erection or *priapism*.[23] We had to put a bed cradle over him to accommodate the great length of his penis, which was closer to 20 than 10 inches long. I was terrified it would go gangrenous from the congestion. All we could do at that time was to keep him on anticoagulants and relieve his pain.

"It's due to thrombosis in the *corpora*[24] *cavernosa* and *spongiosa,* which are normally filled with blood only during erections. In this condition they are filled with clot, so blood entering via the artery can't get out again, like in a massive venous thrombosis in the thigh —*phlegmasia cerulea dolens.*[25] The penis gets progressively bigger and tighter, to the limits of the fascial sheaths. The end result is a huge purple phallus—two or three times the size of a normal erection. In vascular terms, this is an example of a 'compartment syndrome,' a surgical emergency. If treated in those terms it would really need all the corpora to be sliced open from end to end—a terrifying thought— like slicing a blood-filled sponge.

"This case did eventually resolve and shrank down again in a couple of weeks, leaving him with a permanently flaccid organ. What do you do for them now, Jake?"

"We also don't see that many, but the experts are trying to suction out the corpora and wash them out. I'm afraid, as in your case, that erection may be the patient's 'Swan Song.'"

"On that sorry note I must be going," I said. "I loved the 'Bull Session,' if that's the right phrase when Eve is here. Bye, everybody."

[1] East Rand: The 'Rand' or Witwatersrand is the 6,000-foot high ridge of hills where gold was found. Johannesburg is at its center. Cities on either side are either on the East Rand or the West Rand.

[2] Forceps: A pair of obstetric instruments with curved metal blades and handles that can lock together. Used in difficult deliveries only, to help get the baby out. They are placed round the baby's head. (Now largely historical and very rarely used.)

[3] Middelmannetjie: Afrikaans, lit. 'Small middle man.' The strip of grass and low bushes growing between the tire tracks on many country roads that carry little traffic.

[4] Percussion note: Percussion is a basic physical sign. One finger is placed on the skin and the middle finger of the dominant hand hammers or percusses on it. A hollow sound means gas, a dull one means something solid or liquid. Very important in the days before ultrasound, CT scans and MRI.

[5] Pseudocyesis: False pregnancy, often of psychological origin.

[6] Kraal: The name for a collection of African huts. Also used for an animal enclosure on a farm. The word is part of the Afrikaans language, but I'm not sure of its derivation. Pronounced: 'Krahl,' as in Ahh!

[7] M.R.C.O.G: Member of the Royal College of Obstetrics and Gynecology, a British higher qualification, equivalent to American Board Certification in O. & G.

[8] Consultant: Specialist in the field. Equivalent to the American usage: 'Attending Physician.'

[9] Android pelvis: 'Pelvis like a male.' The bony pelvis is often narrow, as in men. This makes a narrow birth canal, with difficult childbirth. It may cause prolonged labor and other problems, such as V.V.F. See # 12.

[10] Symphysiotomy: Cutting the cartilage between the two pubic bones during labor, to stretch the bones apart and allow easier passage of the baby's head. No longer used, because it makes the pelvis unstable.

[11] Lower segment cesarean section: The older 'classical' Cesarean used a long vertical cut through the thick muscle in the body of the uterus. The scar could often rupture during subsequent labors. The newer lower segment procedures are done through a horizontal cut, lower down on the organ. The wound heals better, with less chance of rupture in later pregnancy or labor.

[12] Vesico-vaginal fistula: A hole between the bladder and the vagina. It usually results from prolonged labor against a very small pelvis, which causes pressure and death of the tissues, allowing the hole to form. This produces a constant urine leak through the vagina and urinary infections, with very severe discomfort and danger to health.

[13] Locum tenens: A doctor filling in for another one. Usually shortened to 'locum.'

[14] M.B., B.Ch: The British or South African qualifying exam in medicine, equivalent to the American M.D.

[15] Cow dung floor: In the tribal areas of South Africa the floors of huts and courtyards or verandahs are often made of cow dung and mud, laboriously smoothed by the women's hands and allowed to dry.

16 <u>Drop</u>: The bead of pus that comes out of the end of the penis in gonorrhea. Self-diagnosis by the patient.

17 <u>Fungating</u>: Like a fungus. Used about cancer growing through the skin, exposing the rough, ugly surface of the tumor. This penile cancer had spread to the lymph nodes in the groins and then grown through the skin.

18 <u>Swaziland</u>: A small independent African country almost surrounded by South Africa. It lies sandwiched between Transvaal, Natal and Maputo (Mozambique). The Swazi people often live or work in South Africa.

19 <u>I.U.D</u>: At that time the Intra-uterine contraceptive device was regarded as a good answer for fairly foolproof contraception. However, one variety proved to be dangerous and they have largely fallen out of favor, particularly with the advent of the contraceptive pill and other modern hormonal methods of contraception.

20 <u>Doek</u>: A cloth head covering, often used in South Africa by black women. It is worn like a small turban.

21 <u>Orbicularis oris</u>: The circular muscle that surrounds the mouth, underneath the lip margin. It is responsible for 'puckering' or whistling and is also involved in expression and speaking.

22 <u>Lateral Fornix</u>: The top of the vagina, to one side of the cervix.

23 <u>Priapism</u>: From Priapos, the Greek god of gardens and male generative power. Priapic=phallic.

24 <u>Corpora cavernosa and spongiosa</u>: The spongy parts of the penis responsible for erection. When sexual stimulation occurs, venous valves close off and allow these spongy bodies to fill with blood, making the organ stiff and erect. Later, the valves relax, the blood drains out again and the erection subsides.

25 <u>Phlegmasia cerulea dolens</u>: Literally 'Inflammation of the vein, painful and blue.' It is due to tense thrombosis in all the veins of the thigh, totally blocking venous outflow. The leg becomes huge, tense, painful and blue. Very bad cases may lead to gangrene and limb loss, or a permanently swollen leg.

Variety is the spice of life—and death—at Baragwanath Hospital. No day passes without bringing something new—be it amazing, comic or tragic—often a mix of all three.

Ward rounds start early. I lead them until the new fourth-year students arrive. The unit goes from bed to bed, with the ward sister taking notes and the unit clerk acting as interpreter and 'gofer.' Two sixth-year students form an integral part of the team with the three house surgeons helping them write in charts, draw blood, and do other 'scutwork.' The registrar organizes the work—discharging patients, preparing others for surgery and doing necessary chores. Teaching is part of the routine.

We start on the female side because of my interest in a young girl transferred from Dr. Watson's medical unit for surgery. Thandi is a nineteen-year-old patient with very high blood pressure (called *malignant* hypertension,[1] for good reason). It has caused severe damage to the retinas behind her eyes. If her pressure is not controlled she will go blind, and ultimately die of kidney failure or a stroke. The medical unit has been unable to reduce her blood pressure with any available drugs.

After several weeks of care and investigation in Ward 23, arteriograms[2] have shown severe narrowing (stenosis) of the origins of the kidney arteries and many other large blood vessels where they come off the aorta. This is the rare condition named 'Takayasu's disease' or 'aortic root arteritis.' It is often called 'Pulseless Disease,' because of poor blood pressure in the affected vessels. The cause is unknown. It is seen in Japan, where it was named, and in young black women, but rarely in whites.

Narrowing of the arteries to the kidneys greatly reduces their blood flow. They respond by secreting a hormone[3] that raises blood pressure in an attempt to get more blood to reach them. This causes the malignant hypertension that is so dangerous if not controlled. Fortunately, renal artery stenosis is one of the few causes of high blood pressure that can be treated by surgery.

In this complex operation, a piece of vein is removed from the patient's leg for use as a graft. The abdomen is opened through a long incision, and the aorta is exposed, in the center of the body, behind the internal organs. The artery to the kidney is found and clamped and a side clamp placed on the aorta. The harvested vein or a fabric tube is stitched on as a bypass, to take blood from the aorta to the renal artery beyond the blockage.

Thandi's father has come to discuss the procedure and sign informed consent. He sits at her bedside, an older man with grizzled hair, a Basuto blanket draped over his shoulders and a shiny, gnarled walking stick in his hand. Thandi sits in bed with a bright smile. The whole unit is gathered round.

"Eh Madala!"[4] I greet him.

"Inkosi,"[5] the man answers.

I speak through the interpreter: "Your daughter, Thandi, is very ill and she could die."

"Eh Dokitela, I understand," the father responds.

"We can help her with an operation. I will tell you about it."

I then explain the disease and the procedure in as much detail as I think the father can handle. The interpreter does a good job and I explain more as needed. Thandi and her father nod their heads as they listen—she has heard this many times.

"Do you understand, Madala?" I ask. "Thandi has a very big problem. If nothing is done she will go blind and die of this illness."

"Eh Dokitela," he replies. "It is indeed a very big sickness for one so young."

"We can help her with the operation I told you about. What shall we do?"

"I will take Thandi home and slaughter an ox, as is the custom," the father replies.

"But she will die!" I cry out in horror.

"That may be God's will," the father answers.

Thandi cries softly, but she will not disobey her father. She is secretly glad to avoid the surgery, which she doesn't really understand. She sees mostly the pain and the risks involved. She gets out of bed and fetches her clothes.

The members of the unit chatter in dismay. I stand quietly for a few moments, trying to hide my frustration. What a waste of time and mental energy for all. But I know that using medical logic with a country-bred person such as this will do no good. The old man's mind is made up. Facts will not change anything. I have failed at this several times before. Such patients don't come back until they are dying. I can do no more.

The next patient, Gertrude, cheerily greets the group. She is an attractive young woman with *lymphedema*[6] of the legs, commonly known as elephantiasis. The foot of her bed is raised high on wooden chairs to give maximal gravity assistance in reducing the swelling. Her legs are bound in strong elastic bandages. A student nurse unwraps them.

In contrast to her normal upper body and arms, the lower limbs are huge, mostly below the knees. The calves are bigger than the thighs and the ankles even thicker. Each leg must weigh seventy pounds. There is an irregular granular knobby appearance around her ankles, rather like moss. These lumps become bigger further on down the foot. On the big toes they are like hairy walnuts. The lower legs look like those of an elephant. The pressure bandages have left deep marks imprinted into the swollen tissues. Her legs remain grotesque despite this intensive treatment.

"Good morning, Gertrude," I greet her. "It's a lot better, isn't it?"

"A little better Doctor, not a lot," she answers. "But will it never go away? I have been lying upside down for a week now. I must go home to my children."

"Gertrude, you must either do this, or have an operation. If you sleep like this and keep the bandages on in the day, your legs might stay as they are now. But I don't think they'll get any better. I know it's hard to keep the bandages on and to sleep that way."

"Doctor, I cannot stay like this! What can I do? Tell me about the operation."

"OK, Gertrude. But don't do what that old man did. I can't waste my time again."

"No, Doctor. He is an old man from the country. I'm sorry for Thandi, because I know you could help her. She told me she wanted the surgery, but she was scared. If I want the operation I will tell you, or I will go home and first try what you have taught me."

"Well, Gertrude, it's a big operation. It takes many hours. I'll do one leg at a time. You won't feel pain because we will put you to sleep, or just make your legs sleep. I know I can help you, because I've done the operation before. If you don't like the first leg you can stop at that time, or you can go home and come back later." I paused.

"Go on, Doctor, tell me what you have to do."

"We will hang up your leg, as high as this, so we can work all round it, and put a tight rubber bandage round the top, so you don't bleed. I'll cut from your knee to your foot, right through the skin and fat, down to the red meat. We lift the fat off the meat, and slice most of the fat off the skin. That leaves two thin flaps of skin and fat, connected to your leg at the back, where the blood comes in. Do you know what a Swiss roll or a jam roll is, Gertrude?"

"Yes, Doctor. Where I worked the white children loved to eat that kind of cake."

"We will make a 'Swiss roll' of your leg, by rolling the longest flap of skin inside. Its edge will lie next to the veins in the middle, among the muscles. The water will drain in a new way along the vein. The leg will look thinner and better straight away because we take away so much fat. It is called the 'Swiss Roll procedure' or the 'Thompson operation.'"

"Mister Hunt, if it will help me, please let us do it!" the patient begs.

"There is another operation," I tell her. "But it gives a *very thin leg*. That looks funny under the fatter thigh—like *Kiewiekie*[7] legs—and there can be ugly scars."

"Doctor, you like the first operation. Do what your heart says. When can you do it?"

"On Wednesday. We must first get Intake over. Tell your family, but you must stay here, getting ready for the surgery. We'll do the fattest leg first."

"Thank you Mr. Hunt! I will be here."

The next patient is sleepy from heavy sedation. A nurse takes bandages off her hands, revealing septic, oozing fingers and thumbs. Two fingers are black and wrinkled.

"That looks like biltong[8] now," I comment. "You students missed seeing her. This woman is a psychotic from the mental hospital. She forced and screwed thirty rings, washers and nuts onto her fingers and toes, making a ghastly mess. Lord knows where she got them. We cut off the hardware last intake day. Those hands still look horrible, despite twice daily hand baths. She will lose parts of her fingers. We'll tidy her up on Wednesday. She can't legally sign, so you guys must get consent again from Sterkfontein Hospital.[9]"

It's nearly time to meet the new fourth-years and I hurry through the rounds, discussing only one more patient. Martha is a forty-year-old with a hole in her chest wall where her breast had been. The breast disappeared from cancer before she came. I have seen a penis and other organs destroyed by cancer, but never a breast. I am resigned to seeing these sights but I've never become hardened to them. They still distress me.

The nurse uncovers the chest and we see a bright red, four-inch diameter ulcer, with an irregular, rolled edge.[10] There are reddish-gray round lumps along the border, like beads.

"It's amazingly clean," I tell the unit. "That's bare muscle and rib in the bottom of the ulcer. There's just no breast. Strangely, we can't find any distant disease. A patient with a cancer so advanced is sure to have systemic[11] spread. So she needs chemotherapy. Most cancers in our patients are too advanced to be cured by surgery alone. But there are so few oncologists that we don't have one at Bara yet. I give the chemotherapy my patients need.

"I figured out as a surgical oncology research fellow that tumors don't metastasize[12] (spread) until they reach a centimeter in diameter—half the size of a thimble. How many cells do you think that is?" I ask the unit at large.

"A hundred thousand," one of the students volunteers.

"A few more," I said. "It's about a billion cells. I'm convinced that surgeons can only 'cure' cancers smaller than that, in other words, before they spread. We never get them so tiny, so in our patients the cancers have already got away before we see them. How many cancer cells does it take to kill a mouse—or a person?"

"One," George Pappas, the other student, replies this time.

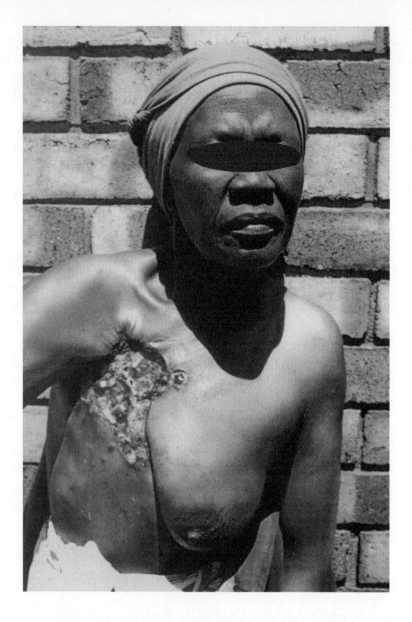

PATIENT WITH AUTO-AMPUTATION OF BREAT BY CANCER.
IN SPITE OF THE ADVANCED STAGE OF THE CANCER,
WE COULD FIND NO OBVIOUS SPREAD BEYOND THE CHEST WALL.

"Absolutely right. Good thinking. As a Fellow, I did cell dilution experiments, until the cell suspension was clear, like water. Theoretically there was one cell per dose that I used. A third of the mice developed fatal tumors. Assuming one out of three doses had no cells, one or two cells must be enough. That's the rationale for much oncology, particularly with adjuvant chemo- or radiation therapy: *Shoot for a cure while there are only a few cells.*

"I've had decent disease-free survivals only since I've added chemotherapy to surgery. Most of our patients are not sophisticated enough to accept long-term or repeated treatment. They often don't return until the tumor recurs and there is a big lump, bleeding, ulceration, or obstruction of something, like the bowel. Then it's the last inning of a losing game.

"I know I've got only this one chance at cure. So I don't pussyfoot around. I aim to send them home cured the first time. I've adapted 'CAMP,' a powerful four-drug regime. The A is for Adriamycin,[13] the most effective drug against breast cancer. I know it's potentially toxic to the heart. But these folks have better hearts than white people, with less artery disease. So I use a dose known to be safe for whites. It should certainly do no harm in black patients."

"But Mr. Hunt, haven't you shot your bolt?" asks George. "You can't use Adriamycin again."

"That's very perceptive, George," I reply. "You must have been doing chemo at the Gen.[14] You're right of course. But that's my point. If the patients won't return until they are dying from untreatable disease, why not use the best drugs first and try for cure?

"These drugs really work for them. For example, I recently had a patient with recurrent[15] breast cancer, a year after surgery (without chemotherapy). She had a big 'cauliflower tumor'[16] where this lady has an ulcer. I gave her my CAMP regime before radiation. The tumor literally 'fell off,' leaving a hole where cancer had eroded and replaced her tissues. Closing that hole was a surgical problem, but all visible cancer had gone.

"Some more points to ponder. If you even mention radiation or chemo to whites, they get nauseous. The blacks don't seem to notice it—whether they're tougher, less psychologically influenced, or just different—I don't know. They don't lose their hair as easily as the white people do, not does their bone marrow take such a knock. It's time someone researched it. Perhaps you'll do it one day, George."

"Thanks Mr. Hunt. I really am interested. I must talk to you," the student replies.

"Any time, George."

"Folks, I must go and teach," I tell them. "I'll see you at teatime. Go on with the males, Peter. I'll be doing baby classes in Ward Five. You can have the students after tea."

I thoroughly enjoy teaching. In the male ward I greet ten eager new white-coated students on their first surgical rotation. They are mostly white, but include an Indian and an African. There are three young women. This is typical of the current student mix. I welcome them to Bara and ask their names, which I will try to remember.

I draw privacy screens around bed one and the group and I greet the patient, who agrees to be examined.

"We try to turn out doctors who are ready to practice after their houseman year," I tell them. "That means you must learn to diagnose using your eyes, hands and brains. So you'll be taught to examine patients correctly and to use your intelligence. I teach by asking questions—the Socratic method. But I won't hound you—maybe just embarrass you a bit.

"The groin hides some interesting anatomy, as you're all aware. It also often requires surgical care. I'll bet most of you will see one in your finals, so it's worth paying attention.

"Mr. Green, can you see anything wrong in his groins?"

The student comes forward and pokes around for a while, looking blank.

"It all looks pretty good," the student says, rather cautiously.

"I don't think you've opened Ham Bailey's book on physical signs," I say. "It's required reading. You might not need me if you study it. Now stand him up."

A large lump now appears in his groin and slithers into the scrotum with a gurgle.

"*Lesson one*: always examine groins both standing up and lying down."

I make the patient lie down again and the lump disappears.

"That's a hernia—take my word for it now. Since it's his inguinal region,[17] it's an inguinal hernia, but what kind?" I ask. "I want two answers from anyone."

"Indirect," says Pillay, the Indian.

"Very good! But why? How can you tell?" I ask him.

"Just guessing—one out of two," Pillay confesses.

"Then you can work it out for us, Mr. Pillay. This is *lesson two*. Find the center of his groin, midway between the two bones at the front of the pelvis. That's over the internal ring.[18] That's right; mark it with a pen. Now make him cough or strain."

The patient coughs and the lump pops out under the mark and soon goes back inside.

"You see what happened," I say. "Now press in firmly where you marked it and let him cough again.

"As you see, nothing comes out. You've blocked the internal ring, so nothing can enter the inguinal canal. That means it's an *indirect* inguinal hernia. A *direct* hernia would come out, because it comes through a different opening, next door. You must believe me for now, but study the anatomy tonight and you'll understand. We'll see plenty more groins.

"Now, what happened when he lay down?" I ask the group.

"It went back inside," one of the girls pipes up.

"So that's my *last lesson*. What do you call that phenomenon —a disappearing act?"

They mumble a bit, but no one is brave enough to speak.

"The third answer I want is that this is a *reducible* hernia," I tell them. "It comes out when he stands, goes back in or *reduces* when he lies down. So that's the complete diagnosis, which I would expect in the final exam—all the key words—*'a reducible indirect inguinal hernia.'* It matters because hernias can get stuck outside and become *irreducible* or even *strangulate*,[19] causing bowel to die. But we won't discuss complications or treatment now. You've got a couple more years for that.

"Surgery's not too hard, is it? It's just like plumbing."

I thank the patient and lead the group to another bed. We go through a similar process on a man with a liver tumor, which is bulging the abdominal wall. The students are keen and able to think. They are a smart group, so I'm satisfied when I take them to tea.

The fourth years join their classmates at a big table. There is an excited buzz as they discuss their new rotations. I get tea and sandwiches and join Unit Five at a smaller table.

"Mr. Hunt, I'm sorry about Thandi," Peter says. "I know your heart was set on doing her surgery and you did a lot of reading. I was looking forward to helping you."

"Well, you can't win 'em all!" I reply. "A few years ago, a colleague was getting consent through an interpreter. It was taking forever, with the patient and the ward clerk chattering angrily back and forth, without ever giving him an answer.

"'Well, what does he say?' said my friend. 'Why's it taking so long? I just want to know if he wants surgery, yes or no. *Come on, Jane*, tell me what he says!'

"Looking down at the floor, Jane answered: 'I was only trying to change his mind, sir. What he says is "Fuck you, Doctor."'

"I now know how my friend felt. As for Thandi, I'm really sorry. She will go blind and die. We must tell Dr. Watson's unit while they're at tea."

I start talking again: "Before we return, I must tell you about a very sad breast cancer patient we had last year. She was slender, spoke good English and was quite educated. She had small breasts; with a large cancer filling each one, so lumpy and irregular that they looked and felt like rocks under the skin. You could easily see the irregularity and I took some pictures. She said 'I have pains in my pelvis.' And she was right. She had metastatic cancer in her pelvic bones and throughout her skeleton. Radiation and chemotherapy did no good. I doubt if even the high-powered chemo at M.D. Anderson would have helped her."

"Why do they leave it so long?" George asks.

"Partly ignorance, and the rest is probably fear of getting the answer," I answer him. "My old-fashioned, farm-born mother might do the same thing. She would probably hide it to the end. I hope I'm not doing her an injustice.

"Only publicity, education, and mammography will help. It's a little better in the whites, but not enough to make them curable by surgery alone. So, George, there will always be plenty of work for chemotherapists and oncologists."[20]

I go over to give the bad news about Thandi to Dr Watson's unit. His team is disappointed, but not entirely surprised.

"Perhaps we just kept the girl here too long, with no tangible result," Dr Watson suggests. "Still, she needed everything we did and we had to try all those drugs. With her terrible hypertension I was unwilling to let her go home. Well, John, better luck next time!"

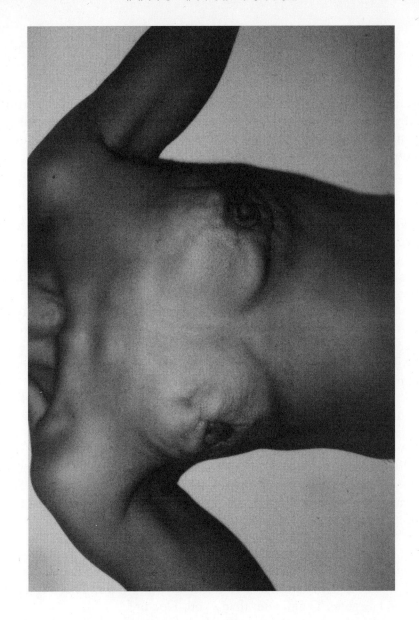

A FAIRLY WELL-EDUCATED WOMAN WHO PRESENTED
WITH HUGE CANCERS IN EACH BREAST.
THE CANCER HAD SPREAD TO THE PELVIC BONE.

I return to Ward Five. The only side room in my unit is on the male side. Princess, an eighteen-year-old VIP from a neighboring African state, occupies it. I look after her myself. When she arrived yesterday I introduced myself and sat at her bedside. While talking I noticed a swelling the size of a basketball in her abdomen.

"Pregnant, are you?" I said, conversationally.

"No!" she pouted angrily. "And I'm not even married."

I apologized as best I could for this major *faux pas* and started asking about the lump. I tried to tie this in with the fact that she had been sent here with a single very bad, but otherwise normal X-ray, which was supposed to show a duodenal ulcer. She had absolutely no symptoms of an ulcer, but confessed that she almost never got her bowels to move properly. The last time was three months ago.

I examined her abdomen and then did a rectal exam. The lump was a mass of firm, impacted stool, as big as a baby. It extended from her rectum right up to her navel, producing a *ball valve*[21] effect. Only gas and a little liquid stool could pass. Nobody could have eliminated that mass unaided, so I understood her problem.

I had just read about a new treatment to empty the bowel, called 'whole bowel lavage.'[22] It appeared to be very logical and safe. I discussed it with her and gathered the ingredients. Princess would have to drink four liters—over a gallon—of Ringer's Lactate,[23] a salty intravenous fluid. I added potassium chloride[24] to each bottle in order to make up for expected losses when her bowels worked. She drank the fluid slowly last night. The ward sister reported success this morning. I'm glad I was not around at the time.

"How did it go, Princess?" I enquire.

"Hau, Doctor, it was terrible! But I am so pleased!" she answers, with the first smile I've seen on her face.

"Look at my stomach! It is like a young girl's. That big ugly lump has gone. Thank you, thank you, Doctor."

"Princess, I want you to stay here for two days so that I can see you are all right," I tell her. "I will come back to show you how to stay out of such trouble. First, you must walk all around the hospital to help teach your bowels to work properly again."

I go to join the rest of the unit in the male ward and tell them of my success with Princess. As Peter Jones goes to join the students, he says over his shoulder: "Mr. Hunt, you'd better call it 'The Royal Flush'!"

"Very good Peter," I laugh. "We'll use it again, so just remember that. Anyway, I must get finished here so that we can get to Outpatients."

The next patient, Samuel Ngeni, is thirty-five years old. He came to Casualty several days ago, during one of my after hours Casualty sessions, complaining of a lump on his left chest for several weeks. He took off his shirt and displayed two big ugly scars, forming a T on its side. In the center of the horizontal scar he had a shiny, tense, pubertal-size breast, not matched on the right side. I thought it was moving, so I felt it. To my horror, it was pulsating strongly, growing markedly larger and smaller with each heartbeat. This was 'expansile pulsation,' typical of an aneurysm.[25] This could be bulging out from the heart or from one of the big arteries in the chest.

Samuel said that both wounds had resulted from operations for the repair of stab wounds in his heart. The midline vertical scar was plainly from a sternal splitting[26] incision and the more recent horizontal incision had been made between the ribs.

The last operation, two years before, was done in another hospital by a surgeon who had once been my assistant. The patient was near death and the operating theater was busy, so the surgery was done in the corridor outside the theater. It saved the man's life. Samuel later had several more operations to the back of his chest, but he knew little about them.

I was alarmed by this unusual story. I was certain this was an aneurysm, due to the trauma. The breast pulsation seemed diagnostic. The skin was shiny, ready to burst.

"You must come into hospital now to let us fix it," I urged the patient.

"I cannot stay Doctor—I must take the keys back to my Boss," Samuel answered.

"You can't do that," I said. "Your breast is full of blood, like a tight balloon. It will burst if you bump it or touch it too hard. All your blood will spray out and you'll die."

"It's O.K., Doctor. It's been growing for a month. I don't think it will burst."

"Well, Samuel, go to X-ray and bring the pictures back. I'll write on your card for you to come to my Outpatients in two days. You must come back or you'll be in big trouble."

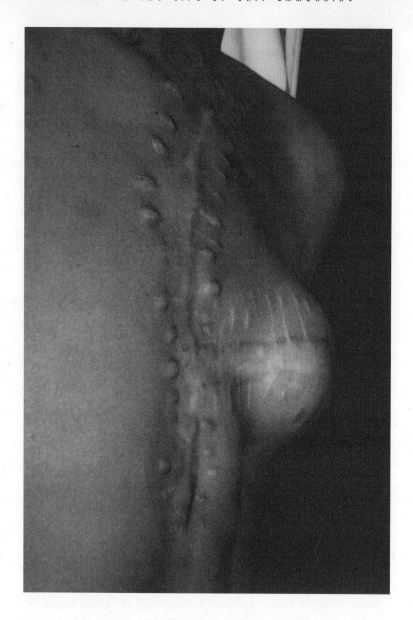

PULSATING SWELLING OF A MALE BREAST.
THIS FOLLOWED 2 OPERATIONS FOR STAB WOUNDS TO THE HEART.
ENTIRE CHEST WAS FULL OF INFECTED FLUID,
CAUSING THE "BREAST" TO PULSATE IN TIME WITH THE HEART.

"I will come, Doctor."

The X-ray showed a 'white-out'[27] of the left chest, with the heart shadow pushed over to the right. This further alarmed me, but I still couldn't change Samuel's mind. I reinforced my warning and planned an urgent angiogram[28] if the patient came back.

Samuel returned, just as he promised, and was admitted. His angiogram X-ray has just been completed and the ward clerk fetched the films during teatime.

"Show me those new X-rays," I ask the Unit clerk.

I hold several films up to the light in turn. The aorta and main vessels in the chest are clearly outlined by the iodine-containing dye given by the radiologist. Their outlines are quite smooth, without bulges or aneurysms. But the aorta is displaced far across to the right side, like a big bow, indicating something is pushing it over. This can still be a large aneurysm of the heart, which will not be shown by these X-rays. I ask for the original straight X-ray and hold it up alongside the others. Something new catches my eye.

"Can you guys see anything there, except for the white-out?" I ask.

No one answers.

"Well, I think this is a chest full of pus and he needs a needle put in it."

Before I can say any more, I find a syringe and needle being pushed into my hand. I realize that I have just volunteered. No one else would dare to do it. It's my baby now.

"Okay, you guys, I'll handle it!"

I tell the patient I am going to put in a needle to see what is inside. Samuel agrees. I clean the chest wall around the 'breast' with Betadine solution and carefully push a needle on the end of a syringe into the chest next to the lump. A stream of creamy-gray pus fills the syringe. I heave a sigh of relief, matched by those of the unit.

"How did you know that, Mr. Hunt?" asks George Pappas.

"Simple observation," I reply. "Look at this X-ray, where you all saw nothing. Don't worry, neither did I, until now. Several radiologists have also missed it."

I point out a lighter gray mark in a corner of the pale gray of the left chest. Suddenly, everyone can see it.

"What's that, George?" I ask.

"A foreign body, I guess."

"Can anyone be more specific?"

Silence reigns.

"Well that's the radio-opaque tag[29] of an operating room pack," I tell them. "The pack must have been left in during that emergency thoracotomy in the theater corridor. Those scars on the back of his chest are probably where they tried to drain pus. The radiologists must have missed seeing that tag every time he was X-rayed. I can see why."

I turn back to the patient: "Samuel, your chest is full of this dirty pus and it must come out. It is too difficult for me to fix. You need an operation by the special chest surgeons. You should be fine. But don't go and get stabbed again!"

"Doctor, I will be good. I now have a child to worry about."

I tell the unit: "I don't mind clearing out blood or clot, but chronic infection scares me. It makes things stick together and bleed badly. I'll gladly leave that to the thoracic surgeons. I would hate to dig that big piece of cloth out of his chest after two years. I'll consult Mr. Williams at lunch.

"This is called 'empyema necessitatis.'[30] The Latin words mean 'a chest full of pus that needs to be let out urgently'—you can see why. The outside swelling is often far away from the opening in the chest wall. In such cases the pus escapes through a long track. In his case the communication is direct. His apparent 'breast' probably pulsates because the opening is right there, behind it. His chest is so full of pus that it transmits the cardiac contraction straight through the hole in the scar. So that makes the swelling look like a breast and pulsate like an aneurysm. It's the first case I've seen and I won't soon forget it. I'm sorry Peter missed all the fun. You guys must tell him and show him the X-rays."

"Well, we've finished most of the acute cases," I say. "I'll take two housemen and George to Outpatients while you two finish up. Peter can join us when he's done."

The unit occupies three rooms. The housemen see follow-ups. I keep George Pappas in my room, where we see new patients and I address any problems. A sea of black faces awaits us in a large open area. Ward clerks and nurses help organize the people. They make sure that the most ill patients are seen first, even though that produces some good-hearted grumbling.

"The Africans are a patient, cheerful and long-suffering people—how else would they have put up with Apartheid for so long?" I comment to Pappas.

Our first patient is a truck driver with a large lump on the back of his neck that he has had for many years. It is as big as an American football. He has to lean forward as he walks. When he drives he must 'park' the mass of flesh on top of the seat of his truck. He has a well-paying job and is anxious to get the lump removed and return to work.

George Pappas examines the lump while I quiz him.

"What is it, Mr. Pappas?"

"I don't know yet," George replies.

"Well, is it benign or malignant?"

"It's very smooth and soft, just like a breast or a ball of fat," George answers.

"Sooo…"

"It must be a *lipoma*,"[31] George decides.

"Good shot!" I say. "Benign or malignant?"

"Aren't they all benign?" George asks. "It really feels good and soft and I can't feel any lymph nodes in his neck or under his arms."

"I agree, it feels benign," I reply. "Most small ones are. Unfortunately, big ones can be malignant. That doesn't show up on 'frozen section' microscopic exam in the operating room, so you don't know until later. I had an eleven pounder in the belly once. It came out cleanly, like a big, soft, yellow basketball. But it turned out to be a *liposarcoma*.[32] He had to have radiation therapy, though that's not too effective over the abdomen. You can't give enough to kill the cancer for fear of radiation-induced bowel damage."

"Well, Shadrack," I say. "You're very lucky. We can cut this off on Wednesday. You need to stay in hospital now, so we can get the skin underneath clean, or you could get infected and not heal properly. You should get back to work in two weeks."

George starts taking a full history and doing a physical examination, which is easily recorded on the simple 'check off' hospital chart. The patient goes to Surgical Admissions.

We see several more cases, admitting only one with a large abdomen full of fluid. After consulting with me, the housemen have admitted a few of their patients. Peter Jones has arrived with the other houseman and the student to lend support. The cases are now being seen at a steady clip and I can begin to see the end of the morning's work. Lunch can't be too far away now.

[1] <u>Malignant hypertension</u>: The most severe form of high blood pressure, which causes severe organ damage in the retina, the kidneys and the heart. Results are blindness, renal failure, cardiac damage and death by hemorrhagic stroke. It is hard to control by using drugs. It is important to find a correctable cause. (Rare.)

[2] <u>Arteriogram</u>: An X-ray examination of blood vessels after injection of a radio-opaque dye into the artery concerned, in this case, the aorta. The dye flows into all the branches, showing the areas of narrowing, obstruction or aneurysms.

[3] <u>Hormone</u>: A chemical substance which is secreted by an organ into the blood stream, with the object of affecting other organs or functions in other parts of the body.

[4] <u>Eh Madala</u>: "Yes, Old Man." A respectful greeting.

[5] <u>Inkosi</u>: "Chief." Another mark of respect.

[6] <u>Lymphedema</u>: Swelling of a limb or an organ due to inability of lymph to leave the limb. This may be from congenital absence or blockage of the lymphatic vessels by disease or repeated infections. In central West Africa, it is often due to a parasite infestation. In this patient the cause is unknown.

[7] <u>Kiewiekie</u>: A plover with skinny red legs, which is seen on the African veld. It noisily attacks people going near its nest, which is made on the ground. The bird's repeated cry as it attacks is "Kiewiekie, Kiewiekie."

[8] <u>Biltong</u>: Jerky. Sun dried meat, used by the Boers under farm and frontier conditions and during 'The Great Trek" or migration northwards in the 1800s. Word derived from 'Bull's tongue.'

[9] <u>Sterkfontein</u>: The regional mental and psychiatric hospital, run by the Transvaal Province.

[10] <u>Rolled edge</u>: A cancerous ulcer frequently has a raised and in-turned edge, <u>not</u> as if it was punched out by a cookie cutter. In this case it also had the 'row of beads' appearance along the edge.

[11] <u>Systemic spread</u>: Spread to other parts of the body, potentially anywhere. Meaning is like 'metastasize.'

[12] <u>Metastasize</u>: Spread outside the visible limits of the tumor. Cancer cells may go to lymph nodes nearby, into the blood stream, or both. Once in the circulation, the cells may settle and grow in the lungs, liver, bones or anywhere else. The knowledge that early spread is so common has led to the modern use of adjunctive chemotherapy and/or radiation.

[13] <u>Adriamycin</u>: Proprietary name for the drug Doxorubicin. A powerful anti-cancer agent, with cardiac side effects at high dosage. Remains a mainstay in many cancer chemotherapy treatments.

[14] <u>Gen</u>: Johannesburg General Hospital. A hospital in Johannesburg taking only white patients. It was the main one in the teaching group.

[15] <u>Recurrent cancer</u>: Cancers will often recur or come back after any treatment, because of cancer cells still present in the body or at the operative site. Hence the need for adjunctive chemotherapy or radiation, to try and eliminate such cells totally.

[16] <u>Cauliflower tumor</u>: A colloquial medical term for a cancer that grows and looks just like the surface of a cauliflower.

17 Inguinal region: Groin.

18 Internal ring: An anatomical ring through which the spermatic cord emerges from the abdomen on its path to the scrotum. It carries the blood vessels and the vas deferens to the testis. An 'indirect' hernia comes through this hole alongside the cord.

19 Strangulate: Bowel trapped in an irreducible hernia may die because its blood supply is cut off. This is 'strangulation.'

20 Oncologists: Doctors who deal mainly with the treatment of cancer by any means, surgical, medical or radiation therapy.

21 Ball valve: A simple valve, with a ball resting above an opening that is too small to let it through. In a case like this, some gas and liquid stool or diarrhea could escape around it, but the ball of stool would remain.

22 Whole bowel lavage: Giving a large volume of liquid by mouth, causing a flushing out of the entire bowel, from above down, clearing it of all stool products. Later, other agents such as polyethylene glycol were added to the solution.

23 Ringer's lactate: A balanced electrolyte solution, resembling the chemical makeup of human plasma. It contains too little potassium for bowel lavage, without adding potassium.

24 Potassium chloride: If the lavage causes a good washout, the patient could lose a lot of potassium in the stool. This was an endeavor to cut such potential losses.

25 Aneurysm: A bulge protruding from an artery or the heart, due to a weakness in the wall at that point. Prone to rupture, spilling large amounts of blood and causing death, if not cured or fixed in time.

26 Sternal splitting incision: The breastbone is split in the middle, using a saw or chisel, and gives direct access to the heart. There was some controversy over its emergency use, as some surgeons felt it was much quicker to enter the chest between the ribs, though full exposure of the heart and big vessels was not as good.

27 Whiteout: Normally, a chest X-ray shows a lot of black, representing the air within the lungs. A 'whiteout' indicates fluid or pneumonia replacing or pushing aside the air in the lung.

28 Angiogram: Another word for arteriogram, #2 above.

29 Radio-opaque tag: All pieces of cloth used as sponges or packs in the operating theater carry some form of radiological identification, such as a metal tag or thread. If a pack is suspected of having been left behind, the use of X-rays should reveal it.

30 Empyema Necessitatis: Empyema means an organ full of pus, e.g. the chest or the gall bladder. Necessitatis implies that the pus has found its way to the surface and must necessarily be drained.

31 Lipoma: A usually benign fatty tumor. They are rarely malignant. If so, they are called liposarcomas.

32 Liposarcoma: Malignant form of lipoma. Poorly responsive to radiation, requiring a high and potentially dangerous dose, especially in the abdomen.

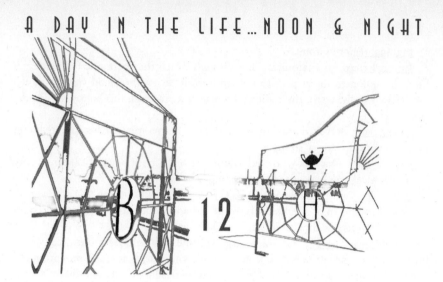

A porter brings in a stretcher with a groaning patient. Mary talks to the man, whose name is Meshack. I examine him and gently touch his belly. His skin is ice cold and sweating and his belly muscles are quite rigid—'like a board.'[1]

"What's going on, Mary?" I ask. "And Staff Nurse, get that porter back here to take him straight to Resuscitation."

"Doctor, this man thought he had trouble with his bowels. You know how they like to go and *boscha*[2] many times a day. Well, he went to an *Inyanga* (herbalist)[3] and got orange crystals for an enema. If you put them in water, the color is very pretty."

"Then what happened?"

"Yesterday his friend used the stuff to give him an enema with a cow's horn..."

"Not that again!" I exclaim.

"Yes, sir. His bowels worked and went on running like water until blood ran out. Then he pushed that thing out in Casualty."

She points to a mushy orange lump lying on a newspaper in a pool of liquid stool. Pappas and I put on gloves and examine the stringy piece of fleshy tissue. I spread it out and say:

"It's the whole lining of his colon! That's a very bad combination, cow's horn enema and *potassium dichromate*,[4] the orange stuff Mary mentioned. They get the crystals from industrial chemistry or photo labs. It's a strong tissue poison, always fatal when swallowed, and often if used by enema. You see what it's done to his colon! I'll tell you about the cow's horn later, George."

"His belly is very sore, Doctor. Can't you help him?" Mary asks.

"Yes, Mary, I'll give him some morphine in Resuscitation," I reply. "Tell the porter to hurry up. Put that thing in a bottle with formalin and send it to the lab."

"Meshack, that enema has made you very sick," I tell him.

"I know Doctor," the patient whispers. "Can you help me?"

"Yes, but you will need an operation to take out your colon—the tube you shit through. It is dead. That's why your stomach is so sore."

"Hau Doctor! How will I *boscha* then?"

"I will make a hole here on your belly, and bring out the end of your small bowel—your *derms,*[5] I say, using the Afrikaans term, and hoping the patient understands.

"You'll wear a plastic bag to catch the shit," I tell him. "Soon it won't worry you. Many people use such bags—even old people. The shit is leaking out inside you now, making you so sick. If I don't fix it you will die. To have the bag is better than to be dead."

"Then, Doctor, you must do it. Please help me."

The porter now takes the patient, while I go through to the registrar's room.

"Peter, there's a messy laparotomy[6] to do after lunch. I'll help you if we are both free. I'm taking him to Resuscitation and I'll set up the surgery. Finish off here and come over so we can discuss it. Then we'll have lunch."

Pappas and I follow the patient to Resuscitation, where I call the theaters to schedule surgery and tell the Anesthetists about the problem. George starts an IV line and takes blood for lab tests and typing. We order large doses of antibiotics and two units of blood, with more on standby.

We now examine Meshack more fully. His pulse is thready and racing, his blood pressure can't be recorded, and his breathing is rapid and deep—'air hunger.'[7] These signs indicate severe shock, so I draw arterial blood[8] for pH and blood gas studies.[9]

The measurement of pH and blood gases is not yet routine in clinical medicine. I have the only modern pH meter in town, locked in the Resuscitation room. I use it to get human validation of my lab research into shock, acidosis and rapid blood transfusion, to see if shocked people react like the animals. I use this knowledge to guide treatment.

Pappas has finished the IV line and comes over to watch. I unlock the box and set up the meter. I draw some of the arterial blood into a fine plastic capillary tube on a pistol-grip handle and dip the tube into a special solution. The needle on a dial moves. I get a reading and transfer it to a big piece of graph paper with curves and lines printed on it—*a Siggaard-Andersen nomogram.*[10] I now draw two oblique, nearly parallel lines, intersecting with those printed on the graph paper. I make a note and call out:

"Hey, Sister! Get a liter of warm isotonic bicarb solution.[11] Give it fast, with a pump!

"I can't sedate him yet," I tell Pappas. "He needs all his breathing capacity to blow off carbon dioxide and compensate for the acidosis. I'll have to leave sedation[12] to the Anesthetist. It'll be only a few more minutes.

"You need not understand this *technique*, George, but you must learn to use the *results*. This should be a lab routine, but they don't have the equipment. According to my animal research, this man is seriously shocked and near death. I've confirmed my findings many times in this room. Believe me, a human being can really become 'as sick as a dog.'

"His pH is 6.9 (normal=7.4) and his 'Base Deficit' is 20 (normal=about 0). His $pCO2$ is down to 25 (normal=40) from the overbreathing. At these levels, which I call 'the point,'[13] I've found that animals and people rapidly deteriorate. Often their hearts or their breathing, or both, will stop. Fortunately, urgent treatment with enough bicarbonate can still bring them back.

"People with cardiac arrest have similar acidosis, or worse, when their hearts are stopped and during resuscitation. Their circulation is shut down. Lack of oxygen causes muscles and liver to pour out lactic acid[14] and potassium.[15] These 'nasties' lie around in the tissues until we get the circulation going, and then they are swept into the blood stream in a big whoosh! That causes severe acidosis, together with a high potassium level—a fatal combination. It stops the heart yet again! It's what I call 'washout acidosis.'[16]

"Such patients need a lot of sodium bicarb," I continue. "Most people give just an ampoule or two. That's only 50 or 100 milli-Equivalents.[17] My old rowing coach said it best: 'It's like farting against thunder.' I'm sure that's why many resuscitations fail.

"To correct the 'Base Deficit,' you must calculate the total body need for bicarbonate. Give them half of it immediately, while you flood them with IV fluids. If they don't soon respond, you add the rest of the bicarb. They'll go on making lactic acid and chewing up the bicarb until they are out of shock, with normal tissue perfusion. So be constantly aware of acidosis in sick patients.

"It's really easy to calculate the *bicarbonate need*: '*Base Deficit' times 1/3 of the body weight in Kilograms.* He weighs, say 70 Kg, and his base deficit is 20. Thus he needs 467 mEq of bicarb. I just asked them to pump in a bottle of 150 mEq of bicarb, and we'll see what happens. He'll need another big line for other fluids and blood, so let's do that now."

While I help George start the new IV line, I comment to everyone: "These nurses know what makes people better. Sister Jane, if you have a stab heart, what fluid do you want us to give you?"

"Hau, Mr. Hunt! Don't say that. It's not funny. But I want only the strong bicarbonate and Plasmalyte B—we nurses all know that. You make those fluids work miracles on these people who drink too much and stab each other to death. I've seen it over and over again. They should work for me, too."

I have designed both those fluids and a few more, based on my research. One of them, Plasmalyte B,[18] is known locally as 'Hunt's Solution.' It is the best-selling resuscitation fluid in the country. The American pharmaceutical company that makes the fluids has provided the pH machine for my use. I am their unofficial advisor, but receive not a penny of compensation or royalty. My reward is intellectual and emotional—I know that I'm really helping people.

"Sister, please send him 'Urgent Direct' to theater," I tell her. "Ask them to put him in Recovery Room and call the Anesthetist. We'll go to lunch first and then meet them there. Let's hope that the bicarb, fluids and antibiotics have perked him up a bit by then."

Peter Jones arrives, and we briefly review the case. I then take Jones and Pappas to lunch by car, since we all need to be back soon.

"What are you planning, Mr. Hunt?" Peter asks as we drive down.

"Well, I'm sure his colon is perforated, with stool all over the belly. That's why he's so sick. His anus is useless, as his colon and rectum are destroyed. So we'll snatch out the dead colon as fast as we can, bring out some living small bowel as an ileostomy and slap on a bag. We'll wash the heck out of his belly and stick in lavage tubes.[19] Then he'll need good intensive care, with circulatory support and antibiotics."

At lunch I find Bob Williams, the thoracic surgeon, hand him a consultation card, and sit down nearby. I briefly tell him Samuel Ngeni's story. Williams' eyes widen.

"That's a first!" he exclaims. "We'd *love* to take him over and fix him tomorrow."

We are sitting with other unit heads. I tell them about Thandi's sad fate and the witch-doctor enema story. They all had their own versions of similar sadness, ignorance, or stupidity. I finish lunch and pick up Peter and George for the drive back to theater.

"Jules, I'm delighted it's you," I say, as I enter the Recovery Room.

"Hullo, John. I wish I could say the same," Brobeck countered. "You find amazing cases. You must have a big neon sign up in Soweto, flashing 'Hunt's on intake.'"

"Sorry, Jules, and it's only Monday. We're also on duty on Saturday, and that's the end-of-the-month payday! Probably Full Moon too! Anyway, how's our customer? I hope you've got him blooming."

"Well, not exactly. But I can measure his pressure for the first time, and he's not overbreathing[20] as much. He's also starting to pee just a little."

"Excellent! Then the dichromate hasn't killed his kidneys. While you get him into theater, I'll take more arterial blood and run over to check his pH. We really need a meter in the theater block, or at least in the lab. Peter, you and George change and get started. Do a long midline incision so we can get the colon out and finish quickly."

After doing the test, I change and enter the theater.

"He's coming back nicely," I tell Brobeck. "The pH is over 7.1 and his base deficit is 10. That's much better, but still serious stuff, so he needs another hundred of bicarb. Jules, why don't you start the blood and order two more bottles? He'll need every bit of it."

By the time I have scrubbed and dressed, Peter Jones already has the abdomen draped and the incision nearly finished. He is about to enter the abdominal cavity.

"Hold your breath!" I say. "George, put the sucker tip near where Peter's cutting, to catch the smell and clean up the muck. That's right."

Peter cuts into the peritoneum and blackish-brown lumpy fluid gushes all over the belly and table. The overwhelming stench of stool and dead meat makes us all stagger backwards. Pappas suctions vigorously, with little success. The sucker keeps on blocking.

"Watch your shoes!" I warn them. "Sister, another sucker please, and lots of warm saline.[21] We'll wash out and clean up so that we can see and maybe reduce the smell."

Jones inserts a self-retaining retractor to open the wound. We pour in jug after jug of saline and swirl it around, while we sponge and wash the small bowel. Pappas and I poke our suckers into all the nooks and crannies of the belly as we carefully wash it out. At last the smell is less and we can see more clearly. The small bowel is swollen, red and inflamed. It fills the abdomen, so we must retract it for Peter to work. The colon is just a shrunken rope of wrinkled fleshy tissue. It tears and falls apart at a touch.

"Mercifully his *ileo-cecal valve*[22] prevented the enema refluxing into the small bowel," I comment. "Now, Peter, you just have to pull out the debris and tie off the big blood vessels. You'll probably find them wherever you see any clumps of solid tissue."

Jones and I start removing dead bowel and tying off arteries with strong thread. The rectum is also destroyed, and we must tie some important vessels deep in the pelvis.

"Now, Peter, for the dirty work. Keep your gloves and gown on. Take a big Foley catheter, go under the drapes and pass it through his anus. When I see the bulb, you inflate it and we'll have our drain and plug in place. I'll place some tubes while you re-scrub."

Peter Jones takes the catheter and crawls under the drapes. Seconds later, on my order, he inflates the bulb and pulls it down till it's snug. While Jones scrubs again, I get three nasogastric tubes.[23] I put one through an incision beneath the right ribs with its tip above the liver, and I stitch the tube to the skin. Peter returns and I help him place the other tubes, one deep in the pelvis and the other one under the left rib cage, near the spleen and stomach. We stitch the tubes in place.

"Sister, please give Doctor Jones a pen. Peter, mark the spot for his ileostomy,[24] on the right, about where you would make an appendix incision. Make sure there's no skin fold—not so easy when he's lying flat, is it? It's a good thing he's not fat."

I approve the location. Jones cuts out a one-inch disk of skin and fat under the mark. He then cuts out a disk of hard white fibrous tissue and finally splits some red muscle fibers apart, exposing the peritoneum[25] beneath. He cuts an X in this layer. I now push a soft-jawed instrument through this opening in the belly wall, grasp the cut end of the small bowel, and pull it up through the skin. It's tight, so I insert four fingers and stretch the hole—the intestine fits better. I pull out four inches of the bowel and turn a cuff of the end inside out on itself, showing the red, ridged inner lining.

"I like about an inch *everted*,"[26] I say. "Sometimes, in an emergency, you can't evert any bowel and must stitch it flush with the skin. But eversion is better—it forms a nice nipple to stick into the bag. That makes care much easier. He'll live with this stoma for a long time, God willing.

"Peter, look under the belly wall at the ileostomy. George, hold that retractor up so he can see properly. That's right. Now, Peter, stitch the bowel to the peritoneum where it goes through the hole, and along the side of the belly. Meanwhile, I'll stitch the stoma to the skin. If we do it right, the stoma won't either drop back in or let lavage fluid leak around it.

"Sister, some more warm saline please. Get a jug with *Ancef*[27] in it for the last wash."

We wash the belly until the fluid comes back clear and finish with the antibiotic. Jones closes the abdomen with several layers of sutures. Because Meshack is so sick and badly infected by stool, he puts in an extra row of very large, thick 'tension stitches,'[28] tied over wide plastic bridges. These should hold the abdomen together if healing is impaired.

"How's the patient now?" I ask Jules.

"Amazingly, he's much better," Brobeck replies. "His vitals are stable and he's really peeing. His urine is very dark, so I hope he doesn't shut down later. But his kidneys should be OK if they're flushed with alkaline urine. I gave him the blood, Peter, so repeat his labs. John, you're the man with the machine—why don't you check his pH again? I'm curious to see how it correlates with his clinical state. So far, what we've got is a blooming miracle."

Peter Jones puts on dressings and then he and I go to the break room to complete our paperwork. A porter and a staff nurse take Meshack to Recovery, where he will spend the night. He is still intubated so the Staff Nurse squeezes a large bag to breathe for him. Brobeck is in the Recovery Room, setting up the ventilator. He will manage the respiratory care and remove the tube when the patient is ready. The nurses untangle the lavage tubes and order the dialysis[29] fluids and antibiotics from pharmacy. I draw arterial blood and go to Resuscitation Room, do the test and return.

"Hey Jules, guess what!" I say. "He's just about 'spot on'—his pH is 7.35 and the base deficit is only 2. They're normal, within statistical limits! Congratulations. I think he'll make it."

"Congratulations to you, John," Brobeck says. "You did it from the start. Both your lines of research came together, as usual. Just a shame you can't make your colleagues into believers. Maybe you've converted Jones and Pappas."

"They'll remember while they're here. I don't guarantee their long-term memory."

Both Registrar and student add their congratulations and reassure me about their belief in both acid-base management and peritoneal lavage. We all go upstairs, change and head for the tearoom.

"Mr. Hunt, tell us about cow's horn enemas," George asks.

"OK. You guys might think today was bad enough. Well, 'you ain't seen nuthin yet.' That horn and the enema at least went into the intended place—the rectum. But some folks can't hit the right spot. So the horn either perforates the rectum or pierces the outside skin. It must be the double curve on the horn—it's difficult to judge direction! In either case, the enema enters the tissues next to the rectum and introduces infection with it. This can of course happen with anything inserted in or around the anus and going into the wrong place.

"Regardless of the cause of the perforation, the result is always the same—a fulminating mixed bacterial gangrene of the rectum, perineum and buttocks, with massive tissue destruction and gas formation. It may involve the scrotum, and can even reach the groins and lower belly. The usual delay in reporting to hospital aggravates the situation. Only the occasional lucky patient lives to tell the tale."

"What do you do for it, Mr. Hunt?" Jones asks. "I've never seen a case."

"Surgery must be super-radical. They need colostomy, drainage, and massive debridement[30] and irrigation of the perineum and buttocks, leaving huge, gaping holes. If you thought today's case was disgusting, this is an order of magnitude much worse. It's one of the most horrible things you can ever see—evil looking, foul smelling and seemingly never ending.

"Of course the bugs involved are wild and wonderful. They include the whole zoo of germs you normally find in the colon[31]—

tetanus and gas gangrene, Gram negatives, Gram positives and anaerobes—the works. So you throw in all the antibiotics you've got."

We finish our tea and disperse. It's after five p.m. Jones and Pappas go to the 'Pit.' I pass through Recovery to discuss the lavage with the nurses and make sure my instruction pamphlet is available. One of the Staff Nurses has done peritoneal lavage before, and she will teach the others. The patient is still intubated, but now breathing spontaneously, with no need for the ventilator. All his vital signs remain stable, and his lab work dictates little change in our treatment.

I now rejoin the unit in the 'Pit,' where they have been working since lunch. As it is Monday, there are four or five patients with fractured jaws, left over from the weekend's fighting. Their hangovers have worn off and they've come to Bara. The housemen have admitted the men, who are not usually much of a problem. The maxillo-facial surgeons will take them over from Surgical Admissions in the morning. They will get their jaws wired together and go home in a day or so. I remember a belligerent man who had his jaw re-broken twice, in two different places, while he was still wired up.

The unit is praying for respite today, because Saturday's intake is looming. So far, we have seen little that requires surgery, except for the usual slew of abscesses that will keep one houseman in Septic Theater for most of the night. Tonight it's Saul Steinberg's turn.

Another houseman, Paul Harley, shows me an old vagrant with an unhealed open wound on his leg. Everyone gathers round. He has a four-inch gash, surrounded by blackish *eschar*.[32] The base of the wound is white and seems to be moving. A closer look reveals that the movement comes from squirming fat maggots. They are over a quarter inch long and half as thick, all actively jockeying for position in the wound.

"Disgusting!" George cries. "How do we kill them?"

"Not so fast, George," I say. "The maggots are doing him a lot of good. They eat only dead tissue, so they clean up dirty wounds really well. A famous Spanish army surgeon successfully introduced maggots into septic fracture wounds for just that purpose."

"How in the world do they get in?" George asks.

"Flies love anything that smells rotten—they settle to feed and if they like it, lay their eggs in it," I reply. "I've even seen maggots in a bad belly wound, next to a colostomy. When the maggots matured the flies flew out. They probably left some more eggs inside!"

"Yuck!"

"We'll have to take him in, clean up the wound with Eusol (hypochlorite)[33] solution and minor surgery, and feed him up. Then get the social workers on the job of disposition. We'll see if Unit Five can do better than a bunch of maggots."

"Thanks for those kind words, Boss," Peter Jones says.

"It's OK, Peter, I have every confidence in my unit. I'll back you guys every time."

We work together for a while, disposing of the patients quite quickly, one to admissions, and another to have a cast put on by the orderlies. A third patient has a deflated lung from a stab-wound that he got during the weekend's Shebeen brawling. Jan de Wet, the remaining houseman, takes him to Resuscitation for a belated chest tube. It never gets too busy, and the work never quite stops. And so it goes on, seemingly forever.

We take a break at suppertime, eat together in the mess, and have a chance to relax and talk. We try and stay off the subject of medicine, but touch on the perennial favorites—politics and sport. The topics blend imperceptibly. Sex doesn't feature tonight.

"Did you guys read about the numbers of Portuguese people[34] coming in from Mozambique and Angola?" asks Saul Steinberg.

"Ja, that will help our White numbers," Jan de Wet answers.

"But, with those territories 'independent,' the world and the U.N. will focus on us more and more," I say. "There's only Rhodesia and South West Africa to go, then we'll be the last 'oppressive regime' left for whipping. In fact, they already blame us for South-West not being independent, even though the government is planning their elections."

"We'll never let South-West go!" de Wet blurts out.

"Famous last words!" Steinberg responds.

"Did you see what those Angolan terrorists are doing to the blacks in South-West?" I ask. "They've bitten or lopped off their ears, lips and noses. It's intended to terrify people into believing they are powerful and must be obeyed. The Cubans are in Angola and Mozambique, with Russia pulling the strings, and providing money and military goods."

"I don't know how the terrorists get past our guys on the border," de Wet says. "It would not have happened when I was doing my army time! But we'll chase those monkeys back in the bush where they belong. You know what they say in Rhodesia: 'If the terrorist goes behind a tree, we'll shoot him right through the tree.' And they do."

"It hasn't done the Whites there much good, has it?" Steinberg comments. "Rhodesia is still under attack. Ian Smith will eventually have to give in. Many of the Whites are leaving. Fortunately, they're mostly coming here."

"I guess Jan was right. We can use more Whites in this country," I chip in. "But the black-white ratio here is at least better than it is in Rhodesia or in the two Portuguese territories. Our numbers are still the inverse of those in America, where blacks are about twenty percent. We have only one white to five blacks. I really think it's just a matter of time before we have a black government here. It doesn't matter what the Government of today thinks, it will happen. Let's hope we all have the wisdom to get there peacefully."

"Never!" Jan de Wet bursts out. "Over my dead body."

"You may be right again!" Steinberg says. "But that would be a rare and final event."

"Thanks for the nice thoughts, Saul," de Wet replies.

"You said the words," Paul answers.

"OK you guys! Enough. You two are OK, at least you've done your army time," I say. "I know you're still in the reserves. But my kids will be facing all that in a few years. Those Cubans don't mind where they put their landmines. I hate to think of my boys out on the border, protecting blacks from other blacks who are backed by Russia, and losing their limbs or their lives doing it. They'll have to defend a system of government that I don't believe in and that I know can't last."

"Thinking of International pressure," Jones chimes in. "I saw in the *Rand Daily Mail* that we're now going to be banned from the Olympic games. The Rugby and Cricket bans were bad enough. We're really getting cut off from the world."

"If anything changes us, these embargoes will," remarks Paul Harley. "We're a sports-crazy country. It'll be the first time many white South Africans realize that someone out there might not like us. They may even understand that we need to do something about it, and soon too."

"I admit, that's a bit of a shock," de Wet says. "The Afrikaans[35] newspapers are even starting to take notice. The country has coped very well with the oil and arms embargoes. We now even invent and make sophisticated weapons and we sell arms to other countries. But *sport*, particularly Rugby, that's just too much for most of us Afrikaners to stomach."

"Yes, I do think it may be a wake-up call," Steinberg says.

"Our friend Jan here excepted, have you folks noted the number of Afrikaans speakers who are beginning to talk like liberals and write politically *avant garde* books?" I ask them. "They're even describing love and sex across the color line. I wonder if it has anything to do with the new Rand Afrikaans University here in Joh'burg. I know some of them studied there. But a few are even from Stellenbosch—Dr. Verwoerd's alma mater."

"But they're so few," Harley says. "They're voices crying in the wilderness. The hard line Nats always get their way. It'll take many Richter scale nine earthquakes to change them."

"I agree with you, Paul, they won't change," de Wet says. "But I confess there are a number of Afrikaner liberals. They come from both those Universities. Their books are having some influence on younger people, particularly those with higher education. Remember though, most of our Nationalist party voters—*Die Volk* [36]—are still humble people from the country and small towns. The 'Afrikaner Liberals' you talk about will either side with the English in the United Party or join one of the small liberal splinter parties, like the Progressives.[37] So they'll still have no political power."

"Well, Helen Suzman of the Progs has been a good influence over the years," I say. "She's the only woman and the only Progressive Party M.P. No real power, perhaps, but she's parliament's conscience. She makes even the prime minister feel uncomfortable. She also has a great international status and wields tremendous influence overseas."

"I know the Nat leaders hate her," de Wet says. "But they also respect her for standing up to them."

"Don't forget that the ANC[38] and the SA Communist Party and several other groups have strong organizations and training camps overseas and in other African states," I say. "Many are based in Russia or Cuba, or are supported by those countries. That's why I'm so concerned about Angola and Mozambique on our borders. They have full, on-the-spot Russian and Cuban support. I'm sure Rhodesia won't be far behind in gaining independence and getting a black government.

"We don't have much gun trauma right now in South Africa or here at Bara," I add. "That's largely because our blacks are not allowed to own guns, and even whites have to have licenses. Can you imagine what it will be like with lots of modern Russian or Chinese weapons smuggled in across the borders and freely available to anybody?"

"To change the subject," Steinberg says. "Did you guys see on the news that the Government wants to trade with Japan? So they declared the Japanese Ambassador and his wife to be 'Honorary Whites'? They forgot about all the loyal Chinese folks who have been here for generations and helped them build the gold mines. Many of those Chinese are now in the professional class. In any case, how are our not-so-bright policemen going to tell who's Japanese and who's Chinese?"

"I had an excellent pair of Chinese housemen last year," I say. "The whole business of racial classification[39] is so crazy and unnecessary. Did you see Molly Reinhardt's article on the subject in *The Sunday Times*? Her punch line was 'Obviously, two Wongs still don't make one White.' A bad pun perhaps, but sadly, only too true."

I look at my watch: "We'd better get going. I've enjoyed the discussion, but duty calls. Saul, you'd better get on with the abscesses in Septic Theater. I'll see you all in the 'Pit.' I'm first going by Recovery to see how our patient is faring."

Meshack is doing well. He is breathing by himself, so Brobeck has taken him off the ventilator and removed his endotracheal tube. He can now talk, and he thanks me for the surgery. Everything is stable, and the lavage fluid is a little clearer. I take a peek into the plastic ileostomy bag—the stoma is good and red. Before returning to the 'Pit' I make sure the night staff can handle the lavage.

The work in the 'Pit' is going on as it was before supper. Nothing has come in for urgent surgery. Paul Harley has early call, and he heads off to his room to relax and sleep, if he is not needed. He will be on call the next day. I stay with the group and go across to Casualty to see how things are going. There is no backlog, so I go to check on Steinberg in Septic Theater. There are only four more cases, none terribly complex, so I'm content to leave him to it.

I return to the 'Pit' and sit around, talking and sporadically working, until 11 pm. I then head to bed and sleep through the night, with only two phone calls from Peter Jones, who took a few cases to theater. Our prayer for a light night has indeed been answered.

Early post-intake rounds show that thirty-one patients were admitted—unusually low, even for a Monday. Many will go to special units, so only fourteen patients are going to Unit Five and we have sixteen empty beds. This gives us a leg up for Saturday's intake.

While de Wet, Steinberg and Pappas finish up in Surgical Admissions, I take the others to work in the Unit and make sure everyone is ready for surgery the next day. I must still take the fourth-year students before I can get to the office and my research work. I'm pleased that the rest of the unit will be able to go home around lunchtime.

In Recovery I find Meshack has largely recovered from the severe insult to his system of the day before. He is sitting up in bed, laughing and joking with the nurses.

"How do you like your new backside on your front side?" I ask him. "It's easier to give enemas there because you can see it now. Remember, no more of that orange stuff."

"Doctor, I know you are laughing at me. But thank you. I have learned my lesson."

"Well, Meshack, you'll need a cork now, not an enema! But you'll find it's not so bad. We'll teach you how to handle the bag, and you'll be able to get back to work. Maybe we should tell the police about your *Inyanga.*"

[1] Board-like rigidity: of the abdomen is caused by severe peritoneal irritation, such as by leaked gastric acid or by peritoneal infection, e.g. stool leaking into the abdominal cavity from perforated bowel.

[2] Boscha: Used by some Bantu tribes for 'bowel movement.' Possibly from the Afrikaans term for 'bush,' as in 'behind the bush.'

[3] Inyanga: A form of traditional healer in South Africa. They concentrate on various medicines derived from plants and animals. They do not throw bones, cast spells or otherwise do what Sangomas or Witchdoctors do.

[4] Potassium dichromate: Bright orange crystals. A powerful oxidizing agent and tissue poison. Used in old black and white photo processes and in some industrial labs. Highly dangerous and not for medicinal use.

[5] Derms: Afrikaans term for intestines. Widely understood in South Africa.

[6] Laparotomy: Opening the abdomen to find the problem. i.e. exploratory laparotomy.

[7] Air hunger: A patient or animal breathing deeply and rapidly in an attempt to compensate for blood loss or acidosis, or both, since they are linked. More oxygen enters, while carbon dioxide is blown off, helping to decrease the acidosis.

[8] Arterial blood: Drawn for pH and blood gas studies. The levels in arterial blood accurately reflect what is happening. Hence the modern term: ABGs or arterial blood gases. Levels of pH and blood gases are linked.

[9] Blood gas and pH studies: These are done together to assess the acid-base balance of the blood. It relates directly to the level of carbon dioxide in the blood—excess carbon dioxide will lower the pH (more acid) and a decrease will raise it, in a complex biochemical feedback. See 'Air hunger,' above, #7.

[10] Siggaard-Andersen nomogram: A big sheet of semi-logarithmic graph paper, used with the pH machine. It carries pre- printed lines and curves, from which the levels of pH and pCO2 are read and the 'base excess' or 'deficit' is calculated.

[11] Isotonic bicarbonate: The name I gave for sodium bicarbonate solution containing the same amount of sodium as 'normal (isotonic) saline,' but with bicarbonate instead of the chloride ion.

[12] Sedation: Giving the patient enough morphine to control his pain could reduce his ability to overbreathe, so his pCO2 would rise and it could cause a fatal fall in pH.

[13] The point: My research in shocked animals was confirmed in bled-out people at Bara. I found a critical point where acidosis and high potassium, which go together, cause cardio-respiratory arrest. Correct treatment can still save such people and animals.

[14] Lactic acid: When muscles lack oxygen, their metabolism changes and they pour out lactic acid into the circulation, causing acidosis (fall in pH.) This uses up the body's bicarbonate to neutralize it, producing a 'base deficit.' This happens in shock from any cause, particularly hemorrhage, and in cardiac arrest.

[15] Potassium: A normal body constituent, present at a low level in the blood, compared to sodium. During anoxia, acidosis or hemorrhage, the liver puts out excess potassium, above safe limits. Together with acidosis, this makes the heart unstable.

16 <u>Washout acidosis</u>: When the circulation is restored by starting the heart or by giving fluids, the excess lactic acid and potassium produced by the muscles and the liver get washed out into the circulation and the true severity of the acidosis is seen. It is better to prevent it or treat it at an early stage.

17 <u>Milli-Equivalents (mEq)</u>: A scientific measure of the amount of a substance, based on its relative molecular weight. More scientifically correct than using say 'ounces' or 'milligrams.'

18 <u>Plasmalyte B</u>: A proprietary balanced electrolyte solution, made by Baxter Laboratories in South Africa, to my formula. It resembles 'Ringer Lactate,' a standard resuscitation solution, but it has bicarbonate ion in place of the lactate. It does not contain calcium because that would react with the bicarbonate to form lime.

19 <u>Lavage tubes</u>: Plastic nasogastric tubes which Jonas and I used to wash out and drain the peritoneal cavity after infected surgery – our system of 'peritoneal lavage.'

20 <u>Overbreathing</u>: 'Air hunger,' above, #7.

21 <u>Saline</u>: Sterile common salt solution in a concentration similar to that found in plasma. It is used for IVs and for dressings. It is also used in surgery for washing and wetting things. It has many other medical uses.

22 <u>Ileo-cecal valve</u>: A non-return valve, situated between the small and large bowel, at the cecum. It prevents colon stool from going back upstream into the small bowel. The colon normally has more germs than the small bowel, so this is protective.

23 <u>Nasogastric tube</u>: Plastic tubes passed through the nose to the stomach for temporary drainage after surgery.

24 <u>Ileostomy</u>: The end of the small bowel is brought out through a hole in the abdominal wall and sutured in place. It acts as an artificial anus and is cared for with a plastic bag stuck to the skin.

25 <u>Peritoneum</u>: A thin membrane that is the innermost layer of the abdominal wall. It forms a closed cavity, like a bag, with the intestines, liver and spleen inside it.

26 <u>Everted</u>: It is modern practice to turn back a cuff of the end of the bowel when making a stoma. The cuff protects the end, and the protruding bowel is easier to manage.

27 <u>Ancef</u>: Proprietary name for an antibiotic often used intravenously and for irrigating solutions in theater.

28 <u>Tension or Retention sutures</u>: An extra layer of very strong, thick sutures placed to close abdominal wounds that are likely to burst because of infection, poor nutrition or cancer.

29 <u>Dialysis fluid</u>: The fluid that is normally used for peritoneal dialysis in kidney failure. It resembles protein-free blood plasma, minus the potassium ion, since potassium needs to be drawn off from patients whose kidneys have failed. It is ideal for the peritoneal lavage system that Jonas and I devised.

30 <u>Debridement</u>: French: The removal of debris. Dead or infected tissue is cut away to leave a fresh, living, bleeding base.

31 <u>Colon bacteria</u>: The normal colon contains a huge variety and infinite number of bacteria. They are beneficial, helping the digestion of food and in one case, making a vitamin. If they get outside the colon, as from a perforated bowel, they cause serious or fatal infections. 'Gram positives and negatives and anaerobes' are generic terms for some of these bacteria.

32 <u>Eschar</u>: Hard, dead tissue, usually black, like jerky.

33 <u>Eusol (Hypochlorite)</u>: Sodium hypochlorite is a strong oxidizer and bleach. A dilute form is used for wound dressings. It was once called 'Eusol'—'Edinburgh University Solution' and was known at Bara by that name.

34 <u>Portuguese</u>: The Portuguese overseas territories became independent in June 1975. Many Portuguese people left Angola and Mozambique, often settling in South Africa, their erstwhile neighbor to the south and west.

35 <u>Afrikaans</u>: The largest section of South Africa's white population. Of Dutch, French and German origins. Also the name of their language, which has the same roots. It was an official language, along with English.

36 <u>Die Volk</u>: Literally: The People.  Used by Nationalist politicians in a purely political (patriotic) sense.

37 <u>Progressive Party</u>: A small political party with advanced and liberal views, more so than the main opposition United Party. Mrs. Helen Suzman, their sole elected Member of Parliament, represented Houghton, a wealthy and largely English/Jewish neighborhood, with a high overall level of education. Our family lived in the area.

38 <u>ANC</u>: African National Congress, a black political organization which was banned by the South African Government. It had many active members both within and outside South Africa. It became the governing party in South Africa in the 1994 elections, with Nelson Mandela as its head and President of the country.

39 <u>Racial classification</u>: A foundation of the Apartheid system. Every person had to be classified into groups by color: White, Black or Bantu, Colored, Indian, Chinese etc. These classifications were entered on all identity documents and governed all activities and places of residence of the people concerned. A major motivation for the laws was the preservation of white jobs. Many other laws, such as the Group Areas Act, were based on the concept of racial separation. Public facilities, such as toilets, trains, buses and cinemas, were also segregated by skin color. The concept went further, to prevent racial mixing, intermarriage and even sex across the color line.

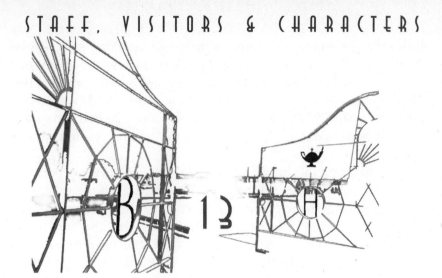

Baragwanath Hospital ran well due largely to the skill and dedication of its staff. This was true at all levels, from the Medical Superintendent and administration, through the black nurses and the largely white doctors, to the attendants in the boiler-room or mortuary. They all gave of their best for the overall good of the hospital, its patients and the community.

The majority of the nursing and lay staff were black South Africans, inhabitants of Soweto and the surrounding areas, with firsthand knowledge of the patients and their problems. Some were born at Bara and many would deliver their babies there. Most of them had been patients of the hospital—or would be at some time. It was estimated that a Soweto resident had an annual five percent chance of being a victim of trauma or assault. No matter what, Bara would take care of them.

The nurses formed the core of the hospital. They were all African, from one of the nine Bantu ethnic groups, the largest being Zulu and Xhosa. Their home languages depended on their tribal origins, but they all spoke English—the language in which their teaching was conducted, and in which the hospital did most of its business. Some Matrons,[1] or Chiefs of Nursing, were white, but African women were steadily climbing the career ladder and entering these senior positions.

The student nurses came from a variety of family backgrounds and home conditions. The majority of their homes were without modern amenities, even such simple ones as electric lights or indoor flush toilets. Cooking and minimal heating were done with coal or wood stoves and paraffin-burning appliances, such as the ubiquitous 'Primus Stove.'[2] Battery-powered transistor radios were common, but telephones or television in the home did not exist. A television service was initiated in 1972, available mostly to whites. At that time most homes in Soweto did not have electricity for lighting, let alone to run television.

Considering this background where they couldn't pop bread in the toaster, call their friends, watch TV or even flush the toilet, the nurses adapted extremely well to their totally different environment in modern nursing. They coped admirably with the constantly advancing electronic technology, the complex drugs and the changes in nursing techniques. In most cases they were the first family members to have any post-high-school education. Bara nursing graduates numbered many thousands and were arguably the largest and most concentrated group of educated black Africans on the continent. Many could not find marriage partners of equal educational background.

The nursing students lived in a large Nurses' Home on the hospital grounds, next to the nursing school. Their course of study involved much practical training in the wards, with ample time off to attend lectures. Accommodation was made in the program to allow pregnancy and delivery without penalty to the nurse's education. Graduates became Staff Nurses and could then live where they chose. After a few years in that grade, promotion to Sister[3] followed, usually in charge of a ward or department, or as teaching staff. The next step up was to Administrative Sister or Matron. I always joked with my Staff Nurses and Sisters that I was scared to teach them anything because when they became really good they would be spirited away to teach in the Nursing School or to do Administration.

In addition to the teaching given by the senior nurses, all heads of medical units in Baragwanath added their skills and gave lectures in their own subjects to the nursing students. These teaching sessions gave the doctors some insight into the minds and thought processes of the students, which they might otherwise not have obtained. I did much teaching and I followed the careers of many of the Sisters, right from the time when they were student nurses in my lectures or on my surgical unit.

The nurses who did specialized work, such as in the operating theaters, running the heart-lung pump, delivering babies, or in the premature baby unit or pediatric 'Drip Room,' all went through the same basic training. After graduation they worked as staff nurses in their chosen area, where they received in-service teaching and on-the-job training. These methods produced excellent nurses. I would have backed my operating room nurses against those in the white hospitals at any time. I heard the same boast from many of my colleagues in other disciplines.

The administrative staff and those with technical positions in radiology, the laboratory, pharmacy, dietary and physical or occupational therapy, were mostly white South Africans.[4] As black people became trained, they were given many of these positions. The clerical staff who had contact with the patients were black South Africans and spoke the languages of the patients. Many employees in administration were Afrikaans speaking whites, which was perhaps fortunate. Afrikaans was used for most hospital dealings with the Transvaal Provincial Administration, which controlled the hospitals and their purse strings.

Doctors who worked at Baragwanath did so for many reasons—as varied as their numbers. Medical students from Witwatersrand University learned about the hospital as they rotated through the hospital departments during their clinical teaching. When they graduated, they had to do a year of 'Housemanship' before obtaining permanent registration as Medical Practitioners. Many chose to do these jobs at Bara, because of the wide range of experience available. Some young doctors chose Bara for humanitarian reasons, wanting to serve where they were most needed. Others were in the forefront of the ideological struggle against Apartheid and for the uplifting of the Blacks in any possible manner. It was another way they could get involved with something close to their hearts.

Baragwanath was a major teaching hospital of the University, involved in both undergraduate and postgraduate training. It was well integrated with the Medical school. The senior members of hospital medical staff had dual appointments, with University titles.

The Registrar grade was the basic post-graduate teaching position. Young people wishing to train in any of the specialties usually passed through transitional posts at Senior House Officer level before starting as Registrars. Registrar training took three to five years, not all of which would be spent at Bara. Rotation through the other teaching hospitals was required in order to complete the educational experience. Many trainees were alumni of the university and of the hospital. Some of them came from elsewhere in South Africa, while a few came from other countries, either as immigrants or visiting or exchange students. The majority of the doctors at Bara were white. But, as the number of Bantu and Asian graduates rose, their representation on the staff also increased.

Colleagues practicing elsewhere often regarded as slightly crazy anyone who remained on staff at Bara after surviving the mayhem and chronic overload. I sometimes felt there was more than a grain of truth in that belief. But, like most other senior members of staff, I chose to work there because I liked it. The Baragwanath Hospital doctors were all dedicated to the care of the people they served and to the teaching of future generations of doctors. This, despite the knowledge that far richer financial rewards were available in private practice and that a perception of superiority adhered to those teaching doctors who worked in the 'white' University hospitals—the elitist 'Ivory Tower' mentality.

Because of its unique nature, Baragwanath Hospital regularly received a number of visitors. Many simply toured the hospital, or visited at the end of the year, as the external examiners for the sixth year students. A number of doctors came to work there for periods of a year or two in order to experience the uniqueness of Bara and take advantage of the wonderful experience it offered. Visitors of all stripes never failed to be impressed by the hospital, its service and the huge scope and variety of its patient care activities.

One of the more notable visitors, who came for a year to work in the pathology department, was Dr. Albert Zuckerman, from Barnes Hospital in St Louis, Missouri. He was a world-renowned Surgical Pathologist, with many honors, books and articles to his credit. He had helped arrange my surgical oncology fellowship at Barnes. I often recalled one of Dr. Zuckerman's first comments after arriving at Bara:

"If I lived here, I would start writing a book about Baragwanath the next day."

He clearly recognized the immense opportunities for study and research offered by the unique social and ethnic mélange of Soweto and its surroundings, by contrast with the socially and economically privileged white population of nearby Johannesburg. He made many contributions during his stay at Bara and continued with cooperative projects long after his return to Barnes Hospital.

As a result of my visit to St. Louis, a Chief Resident named Geoff Lilly came out to Baragwanath for a year after he graduated. He worked in the Surgery Department and learned a great deal about the problems of the doctors and their patients. At first, the complete change of pace and the lack of his usual support systems provided him with a challenge. But, soon learning to 'think on his feet,' he became an 'Action Man' with the best of them. He returned to Barnes Hospital, becoming a leading transplant surgeon.

I remember with affection a Belgian doctor, Hendrik van Warmelo, and a German, Heinrich Mueller, who worked in my unit together. Hendrik was soft-voiced, gentle and rather reserved. Though constantly amazed by the challenging cases he saw, he was very efficient and never failed to get the job done. Heinrich was equally efficient, with the advantage of a great, outgoing personality. He wore a Royal Air Force-style mustache. I could always tell what kind of night it had been by looking at the normally well-kept mustache. It drooped only after really bad nights. On one such occasion I asked Heinrich how the night had gone.

"Mister Hunt, we admitted only those who came in 'Head under arm,'" Heinrich answered. He did not need to say more. That explained well the flood of desperate cases they had seen.

Both Hendrik and Heinrich were involved in my peritoneal lavage work and were co-authors on two papers. Heinrich helped me prepare for a lecture in Germany, so that I could deliver my introduction in German, before reverting to English and my slide show. That ploy was very well received at the German meeting. He translated the paper for publication.

Parting from Heinrich and Hendrik was hard on us all. However, there was a constant stream of visitors, each bringing something new to the party. One Dutch doctor fell off a horse and broke his wrist. He decided to get his friends at the hospital to fix it for him. (Treating whites was illegal.) They reduced it with Xylocaine, both injected into the fracture site and so-called 'intravenous Xylocaine,' where the circulation was temporarily cut off and the local anesthetic solution was injected into the veins below the block. The anesthetic did not work as planned, and the procedure was agonizing. He soon decided not to use that technique on future patients.

Another visitor from the USA was a unique person. Bill Wilson had obtained his F.R.C.S. diploma in Scotland before coming to Bara. It was most unusual for an American to obtain a British qualification. He worked in my unit and we became quite friendly. He was an extremely valuable and resourceful member of the team. While he was in South Africa Bill considered settling there or in Rhodesia. While at Bara he met a young South African pediatrician. They married and returned to the States to live in Florida and raise a family. He joined the staff at the VA hospital and his wife, Patricia, became the tropical diseases expert at the University.

Several Portuguese doctors came as immigrants after the independence of the two neighboring Portuguese territories. Two were from Mozambique. Alberto Diaz worked in Unit Five for a long period and became heavily involved with research in the University Department of Surgery, so he was rapidly assimilated. The other, Armando Da Cunha, was one of the thinnest people I had ever met. He had great facility in using a fiberoptic endoscope,[5] or duodenoscope. He was allowed to spearhead the Surgery Department's endeavor to perform the relatively new technique of E.R.C.P.[6] This involved using the side-viewing scope to pass a fine catheter into the bile and pancreatic ducts in order to get tissue samples and take X-rays. He became very adept at it and was soon showing excellent pictures at surgical meetings. The technique is now routinely used in gastroenterology. He was also easily assimilated into the community.

Baragwanath has had more than its fair share of odd characters on the medical staff. Because of its unique nature and its great size, the hospital was able to accommodate a wide variety of people and different personalities. The strange ones were not confined to any age, sex, or ethnic group. Some stayed until they were detected to be abnormal, others became unusual characters with age, while yet others had been strange from birth and were unlikely to change. Some were overt or even clinically obvious psychotics. Most of them seemed to function within the broad framework of accepted normality most of the time.

When I returned from my Fellowship year in the USA, I found a doctor called Toby working in the unit. I would normally have opposed his appointment because of my preconceived ideas of him. Owing to a severe shortage of staff, I had no option but to keep Toby on and get to know him. In this case, 'familiarity bred content,' or at least tolerance.

Toby had been a few years ahead of me in medical school and was years my senior. He had become 'a legend in his own time.' Stories about him would fill a book. He was among a group of older World War Two veterans, most of whose peers had already graduated. This group had trouble passing their exams—and the reason was not hard to find. They spent almost all their time in the cafeteria gambling— Poker and 'Klaberjas' being their favorite games. The stakes were high. One man staked and lost his Ford car. It was said that Toby once needed money to pay his debts and continue gambling. He persuaded his dear old businessman father to part with fifteen thousand pounds, ostensibly to buy him an X-ray machine that was 'required for his course of study.'

Toby had somehow eventually managed to graduate, and while I was overseas doing my F.R.C.S., he had even specialized in another field. He had a problem with some regulations and had to repeat part of his training. To fulfill this obligation he had ended up filling an empty slot in Unit Five at Bara while I was away in America.

Toby was a good-hearted soul and a great talker, so I always knew what was going on. I needed a car on my return to South Africa, so Toby found me an excellent buy through a friend in the business. Toby asked for a day off per week to do a 'Scrap Deal.' He had access to buildings that were being demolished. He employed an African man who he said was able to 'smell copper' anywhere. This man stripped out all the copper wire and pipes, which Toby sold at a great profit, since the price of copper was high. He made more on his weekly scrap deal than he or I earned in a month at the hospital.

The scrap deals were done on Tuesdays. On Wednesdays Toby's body was back at work, but his brain was at the racetrack. He was almost useless until five in the afternoon. Wednesday was horseracing day, and Toby spent the day on the phone placing bets, until all his newfound money and his credit were exhausted. Like most gamblers, he lost more than he won. So the scrap deals continued.

One intake Wednesday, I overheard Toby spending time trying to persuade our two young Afrikaans female house surgeons to join him in betting on the horses. He was being his most persuasive, repeating over and over the mantra 'You can't lose.' Finally, during lunch he convinced them to part with their money before one o'clock, the time the big race was due to start. He apparently placed their bets by phone and kept them excited listening to the race on the radio. The horse lost, to their great chagrin. Toby let them suffer for a while, and then returned them their money, saying that he was just seeing how far they would go! He taught them a lesson that he never learned.

Toby's fund of stories was endless. When he was in the South African army in North Africa, he and a buddy created an illegal enterprise that would find anything for anybody—at a price. Whether the demand was for cigarettes, whiskey or willing young women—Toby and his friend could satisfy it. Their peers consequently held them in very high esteem.

Toby particularly relished telling stories of the antics they went through to satisfy their customers' many desires. One of their standard techniques involved taking armored cars out on long 'patrols.' The young women would be brought in after dark, hidden somewhere in the car. The cars could equally conceal a lot of otherwise unavailable luxuries. He had enjoyed the process as much as the rewards. His capacious belly used to shake uncontrollably from side to side as he told his tales.

Toby was a large, gruff person. Despite his paunch, he looked as if he would pack a powerful punch. He did not suffer fools gladly. A rather small, loud-mouthed doctor gave him a hard time once too often. Toby lifted him by the collar of his white coat and hung him on a coat rack, with his limbs flailing wildly around. He gave Toby no more trouble.

Yet another character came to Baragwanath during this period. I learned a lot about him from Toby. His name, apparently, was Charles Nixon. He was from another country and seemed to have all the right credentials: he claimed to have the Fellowship diplomas of the Royal Colleges of Surgery of both London and Edinburgh. He said he was an Olympic swimmer and had represented his country in Cricket and other sports. He casually mentioned several other honors.

He had somehow obtained a Registrar position at Bara and was rotating through the surgical units, as did all the trainees. Nobody liked him, except for a quiet young lady with whom he became increasingly friendly. I had not yet had Nixon in my unit, but intuitively did not like him because he would talk softly about his many triumphs and abilities, while continually rubbing his hands together as if he was washing them or anointing them with oil.

"Smarmy," I thought.

The debunking of Nixon's stories began before I returned to Bara. At the time, one of the housemen at Bara was also a Springbok[7] Cricketer. To be hospitable, one Sunday he invited Nixon to a sports and social club to play Cricket. As the game progressed, it turned out that the visitor could neither bat nor bowl, which embarrassed his host considerably. Hearing this, Toby was at the hospital swimming bath the next weekend and spotted Nixon sunning himself alongside his young lady friend. He invited Nixon into the water—it was hard to resist Toby. Nixon tried to dive in and nearly drowned. He could barely do the dog paddle. Toby was satisfied.

As time passed, it was apparent that Nixon's surgical abilities were also seriously in question. Each surgical unit in turn was only too glad to be rid of him. Mercifully, it never became my turn to have him in my unit. One day a large write-up appeared in the local paper about Nixon's impending marriage. A week or two later, on the day the nuptials were to occur, the paper reported that his previous marriage in his native country had not been dissolved. His new intended bride was not aware that he had ever been married. I don't know how that issue was resolved, but I remember Nixon leaving Bara soon after.

At the end of that year, at the examiner's luncheon meeting, I heard from Professor Joubert, the head of surgery in another city, that Nixon was working somewhere there, with less than spectacular results.

A year later, again at the examiner's luncheon, I asked a friend of mine, who was head of surgery in a third city, how things were going.

"Wonderful, John. I'm so pleased. I just got a new surgeon. He sounds very good."

"Who's that?" I asked, curious. The surgeons all knew each other.

"His name is Nixon, Charles Nixon. He's got a double Fellowship and a whole lot more. He comes from Hennie's place."

"Congratulations!" I said, sarcastically.

"Congratulate me!" Professor Joubert said. "Thanks for taking him off my hands."

The rest of the examiners all dissolved in uproarious laughter, as they had all heard of Nixon's reputation. My friend was covered in confusion and embarrassment. He confessed he had not picked up the phone to check with one of Nixon's prior employers and had obtained no written testimonials. He had been too keen to fill the position, which had been vacant for a while. I later heard that it took him a long time to get rid of Nixon.

Two much sadder individuals with occult or overt psychiatric problems passed through the medical staff at the hospital. A British doctor called Richard Asher wrote beautifully on a variety of medical subjects. He once published an article including a picture of a person with 'a schizophrenic grin.' Since my original interest was in psychiatry, I read the article with close attention and thought the description and the picture were perfect.

Not too long after that a new surgical trainee came to the hospital. I thought immediately that the person's smile fitted Dr. Asher's picture to perfection. As the days passed, it became apparent to me that this registrar was indeed not quite normal, and was rapidly shunted from unit to unit because of personality clashes. When it was my turn, I tried hard to understand and get on with the young doctor and to impart some knowledge. But by the end of each day Unit Five's entire staff had raging headaches from the continual stress of trying to deal with the person. One young woman doctor just couldn't take it and left the unit in despair.

I went to a much higher authority and revealed the situation, saying in essence: "This psychotic doctor has the brains to pass the exam and to graduate, and will do so, but should not be allowed to continue in training or to practice surgery due to bad psychiatric problems. I think you should take over the training and assessment so that you can take appropriate action."

Unfortunately, no one listened. I was told that no person could be both crazy and pass the exam at the same time. Also, no other surgeon would go on record about the situation, and some even gave glowing assessments. The trainee remained in the program, passed the exams, and finally graduated, as I had predicted. During a subsequent career, that person did some very unusual and harmful things. For example, screwing a patient's forearm to the armboard while trying to fix a fracture, driving a nail right through the collarbone into the esophagus, and many more. My conscience was clear, but I was sorry for the victims. I remained convinced that some day something very bad would happen, but heard of no major disaster. The doctor eventually emigrated without being exposed, or treated for the psychosis.

The other individual was an older, very pleasant and well-experienced anesthetist who was not obviously abnormal. The surgeons often wondered what the story was and why this person was working at Bara. One day this anesthetist gave the anesthetic for one of my favorite patients, who was having her esophagus removed for cancer, after full treatment with radiation and chemotherapy, in the hope of complete cure.

Unfortunately, after surgery, the anesthetist removed the patient's endotracheal tube and transferred her over a long distance to the ICU with no possibility for her to get oxygen. She should have gone to the nearby recovery room with both the tube and oxygen in place and been put on a ventilator. She suffered a cardiac arrest in the ICU elevator. Her short stay in the unit started with my registrar doing external cardiac massage on her newly operated chest wall, compressing the heart repeatedly against the newly sewn junction of upper esophagus to stomach, high inside the chest. Needless to say, the patient died.

The secret only then came out that the anesthetist was a schizophrenic, on medication for years, but had not taken any for several days. The anesthetist's services were hastily terminated.

The pathology examination of the patient's excised esophagus showed that the cancer had been completely eliminated by the treatment. The tragic irony was that the patient would have been cured of her cancer and could have had a long-term survival, which until then was virtually unknown at Bara. Even in death, she helped justify my research.

While I was a student at Bara, I was amazed at the abilities of one of the anesthetists. He was often alone on night duty and would stick spinal anesthetics into three patients in rapid succession so that surgeons working on the lower limbs could occupy all the theaters. He could then sit idly in the Doctor's room and smoke to his heart's content.

At the same time, one of the subspecialty surgeons was a big, burly and aggressive man named Jan Swart. He often showed his anger during surgery by throwing large instruments through the plate glass theater window. He was disciplined for that and for his rudeness to the staff. He loved boasting of his sexual escapades. His favorite saying was: "You know you're enjoying it when your toes are curling and the dorsal vein (of the penis) is standing out like an anaconda."

He was fond of showing off his body and muscular development in an intimidating manner. One day my young uncle John, an ex-service-man who played championship tennis and kept himself very fit with a variety of exercises, walked into the change room from the shower with no shirt on. Swart, who had not met him before, commented: "I don't think I'll tangle with that gorilla."

On one occasion Swart, to get himself a few days of leave, sent word that he was ill with a heart attack. Unfortunately for him, a buffalo gored him while he was hunting. He then really landed in hospital. Ironically, Swart suffered a heart attack a few years later.

When I was a houseman at Bara, one of the other units had a clash of personalities amongst their house doctors. One of them was an outspoken Afrikaner called Jan, who did not like to be put upon. Another young doctor was quite incapable of doing anything technical or practical, such as taking blood, which was one of our many daily chores. So some of his work spilled over onto Jan, who complained one day: "Crikey, you should see him try and take blood—he jabs a big needle in and out, first up, then right, then left, then down. Nothing happens except a big hematoma.[8] He pulls the Blerry[9] needle out and holds the tube under the arm, squeezes it and some blood drips into the tube, if he's lucky! Then he calls one of us to do the job right."

I found that women doctors were very reliable and frequently smarter than the men. Pregnancy did not harm their work ethic or abilities. One year I had two female house surgeons working together, one of whom was pregnant. They both did an excellent job in the unit. The pregnant one pulled her weight throughout. Near the end of their six-month jobs it came to Christmas and the New Year. A 'pot luck' party was held on an Intake night, the 23$^{rd}$ of December, with everyone bringing a representative national dish. The staff was racially mixed and the foods were delightful, including an Indian curry, Jewish Borscht, English Christmas pudding and much else.

A young single Indian doctor brought only a brown bag containing huge cashew nuts from Mozambique. These were my favorite. I had never seen such big cashews and took one right away and stuffed it in my mouth. It was a complete mouthful—of fire! I had to indelicately spit it out and cool my mouth with ice. I only then learned that the nuts had been marinated in 'Peri-Peri sauce,' a very strong hot flavoring from Mozambique.

Next day, the young doctor's baby was born and she took the week's leave, which was her due. She finished her obligatory year of housemanship and could register as a Doctor!

I will always remember that Christmas because it showed Bara's staff at their best. A rich mix of talented people from diverse cultures, all working effectively to treat Bara's challenging patients. Only later, with the Soweto uprisings, would come stress and rupture. Not even Bara, with its unique learning and nurturing environment, could hold against the fissures of long held resentments and primal angers against social inequities.

[1] <u>Matron</u>: Chief of Nursing. The term was a holdover from the British system, used in South Africa.

[2] <u>Paraffin</u>: Kerosene. Used for much heating, lighting and cooking in South Africa's rural and poorer areas.

[3] <u>Sister</u>: The head of a Ward or Nursing Unit. Also British terminology.

[4] <u>White South Africans</u>: Most South African whites were born in the country, being at least the 3rd or 4th generation of their family in South Africa. The two broadest groups are those of English and those of Afrikaans origin, hence two languages. The Afrikaans people and language are largely of Dutch, German and French extraction. Their forebears go back to 1652, when Jan van Riebeeck established at the Cape of Good Hope a victualling station for the Dutch East India Company.

[5] <u>Fiberoptic endoscope</u>: A relatively new type of instrument at the time. It combined ultra-bright quartz lighting with the ability of fiberglass to transmit light and to bend at the same time. These scopes were used to examine many internal organs, such as the esophagus, stomach and duodenum and the colon. Those for the stomach are called 'gastroscopes,' longer ones duodenoscopes, and so on.

[6] <u>E.R.C.P</u>: Endoscopic Retrograde Cholangio-Pancreatogram. A duodenoscope with a side view is passed beyond the stomach into the duodenum. A fine catheter is passed through the scope into the lower end of the bile duct, and X-rays are done or samples of tissue are taken.

[7] <u>Springbok</u>: A South African representative in sport of any kind, such as Cricket or Rugby. Named for a small, fleet-footed and graceful South African antelope, which has become the national symbol.

[8] <u>Hematoma</u>: A collection of blood in the wrong place, e.g. under the skin, as here. A bruise.

[9] <u>Blerry</u>: A rather crude Afrikaans pronunciation of the English swear word 'bloody.'

Delivering babies and providing pediatric health care for the black population of South Africa presented even more challenges than did the care of adults. In the rural areas, known at times as 'Reserves' or 'Homelands,' white people were scarce, and there were few sizable population centers or industries. On large white-owned farms the living conditions for black workers and their families were little better. Healthcare in such rural areas was virtually non-existent, with few doctors, nurses or clinics available. Mission Hospitals of various denominations did a good job, but such places were few and far between. Distances from major hospitals were great, and transport facilities primitive in the extreme.

There were few employment opportunities, so survival was by subsistence farming, done largely by the women. Many able-bodied young men were recruited by the gold mines to work on contract for periods of years at very low wages. Some men chose to go to the cities and seek work in industry. The little money such migrant workers could send back home provided only a meager living for their families. Women often went to the cities themselves to try and augment family income by working as domestic servants or in other service jobs, leaving their children under the care of the grannies. The residual population thus consisted largely of older women, children and old men, who could no longer go to the mines or cities in search of work. Contraception was almost non-existent and was scorned by the men. Once a year the migrant workers returned on vacation to make more babies.

From the tourist viewpoint, many houses and villages in the rural black areas were certainly picturesque. The people did incredibly well with their natural resources. In most country areas the Africans constructed their homes from locally available materials—stones, sun-baked clay bricks, woven tree branches and reed or buffalo grass thatching. Floors were of bare earth or sometimes made from a hardened mixture of mud and cow dung. This material was also used to plaster holes between the stones or tree branches used in construction. Without window glass and conventional doors, ventilation was poor and the huts were freezing in winter. In some areas the women decorated the huts with brightly colored designs. Though such houses were traditional and part of the tribal way of life, by no stretch of the imagination could they support an adequate, healthy standard of living.

The burning of ever more scarce wood provided cooking and some heating. As plumbing was non-existent, toilets were simply patches of open ground, behind nearby bushes. Hence the use of the word *boscha* for a bowel movement, from the Afrikaans word for bush. Fresh or running water were unheard of luxuries, and neither electricity nor telephones were available. The few transistor radios used dry cells.

Poverty and lack of education were the background for malnutrition and a wide variety of socio-economic ills. Tuberculosis was endemic in South Africa, particularly among rural African people and the equally poor urban black population. This airborne disease, which is transmitted by coughing and sputum, spread rapidly under the close living conditions in these areas. Since the uneducated people did not understand the cause of TB or its prevention, it was seldom detected or properly treated, and its ravages continued to spread.

With no community knowledge of even elementary hygiene, other infectious and parasitic diseases were equally widespread. Bilharzia, or *Schistosomiasis* affects the urinary tract, causing bleeding. It comes from parasites living in snails in infected streams or other water and is contracted by wading or swimming in water containing the snails. Infected people passing urine into the streams perpetuated the disease. In some areas passing blood in the urine was so common that boys regarded it as a rite of passage, like menstruation in girls. The disease is hard to eradicate and has horrible complications. Mercifully, two other parasitic diseases, malaria and yellow fever, are not major scourges in South Africa, though malaria is seen in more tropical areas, where the Anopheles mosquito vector is present.

Natural childbirth was the order of the day under tribal conditions, with older women doing the birthing. Only prolonged or obstructed labors led to some form of transportation to hospitals many miles away. Thus many mothers and babies died during or after delivery, or suffered severe complications.

Another unfortunate result of tribal home delivery and traditional beliefs was the practice of placing cow dung on the umbilical cord stump of the newborn baby. Infection was not obvious until the infant started to jerk and develop spasms, could not breathe adequately and died, or was brought to a hospital days later with full-blown tetanus. The only treatment was heavy sedation and paralyzing of the muscles in spasm, penicillin and the use of a ventilator or some form of respiratory support. At that time, neonatal intensive care units did not exist and newborn respirator care was unsophisticated. Most babies died.

Many tribal women breastfed their babies for up to eighteen months, both because it was easier and cheaper than other forms of food and in the mistaken belief that it prevented conception. The youngest child was often carried on the mother's rump, wrapped tightly in a blanket, with hips widely splayed and legs around the mother's waist. Both Ann and I had seen women feeding such children on their backs by throwing one long and floppy breast over a shoulder and allowing the baby to suckle. The second breast was soon thrown over the opposite shoulder to pacify the hungry baby and stop the crying.

One curious advantage of this system of transport for the baby was perhaps seen in the apparent rarity in blacks of the disease 'congenital dislocation of the hip' or CDH, fairly often seen in white children. The therapy for this condition involved placing the baby in a plaster of paris splint, with the hips and legs widely splayed apart or 'abducted,' just as the black babies' legs were while on their mothers' backs. Since the babies practically lived in that position and seldom saw a doctor, it is not clear whether they had the condition and got cured or if they were perhaps just not genetically programmed to have CDH.

Women carrying their babies in this manner still went about their daily tasks, whether working in the home, tilling the fields, walking miles to fetch water, or going to a distant store for provisions. They often returned from the stream or the store with their water or other burdens balanced securely on their heads! It was quite awe-inspiring to see a line of such women walking single file on a country path, each one carrying something on her head.

During our honeymoon, Ann and I drove through Pondoland and the Transkei, the Xhosa-speaking area of the Eastern Cape. We saw some tiny thatched huts half a mile away, across the dry grassy open veld. Many children of all ages came running up to our Volkswagen Bug from the huts, seeking handouts of money, food, clothes or candy. The younger ones were usually naked, with G-Strings or other scant coverings. Their bellies bulged, probably from protein-calorie malnutrition, known as *kwashiorkor* or 'Red Boy,'[1] from the thinning red hair such children developed. Their navels were often prominent, from untreated umbilical hernias, sticking forward for an inch or two, like short penises.

I once did a *locum tenens* job in Zeerust, a small town in the western Transvaal, near Botswana. I worked for Dr. Willemse, who, in addition to his private practice, had the Government appointment as District Surgeon. This meant that he had the task of looking after the poor people in a large area of several hundred miles in each direction. As part of this job I attended clinics and saw patients in far distant rural African areas. Ann sometimes came along and used to enjoy the 'bare bottom parade' when the resident nurse got a row of howling babies prepared for me to give them their regular shots of long-acting penicillin.

The people there were poor and underfed, though their village had fertile soil and a great stream of fresh running water—a rare commodity in Africa. I asked about this and was told that the chief was an indolent man who had often been treated by Dr. Willemse for venereal diseases. Tradition and tribal law prevented the people from planting their crops until the chief had planted his, but he was too busy sowing his wild oats. So the people's seeds were planted too late to come to fruition before winter set in.

One day after the clinic visit, I took Ann and Petrus, my interpreter and guide, on more calls that had come before I left the office. I had a box of common drugs and syringes in the trunk of the car. Our first call was to see a very ill little boy at a black schoolteacher's home a mile or so away. We found the wife weeping because their first child had just died. Now the couple thought that their second boy had the same disease. I listened to the story and examined the child, who was semi-conscious, with a fever and a stiff neck. I had to agree with the parents—the child probably had meningitis, which could easily prove fatal.

The week before, the parents had refused to allow Dr. Willemse to take the first child to the new hospital for a spinal tap. I now had better arguments than my boss had and could convince the family to let this boy come with me for treatment. The hospital had then been open for two weeks, and I promised to take care of him myself. The parents agreed that he could go with us. I gave him a shot of penicillin before leaving. The mother was extremely grateful and gave everyone a cup of tea in her tiny, but impeccably clean, home. The parents would have to find their own transport to the hospital, seventy miles away.

I did two more calls before returning to town. The first was to a very poor home, where we found a painfully thin four-year-old boy, with a cloth over his face. I removed the cloth and flinched. Ann turned her head away. She would never forget the sight. We saw something I had certainly never seen before and which was probably known to very few people in the world. The front of the child's jaw and his whole lower lip had fallen off, as if cut by a knife. Most of the teeth and gums were exposed on the surface. It was quite clean and white, not bleeding. This was the condition of *Noma*,[2] due to malnutrition, but not well understood. We also packed this pathetic child into the car for transport to the hospital.

I next saw a sixteen-year-old girl, writhing in abdominal pain. This had gone on for a few days despite visiting the witchdoctor. Her father didn't want her to see a regular doctor. Other relatives insisted, so we finally got the call. The girl was very ill and I felt a large, round, tender lump in her belly. I diagnosed a twisted ovarian cyst and explained the need for urgent surgery. After an hour of heated discussion they let me take her to hospital—hers would be the first operation done there. But I knew she would die if she stayed at home.

I was now very pleased that Dr. Willemse had insisted that I take the spare practice Dodge sedan for these trips. My Volkswagen Bug would certainly not have coped with the load, nor with the rutted and potholed dirt roads. I felt very sorry for the girl with the sore belly during the bumpy trip on a dirt track back to the corrugated gravel highway.

Once back in Zeerust, I dropped Ann at the hotel, then took Petrus home. The hospital admitted the three patients, two to my care—the boy with meningitis and the girl. I was not surprised to hear the next day that the boy with Noma had died.

I still had work to do that night. First, I had to set up surgery on the girl. I needed an anesthetist, and the friendly rival group of doctors assured me that their youngest member had trained in my hometown and was a 'Puik Narkotiseur' (Ace Anesthetist). Since I knew the town and its hospital, I had my doubts. The doctor had completed only a year of housemanship in a general practitioner-staffed hospital. Since I had no alternative, I arranged to do surgery as soon as the theater was ready. I had been qualified about two years myself and had opened only a few bellies for appendicitis, though I had been part of much major abdominal surgery. None of the other doctors in town had seen an operating room for fifteen or twenty years, so I was to be the surgeon! I could feel my heart practically in my mouth, pounding away as fast as it would go.

While the nurses readied the operating room, I attended to the child with meningitis. I set up an IV line and did a lumbar spinal tap. The spinal fluid was cloudy, so I started intravenous penicillin right away. I greatly missed the side room at Baragwanath to do a Gram stain. Many days later, the lab in faraway Pretoria confirmed the diagnosis on the CSF. The boy had a stormy course, but ultimately survived, to the great joy of his parents.

By seven o'clock all the participants in the operation were in the operating theater. Dr. Willemse came to help and learn about surgery. The scrubnurse had rotated through an operating room in Krugersdorp, another small Transvaal town. She was barely qualified to hand out the instruments, and didn't know their names or uses. The Matron or Chief Nurse was there to help out as a 'runner' and trouble-shooter. She had volunteered to come out of a comfortable retirement as a farmer's wife to help start the new hospital. I found out that the anesthetist was about my age and had qualified a year later from Pretoria University.

The patient was wheeled in and placed on the operating table. The Anesthetist started while my boss and I went to scrub and then joined the scrubnurse in the theater and put on our gowns and gloves. The patient already had an endotracheal tube in place, so I scrubbed her belly with antiseptic solution and placed the drapes. The Anesthetist said I could start. The nurse handed me a knife with the blade pointed forward, so that I could have cut myself if I had grasped it. I declined to take the scalpel from her and realized this would be a long battle. I explained the correct way to hand instruments. I was met with a sulky scowl and a grunt, even though I spoke in Afrikaans, the nurse's native language.

I cut into the skin and noted little bleeding. At first I was pleased that it might be a fairly bloodless procedure. But as I worked I wondered why there was not more bleeding.

EKG and pulse monitors had not yet been invented and we certainly didn't have one, so I couldn't see for myself what was going on.

"How's she doing, Doctor?" I asked. "I'm worried that she's not bleeding very much. How's her blood pressure?"

"She's OK, man. Just 'Piekfyn,'"[3] the Anesthetist replied. "But I'll put up a drip anyway."

"You mean you don't have a drip?" I asked.

"No man, I wanted to get you started, so I didn't have time."

I had a sense of foreboding, but continued the procedure. The muscles jumped when cut or touched with the cautery, so I felt a bit better. I cut into the peritoneal cavity and asked for a sucker, which took forever to arrive. I suctioned out some blackish bloody fluid, exposing the big black cyst. To satisfy myself, I felt for the patient's aorta behind the cyst, against the backbone. I found no pulsation. I pushed my hand and arm upwards through the incision in the lower abdomen to feel the heart from below. It was not beating.

"What the hell's going on?" I yelled. "She's dead. She's been dead all the time! Why didn't you tell me? I could've massaged her heart."

With that, I took a knife and slit her belly open from the top of the incision to the rib cage. There was still no bleeding. I thrust my hand upward and started to massage the heart from below. I asked the Anesthetist to give adrenalin into the intravenous line, but he now confessed that he could not start an IV in the collapsed patient.

"Then stick the needle into the heart, Doctor!" I shouted.

He did so and injected the drug. I continued the massage for a minute or two. It took me a little while to realize that the dice were just too heavily loaded against us—first by the patient's being extremely ill before we started, and then by the delay in diagnosing the arrest and the conditions under which we were working, not to mention our own inexperience. The case would have taxed a far bigger institution. I also realized that the patient must have been dead since near the start of the case—probably five or ten minutes. Hearts could not be restarted after more than a minute or two of arrest.

I shared these thoughts with the others. We all discussed it and decided the patient was dead. So we ended the case and I sewed up the long wound.

The Anesthetist was shattered by what happened to his first case in the community. On New Year's Eve I saw him communing with a large bottle of brandy in the hotel bar. By that time he was barely able to speak. I could also not really take the death in my stride. But having come from a larger hospital, where illnesses were more severe and often ended in death, I soon put the events in perspective. Considering the distances involved, I knew the patient could not have made it to a larger hospital. At least we had tried.

Mrs. White, the Matron, and I liked each other. She invited us to her farm for New Year's Day. This is midsummer and a time of great celebration and neighbor visiting on South African farms, with tennis, horse riding, children's games, beer drinking, much traditional cooking, *Braaivleis* [4](barbecues), and the devouring of watermelons grown on the farm. All this went on until nearly sundown and we met many farmers and their families. We had a great time; very nostalgic, since many of my childhood vacations at Christmas and New Year had been spent on a similar ranch belonging to my uncle.

At sundown, as guests took their leave, Ann spotted something in a display case on the verandah. About a foot long, it was a smooth, rounded stone, with a blunt point, like a big carrot. It tapered from two to four inches diameter, and was clearly an artifact. Always fascinated by archaeology, she waited for the guests to go before asking our hostess about it.

"I'm sure you found this on the farm," she said. "What's the story behind it?"

"Do you really want to know?" Mrs. White asked the obviously very young bride.

"Yes, I love archaeology!" Ann bubbled.

"Well, it's a circumcision stone, used for ritual female circumcision by some tribes."

"I guess they must stick the sharp end in the vagina and cut off the labia against the stone," I interjected. "I know they don't have anesthetics."

"That's right. I think they still do some around here. No one discusses it much."

"Ugh!" said Ann. "I guess I shouldn't have asked."

The end of childhood is marked in many ways in Africa, some more brutal than others. Further north in Africa, the inductee into manhood proved his ability to survive in the jungle and bring back proof of his hunting ability by killing a large animal, such as a lion, using spears or bow and arrow. In South Africa, big game was less common, but ceremonies still occurred. Schools were held for groups of adolescent boys or girls in secluded areas, far from home. The witchdoctor and selected elders indoctrinated them into the mysteries of adulthood and the boys had to prove their manhood. They were circumcised as a group, with very crude dressings applied to the cut area, often causing severe infection, requiring hospital care. As part of the ceremony they had to bury their foreskins, along with their childhood. I once saw a whole 'Circumcision School class' brought to Casualty with serious infections. All were admitted. In recent years some youths refused to attend these schools, causing increasing requests for adult circumcision at Baragwanath. Female circumcision was a less frequent practice in South Africa than in some other parts of the continent.

Against that background it is easy to see that Baragwanath Hospital faced a monumental task in caring for a population that was steeped in poverty and many of whom had recently been exposed to the ignorance and superstition of the tribal way of life. The Department of Pediatrics had a stellar international reputation for the work they did to ensure better and ever-advancing standards of child care. They were constantly involved in outreach and research and introduced many innovations to patient care. My exposure to the department came from surgical consultations and Pediatric burn care and living daily in the same closed medical community. I developed a good insight into their activities.

Like most departments at Bara, the Pediatricians ran permanent daily clinics and outpatient departments with very adequate and active triage. There was far too great a demand for their limited facilities, staff and beds for them to have been able to get by with less effort. They evolved many unique solutions to their problems. These differed with the seasons and the diseases then prevalent, such as pneumonia in winter and diarrheal illnesses in summer. Malnutrition was always present and required its own management. Education of the parents and grannies took center stage at all times.

During the hot summer months gastroenteritis, typhoid and amoebic or bacillary dysentery took a severe toll, especially on infants. Initial outpatient screening of patients with diarrhea led one of three ways: Serious cases with specific provisional diagnoses were admitted for investigation and treatment. Patients with milder disease, without serious dehydration and with an intelligent mother, would be sent home with medications, dry skim milk and vitamins, after the mother or granny had received adequate teaching.

Babies in the third, and by far the largest group, had severe dehydration but only moderately bad disease. They were admitted to the 'Drip Room' for fluid replacement, observation and regular reassessment. There were often thirty or forty infants receiving drips at one time. The doctors admitted to the wards babies who deteriorated or failed to respond to IV fluids.

In the 'Drip Room' were three or four long, narrow tables covered in babies. The work surface on which they slept had low partitions, about nine inches high. These separated individual stalls, fifteen inches wide, with thin mattresses. There was an overhead rail on which the IV solution was hung, with a tube leading down to the baby's head. The mother was in attendance, standing at the foot end, watching and caring for her child. The doctors and nurses had free passage across the head end, for patient care and assessment.

These highly skilled nurses did the care, setting up IVs in scalp veins with great facility, changing the IV solutions according to the doctors' orders and watching the babies' progress. They soon developed a sixth sense for when things were not right and alerted the doctors very quickly. They also had the task of teaching the mothers the elements of good hygiene and proper nutrition. Much of the diarrhea came from a lack of basic personal and home hygiene and sanitary facilities. Simple hand washing might not have been practiced or even available in the home. The need for clean water supplies was always emphasized.

One of the more pernicious forms of ignorance came from poor grannies who fed babies on 'mielie-meal milk,'[5] which was the milky fluid left when ground corn or 'grits' was soaked in water. There was no nutrition in the fluid—it just *looked* like weak milk. A diet consisting only of corn was also dangerous as it lacked two essential amino acids needed by the body to build protein, and it also provided inadequate preformed protein. The end-result could be Kwashiorkor or even pellagra—both severe deficiency diseases. Diarrhea came with the pellagra. Since many people could only afford corn to eat, malnutrition played a major role in many cases seen at Bara.

The doctors did frequent rounds in the 'Drip Room', assessing each case individually. Those babies who were clearly not thriving were admitted for further investigation and treatment. Some babies would be kept in the 'Drip Room' a while longer for further rehydration and observation. The doctors would discharge any patient whose 'tank was full' and whose mother had been adequately educated. Due to this concentrated teaching there were relatively few repeat offenders. Discharge medications consisted of a form of antibiotic, if needed, and something to suppress diarrhea on a temporary basis. Just as essential was a stock of five pounds of dry skim milk or another protein food supplement. There was little more satisfying than to see in follow up a baby that was once ill, dry and thin, now bouncing and well, with a glossy skin from adequate nutrition.

The other major innovation that had been developed at Baragwanath in Pediatrics was the Premature Baby Unit. This saved lives every day. It was different in concept from any other such unit in the world, both in construction and staffing. The architecture was unique because a standard army hospital ward, like all the others in Bara, was sealed and converted into a giant communal incubator, kept heated to premature baby temperature—well above comfort levels for adults. Thirty babies were housed in separate cribs in this enormous room. There was not a traditional modern incubator in sight. Since all infants are prone to heat loss and preemies are particularly sensitive, the temperature was kept at a level that would prevent even the smallest baby from losing body heat.

The mothers were housed nearby, within easy walking distance of the unit. Premature babies were admitted only if their mothers could and did come with them and performed most of their care.

This criterion achieved two objectives, as with the drip room. The first was to save on staffing requirements, since the mother did the routine nursing, except the most skilled. The second was educational, since the mother had to learn the correct handling of a tiny baby and acquire knowledge of proper nutrition and hygiene.

The survival results were comparable with many obtained in first world conditions. The Premature Baby Unit and the 'Drip Room' were always proudly shown when visitors toured the hospital.

The number of patients dealt with by the pediatricians was staggering. Nearly a quarter of all babies born in the Transvaal province were delivered at Baragwanath. This created a constant flow of patients for pediatrics. Apart from illnesses, these babies all needed immunizations. Doctors and nurses working in clinics in the townships of Soweto helped to lighten the load. Thus the triage and many immunizations were already done. Patients referred in from a clinic needed specialist consultation and admission.

Apart from the endemic diarrhea and problems of prematurity, probably the major illnesses encountered in pediatrics consisted of malnutrition, vitamin deficiencies, anemia, and infectious diseases, including Tuberculosis. There was a flood of pneumonia cases in the winter and diseases due to parasites in summer—diseases due to intestinal worms, such as ascaris lumbricoides,[6] tapeworms of various kinds, threadworms and pinworms. Skin infestations, such as lice, headlice and scabies[7] were common. All these parasites had their own specific treatments, which evolved gradually over time.

Both adult and pediatric surgeons often encountered ascaris worms. These patients had intestinal obstruction due to a mass of worms stuck in the lower (narrow) end of the small bowel. Medication was aimed at 'stunning' the worms and then having them pass out under the influence of a powerful laxative. If that failed, they sometimes had to be removed by surgery. This could bring problems, since any remaining worms could climb out through the stitches in both the intestine and the abdominal wall, with the worm greeting the nurse through the dressings. This forced a quick return to the operating theater.

Their sheer numbers impressed me whenever I saw a large bottle full of worms that had been passed or removed. Some patients with abdominal pain had barium contrast X-rays during their workup. Any ascaris present also had 'barium meals,' the dye outlining their intestines. For many days, fine white lines on the X-rays betrayed their presence.

Ascaris had some other peculiar features. They tended to wander from their usual habitat in the small bowel. Sometimes one climbed up the common bile duct and got stuck there, causing obstructive jaundice and dictating the need for surgery. They could also migrate up the esophagus during sleep and go down into the lungs—quite a bad situation!

Though ascariasis was commoner in the poorer black and colored communities, it was certainly seen in white people. A young white girl staying in our house was having severe, unexplained, intermittent abdominal pain. Visits to her general practitioner had been fruitless. One day she started screaming in the bathroom and ran out. She had just passed a huge ten inch by one quarter inch ascaris worm and had to assist it on its way. I identified it in the toilet bowl. I reassured her it was not a snake. Curiously, treating her for ascaris yielded no more worms. She certainly didn't care—her abdominal pain was cured!

Pediatric surgical cases seen at Bara were often particularly severe and unusual. They were referred in from a wide area because of the expertise required for their management. The diagnoses of such patients included Hirschsprung's disease, infantile pyloric stenosis, small bowel atresia and obstruction, cleft palate and many more. The head of pediatric surgery was also the University Professor and head of that Department. Every week pediatric surgery cases were presented for discussion at the Surgery Grand Rounds in Johannesburg, thus maintaining a stream of continuing education and interest in the subject.

Even though I had pediatric surgical training, the only children I generally dealt with were burn cases, as my adult patients were a full-time job. Towards the end of my career at Bara a very large pediatric burn unit was established, containing thirty beds, reflecting the great need. It was one of the largest in the world at the time.

Pediatric burns are always tragic, often causing deformity from scarring and altered skin color. When the pigment layer is burned off, even though skin grows back in, it will not have a normal color, appearing 'piebald.' Some areas, such as donor sites, where skin grafts have been taken, may become nearly black, further aggravating the appearance.

People of African origin are also prone to develop 'keloid' overgrowth of tissues in place of normal scars. Keloids, or hypertrophic scars, are thick, hard areas, standing well above the skin surface. They are very ugly, and not very amenable to treatment. Sadly, the tendency to form keloid is even worse in the young, possibly associated with the increased levels of growth hormone present during childhood. In certain tribes this tendency is used to advantage in order to make prominent tribal markings on the chest and elsewhere.

One of my pediatric burn patients had a halfway happy ending. Almost an entire family was burned to death in their house. In an argument over a small debt, someone threw in a can of gasoline, lit a match, and shut the door. In the ensuing conflagration the father threw the baby out of a window, to land on the ground outside. Everyone else in the house was burned to death, not even reaching the hospital alive. The baby's burns were relatively minor, and he could be sent home in a few days, to the care of a very good granny.

[1] Kwashiorkor or 'Red Boy': A native name from Ghana for severe malnutrition in infants and children, caused by a diet consisting mostly of carbohydrates, but low in protein and calories.

[2] Noma: From Webster: A spreading gangrene of the lining of cheek and lips that occurs usually in severely debilitated people.

[3] Piekfyn: Loosely translated from Afrikaans as 'Peachy.'

[4] Braaivleis: 'Fry Meat.' Essentially the same as a barbecue.

[5] Mielies or mealies: Maize or corn. A staple in the African diet, eaten grilled on the cob, milled into mielie-meal for a type of porridge, like stiff 'Grits,' or eaten in stamped form, called 'Samp' (Hominy), along with meat, if available. May also be used as a base for beer brewing.

[6] Ascaris Lumbricoides: A roundworm, similar in appearance to an earthworm, but with a much harder outer covering. Usually whitish gray in color and growing to ten inches long. There could be many hundreds in the small bowel at one time.

[7] Scabies: A severe itch due to infestation of the skin by *Sarcoptes Scabii*. It was marked by tiny paired holes in affected areas. The hair had to be shaved, the whole patient covered in greasy medication and the bedclothes decontaminated.

People in many cultures have enjoyed alcohol and recreational drugs since time immemorial. But overuse of such agents has often caused much harm to individuals and to society. South Africa is no exception. Before the arrival of white people in 1652, Bantu tribes made beer from 'Kaffircorn' or millet. They also grew and smoked 'Dagga,' which is similar to marijuana.

Another source of alcohol was the fruit of the Marula tree,[1] a native of many African states. Archaeological evidence shows that humans in Africa ate Marula fruit between ten and nine thousand years B.C. The trees may yield half a ton of fruit that falls and ripens on the ground, where contained yeast lets it naturally ferment into alcohol. Africans made strong beer from the pulp and today a tasty, aromatic Marula liqueur is sold commercially in South Africa. Herds of lucky elephants sometimes get in on the act, seeking out and eating the fermented fruit and having a wild party, with much trumpeting and drunken fooling around, falling and rolling on the ground. It is a really incredible sight.

After seven years as Commander of the new Cape settlement, Jan van Riebeeck produced the first wine with his own hands. In February 1659 he wrote in his journal: "Today, praise be to God, wine was made for the first time from Cape grapes." (The wine was meant to prevent scurvy, but the vegetables and fruit the settlers grew accomplished that goal.) The Cape was well suited to viticulture and became a leading wine producer for Britain and Europe. It continues to produce high-class wines for world markets.

Among the first South African people to suffer the ill effects of Europeans' alcohol were the Khoikhoi, who used to trade cattle for liquor but reacted badly to the alcohol. This, together with Smallpox, was a major factor in reducing their numbers. Historical records show that many early European settlers were also prone to excessive drunkenness.

From the start of Cape viticulture, colored laborers were involved in planting, tending, picking and 'treading' the harvest. They walked barefoot on the grapes, crushing them to extract the juice for wine-making. As part of their wages they got daily supplies of wine—the 'Dop'[2] system—causing much chronic alcoholism. This continued until quite recently.

In South Africa's paternalistic society, black people were for many years denied access to European style hard liquor—'for their own good'. By law they were only allowed to buy 'Kaffir beer.' As with prohibition in the USA, this only made their access to hard alcohol more difficult, but certainly not impossible. Illicit suppliers became rich. In the 1970s a law was passed to allow Bantu people access to 'White People's alcohol.' Much of the pressure for this change was financially motivated, coming from white liquor suppliers. For better or for worse the law did remove one point of racial inequality.

Since 1948, when Baragwanath started to care for the black people of Johannesburg, alcohol-related trauma and diseases have been a major part of its patient load. This alcohol abuse was probably of socio-economic rather than racial origin, since the same pattern is found in underprivileged communities worldwide. All aspects of alcohol abuse were seen at Bara, starting with acute drunkenness and aggression, causing the perpetual trauma treadmill.

This led on to spousal and child abuse and chronic alcoholism. The cycle continued, with job loss and financial hardship, malnutrition and pellagra, brain deterioration and dementia. Aspects affecting the surgeons were recurrent pancreatitis, cirrhosis of the liver with portal hypertension[3] and vomiting of blood. Heavy, prolonged drinking also led to cancer of the esophagus and alcoholic peripheral neuropathy,[4] in which the patients got septic foot ulcers, requiring partial or total amputations. 'Fetal alcohol syndrome,' a recently recognized entity, was probably also a negative force at that time.

I can well remember my first Saturday night at Bara as a fourth year student, three years after the hospital's takeover by the Transvaal Province. In the middle of a flood of alcohol-smelling trauma, a man was brought to Casualty with the end of a two-foot length of rusty one-inch steel rod embedded deeply in the back of his head. He was still clearly alive when the neurosurgeon took him to the theater to remove the bar. I watched the surgery. As the rod was removed blood gushed from the large veins that had been torn. The hemorrhage could not be stopped; the man died within minutes. That case and the experiences of that Saturday night, during my first surgical rotation, so revolted me that I initially turned away from surgery entirely.

Enjoyment of alcohol was dependant on having the money and the leisure to do enough drinking. Weekends were the prime drinking time, causing hospital visits and trauma admissions at Bara to rise six- to ten-fold over weekday levels. The drinking started after work on Fridays, when many people had been paid. After passage of the new law allowing Bantu people to purchase 'hard' liquor, I often saw black men go into 'Bottle Stores' in the white areas on Friday afternoons. They emerged with a 'Half Jack'[5] of cheap brandy in a brown bag. They sat on the sidewalk, heads back, and inverted the bottles over their mouths. They were drained in less than a minute. Their weekend was well under way.

After getting back to Soweto from work on Friday the night was short, so drinking continued for 24 hours on Saturday, bringing the peak of admissions. Some people were paid once a month, causing even further increases in trauma cases on month-end weekends. By Sunday the drinking was nearly over, since the money was finished. Trauma admissions fell again to somewhat above the weekday baseline.

I collected some figures in the early 70's. In March there were five Saturdays, two at month-ends. The month brought 1657 trauma cases. On the three mid-month Saturdays there were about 120 trauma victims, while the two month-end Saturdays each brought 150 to 200 such cases to the hospital. Usually somewhat less than half the cases required admission to the wards—the remainder could sleep in Casualty or go home.

The women of Soweto were well aware and disapproving of the drinking, and the sex and brawling that went along with it. These activities caused much suffering for them and for their families. Many wives used to go to the workplaces of their men-folk and demand some of their pay, to protect the money for food and rent. In any event, the cash was safer with women traveling before the rush hour, since after work on Fridays many newly paid workers were robbed at knifepoint on the crowded trains and buses.

One Saturday at Bara, when Unit Five was on duty, the hard work started in late afternoon. A forty year-old man, David Radebe, who worked at Baxter Laboratories, near Baragwanath, was involved in a severe car wreck caused by a drunk driver. Both his legs were mangled and I went to the operating theater to help sort out the mess.

I kept the end-result of Zephania's limb re-attachment clearly in mind and did not intend to repeat it. I had set very strict criteria for the unit governing salvage of such mangled limbs. The registrar, Brian Jensen, and I scrubbed the leg wounds carefully and flooded them with fluid, until all visible road dirt was gone. We draped big green towels under and around the legs, and then started inspecting the injured areas above both knees.

"You work on the left leg for now," I told Jensen. "I know the knee is damaged, but check on the sciatic nerve."

Jensen found the knee was indeed badly crushed. The leg was hanging only by some very ratty-looking skin and some 'hamstring'[6] tendons at the back, since they were hard and resistant. The artery and vein were destroyed and the major nerves were pulled apart.

"Mr. Hunt, I think this left one's had it," Jensen said. "The top end of the nerve looks like a horse's tail. There's nothing worth saving. I think the wheel went right over it. How about yours?"

"I don't think mine's much better," I replied, as I looked across the table at the left leg.

"Staff Nurse, prepare for amputation, probably both sides," I added. "The right knee isn't damaged, so it initially looked better than yours. Even the vein is hanging in, though the artery is torn. But the sciatic nerve is also gone. This one also has to come off.

"We'll do them at the same time and give him a good pair of above knee stumps."

We completed both procedures within forty-five minutes and returned to the 'Pit.'

In the post-operative period the Physiotherapists did a great job. To let David gain his balance, they used special rounded, backward-facing, rubber-shod metal feet on the ends of short straight prostheses. These made him look only four feet tall. As he learned control, they gradually lengthened the legs. His balance and control improved until he could wear proper artificial legs with articulated knee joints. The Occupational Therapists taught him leatherwork between times. When David Radebe left hospital, he could walk well and drive a small truck. He started a leatherwork business, bought a truck and did better financially than ever before. The therapists truly rehabilitated him and could be proud of their work.

After the amputations we walked back together to Casualty, enjoying the beautiful evening. The sun had just set, leaving a dusky-red glow between towering thunderheads. In the east, a huge golden full moon was beginning to show over Casualty.

"Fine drinking weather," I commented.

"Unfortunately," Jensen replied.

Casualty and the 'Pit' were full when we returned, with the usual mass of cursing, groaning, bleeding and puking humanity. It was dangerous to walk fast, as the floor was slick from vomit and blood. As I entered the Resuscitation Room, something unusual caught my eye. A man lay on his back on a gurney, with a carving knife stuck deeply into his eye socket, alongside his nose. X-rays showed four inches of the blade embedded in his head. Amazingly, he could see with the eye, and I could find no major neurological defect. I sent the man to the theater while I assessed a few more patients.

The four housemen and three students were all hard at work placing chest tubes and IVs fast and furiously—it looked as if it might be a record night. I remembered a hand-made poster painted on a piece of bed linen that I had recently photographed on a wall outside the hospital:

*"Bara by Night" with Zakes Nkosi*
*Plus*
*Crocodiles.*

I thought that one day I ought to see that show. But it could never beat the long-running original, in which I had for so long been an actor. I thought with amusement that the name of the group was rather apt, since Unit Five was 'knee deep in crocodiles and no one could drain the swamp.'

I looked at each patient in Resuscitation and scheduled a couple of stabs in the abdomen for surgery. There were not yet any problems that we had not seen many times before. Everyone was really busy. I then looked in at Casualty. It seemed like a regular Saturday evening. So I went off to the theater to handle the man with a knife in his eye.

I changed and went to theater four, and there I found an unexpected scene. A pool of blood on the floor outside the theater was seeping out from under the door. Inside, the patient was sitting up at an angle on the operating table, with a staff nurse holding pressure on a pad over his eye. The knife was lying on a table nearby. The anesthetist, with more daring than foresight, had pulled out the knife. A pint or two of blood had immediately gushed out of the wound, and much of it still puddled on the floor.

"Why on earth did you pull the knife out, Jules?" I asked.

"I thought it would be a trivial matter and we could save some operating time," Brobeck answered. "I was wrong! I've never seen blood flow like that. It looked like a bucketful. When he bled, I finally got my head on straight. I gave him a *hypotensive anesthetic*,[7] and got the nurses to put a soft pad over his eye and apply pressure toward the nose. We raised the head end of the table, to reduce pressure in the veins of the face and orbit. It seems manageable now. I'm sorry, John, for my bad judgment."

"That's OK, Jules. This just proves you'll do anything to get to use your hypotensive techniques! But you may have saved us some time after all. I'd probably have taken forever to prep him and then pussyfooted around for a while before pulling out the knife."

The situation indeed seemed under control. The bleeding had stopped and the patient was receiving blood. All I did was pack the wound with absorbable haemostatic[8] gauze and suture the skin. I applied eye ointment and a pad, with a turban-type bandage.

Next day I removed the dressing. The man had a black eye, but he could see well. I looked at his pupil with a penlight, and then I moved my finger, giving him commands.

"Look up...Look down...Follow my finger...Left...Right," I said.

As I shone the light, the pupil contracted briskly. The eye moved normally in all directions. The man had not lost an eye muscle or a nerve controlling his eye movements! None of the doctors could understand how this injury had been so benign. The patient would never know how lucky he was.

I looked in on Jensen doing an abdominal stab and then returned to the 'Pit.' I passed by Casualty and heard that a couple of corpses had come in from faction fights at a 'Hostel' in Soweto. This was a frequent problem. In these huge, barrack-like buildings packed with single men, there was often friction between various Bantu tribes, reflecting historical conflicts. Free time and drinking on weekends made matters worse.

The groups most often involved were Zulus, Xhosas or Sothos. Sometimes separate Zulu clans would try and kill each other. The violence often escalated into small civil wars. Fortunately, the men had no access to guns. Sticks, spears and knives were the weapons of choice. Police sought to keep order, with scant success. On the gold mines, faction fights were often so bad that the compounds had to be closed and the inmates sent home. The mine closed down until a new labor force was hired and trained. I was glad the gold mines had their own hospitals, so that their trauma did not come to Bara—there were enough problems dealing with men from the Soweto Hostels.

Hearing of the corpses reminded me of a recent conversation. In one of my moonlighting jobs I did medico-legal examinations on drunken drivers once or twice a week at the District Surgeon's office in Hillbrow. This was next to the Government Mortuary, where all trauma and accidental deaths ended up. While examining drunks one busy Friday night, I started chatting with the senior mortuary attendant. I learned that after a busy weekend there were often more than forty black corpses in the refrigerators by Monday morning, the products of Johannesburg and Soweto violence.

The deaths were due mostly to homicide. Only a small proportion were caused by motor vehicle or industrial trauma. Apart from the occasional tribal faction fights, the violence was not politically motivated. These fatal assaults were largely 'Black-on-Black,' and were usually crime or alcohol-related. I was well aware of this aspect— any Bara trauma patient whose life could not be saved would end up in these refrigerators, awaiting an autopsy on Monday morning. I was glad I was not the 'District Surgeon' who had to do those post mortem examinations. Dealing with the living was punishing enough.

Thirty to forty murders per weekend! It boggled the mind. But as I considered it I realized that the white population of South Africa and the world at large was quite unaware of the frightening statistics that black hospitals faced on a daily basis. The blacks did not know the exact numbers either—they just had to live with the horror and constant personal danger. At that time in South Africa's socio-political evolution, such things were simply taken for granted. The knowledge was not suppressed in any way; it just didn't make it into the white newspapers or other media. The whites, if they ever became aware of it, were happy that the violence was confined to Soweto and not directed against them in their white suburban enclaves.

The Resuscitation Room was still loaded when I returned. One of the nurses ran up and grabbed my arm, pulling me across the room.

"Mr. Hunt," she said. "Come quickly! This man's blood pressure has gone and he can't breathe!"

The patient was having a hard time, breathing rapidly and with great effort. His tongue was blue. His heart was racing and his blood pressure could not be recorded. I looked for an injury and found nothing on the front of the chest, so I rolled him over. At the back of the chest was a small wound, not near any vital structures. The case still made no sense. I rolled the patient back and listened to his chest with a stethoscope. The heart sounds were good, so it was probably not a stab in the heart. I listened to both lung fields and then felt the trachea[9] in the neck. It was pushed across to the left.

"George," I called to a houseman. "Come and listen here, it's a great case for you!"

I indicated the chest, and asked the nurse for a large syringe and a thick needle.

"What do you hear on the right?" I asked. "And have a look at his trachea."

"There are no breath sounds on the right and his trachea's over to the left—so something's probably pushing it across. He must have a tension pneumothorax,"[10] George answered. "I've never seen one."

"Good man!" I said. "Clean up his chest while I get the others to have a look."

The housemen, nurses and students all gathered round and George told the story. He percussed the right chest with his fingers. It sounded like a drum, quite unlike the left side.

"He's really full of air," another houseman commented.

I handed the syringe and needle to George, who looked a bit surprised.

"You made the diagnosis—you can cure him," I said. "Treatment is urgent. Let out the air. He can't wait for an X-ray, let alone a chest tube. You can do that later. Just stick the needle in his chest, three inches below the middle of his right clavicle."[11]

George stuck in the needle and disconnected the syringe. The air literally whistled out under pressure. The patient looked better almost immediately. The nurses gasped.

"Let the air out while this very smart nurse, who called me so quickly, gets a chest tube," I added, patting her shoulder as I spoke. I was rewarded with a radiant smile.

"That's one reason we place so many chest tubes!" I said. "We're lucky it's not more frequent. This is why we put an IC drain in anyone with a chest injury *before* surgery or going on a ventilator. If not, positive pressure breathing would give them a tension pneumothorax, which can be rapidly fatal if it remains undetected."

The nurse connected the needle to an IV giving set and taped it in place. Then she put the end of the tube under water in a sterilized old IV fluid bottle. A continuous stream of bubbles came out. She then fetched the chest tube set and George inserted the tube.

The Hostel rioters now started to come in. Some were still fighting in the corridors, and Security had to keep them apart. Their injuries were fortunately the usual club wounds to the head and stabs in the chest, requiring time and attention, but no great expertise.

As the night wore on, I had one of my recurring fantasies. I always thought Baragwanath was like a giant ant nest, home to countless black ants, coming from all points of the compass, endlessly streaming back to the common hole. The flow never ceased completely; one line always replaced another. Bara absorbed them all.

The stream of patients continued and the Unit was up all night. I stayed with them, operated on or helped with a number of cases and started rounds early in the morning. We took in seventy-three patients—high, but not a record for a Saturday. Many patients went home from Admissions if they were sober. Most would be gone by the next intake on Thursday. One thing that we as surgeons at Bara knew well was how to deal with trauma rapidly. Were that not so, there would have been no room or time to care for regular patients.

The drinking on public holidays depended on their proximity to the most recent payday and whether enough people had the day off. So the load on Bara was intensely variable. Since many industries gave their workers only four universal holidays, the others had little effect on the pattern of trauma.

The difference was in December when the builders, and nearly all of industry, had a holiday for two weeks. This was true at least for the industrial heartland of the Transvaal, stretching many miles around Bara. Many workers got double pay packets and Christmas bonuses or handouts from their employers. Dingaan's Day was the 16$^{th}$ of December and the big payday was the Friday before. The holiday lasted through New Year's Day.

Though that pattern of holidays predated my arrival on the scene, I soon discovered one of the reasons for its continuation: much of the labor force would be drunk for two weeks. I was never sure which was cause and which effect. My study of the figures showed that for December there were 2741 trauma cases—eleven hundred more than in March—a 65% increase. The Saturday before Dingaan's Day brought 300 trauma cases, while Christmas Day brought 500! I checked at the white Johannesburg General Hospital and on Christmas Day they had none!

In the Cape the pattern was different. Work did not start again until after the second of January, 'Tweede Nuwe Jaar.'[12] By long-held tradition that was the 'Second New Year,' when the Cape colored people got to celebrate. The very happy and festive 'Coon Carnival' was held in Cape Town on that day. Troops of Cape coloreds and Malays prepared for weeks and had fancy costumes made. On the big day they dressed up in bright costumes, gathered together, paraded through the streets and ended up in a large sports ground where they held competitions among bands, singers, dancers and vaudeville type acts.

Because of the predictable trauma influx at Bara, surgical staff were prevented from taking leave at Christmas time. In my early years there I had dared to go away a few hundred miles and was recalled by the Chief Surgeon to provide extra help to the unit on duty. Since the units were on duty every fifth day, the same unit would have been on for four Christmases, between Leap Years. So a plan was made to avoid the problem by 'slipping' the hospital calendar one day ahead each year except for Leap Year. As I became more senior in the service, I was able to arrange my vacation around Christmas when my unit was not on duty and take the family to enjoy the school holidays in the Cape. One of the high points of our visit each year was watching the 'Coon Carnival.'

The servants in our household refused to be in Soweto at Christmas. Though they had the day off, they chose to stay in their rooms or the backyard. They knew all about the trauma to be expected. As a sad commentary, one of our Bantu women servants told Ann that if she were walking in the street at any time and a white man was walking near her, she felt perfectly safe. If an unknown black man was anywhere near, she felt threatened and hurried to get away. This applied all year round, not just around Christmas.

It was rare to receive presents from patients. Most of them simply left the hospital without even a smile of thanks. So any gifts I received were memorable. One December I did a lot of work on Mr. Dlamini, a shopkeeper in Soweto, from the same tribe as the Swazi Royal house. He had been in Swaziland, fetching his son from an excellent integrated private high school, where white and black South Africans often sent their children.

On his way back Dlamini was in a rollover accident near a small Transvaal town. He was taken to the local hospital for care. A shard of glass had entered the front of his elbow and he bled quite a lot. He got only some skin stitches and a few aspirins with codeine. His hand did not function and it hurt badly, so he signed himself out of the hospital. He hired a taxi to come to Bara, but the delay from the accident was already over two days.

I could feel no pulse and he seemed to have an arterial and possibly a median nerve injury at the elbow. I explored the arm and found that only the brachial artery was severed. I repaired it and got a good blood flow. But the forearm muscles were already dead from lack of blood supply for two days, so I removed most of them at the same time.

After surgery we could all see that the arm was functionally useless, so in a few days the patient agreed to let me amputate it below the elbow. He was very grateful for the work and for the kindness he had received. He thanked everyone heartily when he left.

A few days before Christmas Mr. Dlamini returned to Outpatients for a checkup and took me aside.

"I've got a present for you, Doc," he said. "Come. It's in my car—next to yours."

Dlamini led me out to the two cars. He opened his trunk and removed a live turkey with its feet tied together, and handed it to his surprised and embarrassed surgeon.

"Thank you, but what am I going to do with it right now?" I asked.

"Put it in the boot[13] of *your* car," Dlamini answered.

I opened the boot, popped in the turkey and shut the lid.

"Merry Christmas, Doc."

"Thank you Mr. Dlamini—I really appreciate this," I answered, rather uncertainly.

I had no plan for such an unusual gift. Fortunately, I had nothing more to do at Bara that day, since the unit was quiet, cleared out for the Christmas rush. We had discharged everyone who could possibly go out. As I drove home, I thought of a plan. I knew that my wife and the children would not tolerate slaughter of the bird if they saw it alive. Ann's car was not at the house—she must have taken the children out shopping.

The maid's husband Alfred was there, staying with her on 'Builder's Holiday.' I bribed him to perform the last rites on the bird, pluck it and remove the entrails. Alfred cooperated fully and he safely disposed of everything that came from the bird in a plastic bag in the trash. By the time the family got home there was a 'gift turkey' in the refrigerator. Alfred was a few Rands richer.[14]

On my last Christmas duty at Bara, a man was rushed in to Resuscitation with several people clustered around the head end of his gurney. I took one look, sent them straight on to the theater and followed the gurney across. The cause of all the excitement was a large garden fork, driven into the back of the man's neck, with one tine in his shoulder, two in his neck and one in his head. He was so firmly impaled that movements of the handle waggled his head. The fork had to be placed on a nearby table to keep his head still, so that the Anesthetist could try and pass a tube.

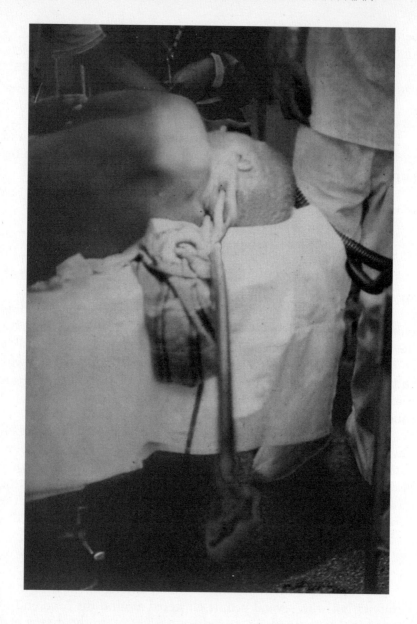

MAN WITH A GARDEN FORK STUCK IN THE BACK
OF HIS NECK & HEAD.
THIS OCCURED ON CHRISTMAS DAY AS HE PROTECTED
HIS EMPLOYER'S HOUSEHOLD FROM BURGLERS.

Before he was put to sleep, the man said that he had been guarding his employer's house during the family's absence. He surprised two burglars, and they attacked him. He grabbed the fork in self-defense, but they got it away from him, pinned him on the ground and stuck it into his neck. He was powerless to even raise his head. His voice was OK, and his yelling finally alerted a servant from next door to see his plight and call the ambulance.

I arranged tetanus shots and antibiotics and then set about trying to remove the fork. While I worked on the handle, a houseman and an orderly applied powerful counter-traction against my pull. By wiggling and pulling and working on one tine at a time, the entire fork finally came out. We disinfected each hole and applied dressings. This was a lucky man, because no vital structures had been stabbed and he developed no infection or tetanus—very likely results from an injury with a dirty garden fork.

As I walked out of my theater, I saw Michael Jonas rushing in next door.

"What's up, Mike? Can't you even say Hullo?" I asked.

"Sorry, John, didn't see you. We've got this bled-out ectopic[15] dying on us here. I guess it's all that pelvic sepsis that screws up their tubes."

"I suppose there's no choosing when the tube ruptures, even at Christmas," I replied. "I'll leave you to it. Remind me to tell you my English ectopic story some time."

Back in the Resuscitation Room I was shocked to hear that one of our staff nurses had gone home at midday and been stabbed to death at her own front door by her drink-crazed husband. She did not make it alive back to the hospital, even though she lived just across the highway in Diepkloof. This news started a wide-ranging conversation among the doctors and nurses about family stabbings.

"You know, Mr. Hunt," Sister Martha said. "The people stand at the bus stops and taxi ranks and talk about how to kill their husbands or wives. They know exactly where the heart is, but they know an even better place—here, in the neck—just above the collarbone. They don't like the belly. It's too slow. They want the person to bleed to death quickly."

"Sister, I thought it was just the men who were so bad," I said.

"That is often so, Doctor. We women will do it only for self-defense. Like Staff Nurse Mary's husband—he should have been stabbed, not she. He is so bad and she was such a good person. She was afraid to go home, because she knew he would be drunk, and she was right. He was really wild."

A porter rushed in with a blood-covered patient on a gurney, interrupting our conversation. The patient reeked of Bantu beer. He was spluttering and vomiting at the same time. His wound was in the low neck, pouring blood. The more he strained to vomit, the more blood spurted out.

We all jumped into action, working fast, taking blood for cross-match, setting up an IV line, calling theater. One of the nurses strapped a big sterile pad over the wound and held it there, to try and stanch the bleeding. These routines were second nature to everyone.

"Sister Martha, why did you have to talk about it? Look what you've done!" I chided her. "Maybe his wife got him. The stab is exactly in the place you just told me."

"No Doctor, I'm sorry, but it wasn't me! Or his wife. He said it was his best friend."

"I've heard that too often before," I answered her. "I'll go back to theater. Send him 'Urgent Direct' please, Sister. Brian and George, come along; I'll need you."

I needed help because these were among our most difficult cases at Bara. We all went up to change, and then waited for the patient in the downstairs lounge, where Jonas was busy writing up his case.

"How did it go?" I asked my friend.

"OK. They are easy cases once you get them here alive," Jonas answered. "Taking out the tube isn't rocket science. It's a bit messy with a belly full of blood and clot. Tell me about your English ectopic."

"Well, as a registrar I had to share duties with an inept colleague who had a great sexual appetite outside the marriage bed. On duty nights we covered four hospitals. His coverage was mostly non-surgical. He went from one hospital to the next, sleeping with a nurse at each one, ending up at our main hospital, where he did some bad surgery and spent the rest of the night with a fourth nurse.

"I don't know what he did with his nights off, but he must have paid some attention to his wife. He came home late one night, to find her on the floor, crawling to the telephone to call an ambulance.

She was nearly dead from a ruptured ectopic. He was about the only doctor I ever met who was relieved of his job for incompetence. I guess some people are bad through and through, and he was one of them."

"That's sad. I've known a few guys like that," Jonas said. "What do you have now?"

"A nasty stab neck—see you in a few hours."

The patient came around the corner and my group followed him to the theater.

"Sister Jane, he has a stab over the clavicle and we're probably going to have to cut a piece out or do some minor orthopedics, so you'll need some bone stuff, like a Gigli saw.[16] Otherwise it's straight vascular work. We'll start as soon as the anesthetist gets here and puts him to sleep."

George and I scrubbed and gowned up, then started cleaning the skin and getting ready. Blood poured out of the wound each time it was exposed, so Jensen held pressure while we sterilized the skin. Once the patient was draped, George stuck his finger in the wound while Jensen went off to scrub.

"These cases are so difficult because the blood vessels lie under cover of the clavicle. You can't get at them," I said. "You'll see, George, I'll work around your hand."

I made an incision along the top of the collarbone and then exposed a piece of the bone well to the outside of the stab and made a little tunnel beneath it.

"Gigli saw please, Sister," I said.

I took the strange piece of rough metal wire cord that she offered and pulled it through this tunnel. I hooked a small handle in each end of the wire and tightened the wire into a V-shape. I then pulled and rocked my hands back and forth, producing a sawing action under the bone. I passed the handles to Brian, who continued sawing until the bone was cut through.

I then stuck a knife into the joint at the inner end of the clavicle and levered the bone out of its socket. With some hard work and 'Bovie'[17] cutting I could then flap up a kind of 'lid,' exposing the blood vessels under the clavicle and on top of the ribs. We could still not see much of the vessels, so George's finger had to stay in the hole, making my life difficult, but saving that of the patient.

Jensen and I started to clean the big vessels by gentle blunt dissection. The subclavian vein lay in front, so we put a tape[18] round it and pulled it aside. We then taped the artery, and clamped it to reduce the bleeding. The blood flow slowed down, and it became much easier to find and tape the vessels beyond George's finger.

"The danger is that the knife may go through both vessels, making a channel between them that you don't see," I said. "We often see an A-V fistula[19] caused in that way, even in people with no surgery. When you see the amount of blood coming out of this hole, you can't imagine such a wound could ever heal without surgery.

"Brian, put some clamps on at both ends and we can give poor old George a rest."

Once the clamps were placed, George removed his finger and we suctioned the vein clear. There was indeed another hole in the back and a corresponding slit in the side of the adjacent artery.

"OK Brian, stitch him up with Prolene," I said. "Use a four 0 suture[20] for the artery and a five 0 for the vein. I'll help you. I've had to do these by myself, with one finger in the hole and working round it with the other hand. No fun, I assure you. I've tried what the textbooks say and removed the center of the clavicle. That gives good access, but it causes a very bad deformity later. Don't do it unless your patient is dying."

Jensen worked away at the suturing, and when he was done, we let off the clamps and held pressure for a few minutes to let the bleeding stop. Jensen and George started stitching up the muscles and skin. They put some small pins in the bone to hold it in place during healing. I then left them and returned to the growing mess in the 'Pit.'

What the day had lacked in big cases, it made up in numbers. Drunken souls kept on streaming in by car, taxi, minivan and on foot. They all required triage and I joined the Casualty officers on the front line, within calling distance, while the Unit manned the 'Pit' and Resuscitation. I could see cases far faster than the doctors in Casualty and could dispose of them better. I was a handy consultant to reduce the cases sent to the Surgeons, and I could write instructions on the cards of the patients I did send. This was the best use of my time, unless I was needed in the theater or Resuscitation for an urgent case.

I soon had a case in point. A man had already been seen in Casualty and sent for abdominal X-rays, both 'flat and upright.' The patient had been drinking for a few days and now had abdominal pain. This had happened before and he confessed that he had been told to give up drinking. On the X-rays there was no evidence of 'free gas' under the diaphragm, which would have shown a perforation. But I could clearly see telltale white spots of calcification in the pancreas. This was recurrent alcoholic pancreatitis. I wrote instructions on the card and sent the man to Resuscitation for an IV and admission by the housemen. Such cases did not need urgent surgery.

Next, one of 'regulars' was wheeled in, vomiting blood. He had esophageal varices,[21] with recurrent bleeding. He had been boozing for the week since payday. He also knew he should not be drinking, but didn't seem to care. I wondered how much of this attitude was a 'death wish.' Certainly, I knew it was hard for alcoholics to quit the habit, particularly under Soweto living conditions. Such cases consume considerable hospital resources worldwide.

This man's future path flashed depressingly through my mind as I accompanied the gurney to Resuscitation. First he needed an IV and cross-match of six units of blood, then transfer to ICU for care and observation. The new Gastroenterology doctor would have to endoscope him, to be sure it was the varices bleeding. If the bleeding didn't stop, he might require injection of the varices, which I could do through a special brass esophagoscope[22] that I had modified for the purpose.

If bleeding became too great, he might need a Sengstaken-Blakemore bag[23] passed through his mouth and inflated in his esophagus. After 24 hours of pressure from the bag he would require a lengthy surgical procedure, to do a complex venous bypass and relieve pressure in the veins. This would all be very interesting, but on this busy Christmas night, it seemed to me rather pointless. If the man was still alive at that stage, he would still remain a chronic alcoholic with cirrhosis, doing himself repeated harm.

The flow of trauma continued unabated until eight a.m., when Unit One took over. The final tally was 512 patients through Casualty and 105 cases admitted. In addition to those discussed, twenty-one stabs in the chest needed chest tubes, seven abdominal stabs had surgery, and some stabs in the neck were being watched. There was one stab in the heart, a paraplegic and a variety of blunt head injuries, long bone and jaw fractures.

As Christmases at Bara went, it was pretty average.

1 Marula tree: *Sclerocarya birrea* ssp. *Caffra*. A fast growing wild fruit tree, native to many African states. Fruits are over an inch in diameter, with a sweet flesh and a large nut kernel. The pulp is edible and is used for jellies, beer and liqueur production. The nut contains edible oil and has a high protein content. Trees can produce half a ton of fruit in a year. The tree is also host to the edible Mopane caterpillar—a local delicacy!

2 Dop: A small or not-so-small measure of alcohol given free to vineyard laborers as part of their earnings.

3 Portal hypertension: Scarring of the liver in cirrhosis causes narrowing of the portal vein going through it. The pressure rise causes *varicose veins* in the esophagus, which may bleed heavily, causing death. See # 21.

4 Alcoholic peripheral neuropathy: Many chronic alcoholics developed severe nerve damage in the feet, with near total anesthesia, so they did not know when they had an injury. They developed horrifying, infected, smelly ulcers on the feet, requiring repeated partial amputations. The disease is similar to diabetic neuropathy.

5 Half Jack: Hip flask. A flat bottle containing 375 milliliters—about the same as a can of beer or Coca Cola.

6 Hamstrings: Muscles at the back of the thigh, with long, hard tendons, which flex the knee. 'Hamstringing' meant cutting these tendons.

7 Hypotensive anesthetic: Specific drugs were used to lower the patient's blood pressure, so that he/she would bleed less, improving working conditions for the surgeon.

8 Haemostatic gauze: A ribbon or a square of special woven material that makes blood clot and can be left inside the patient for the body to absorb later.

9 Trachea: The breathing tube above the lungs in the neck. Pathology in the chest may cause it to shift. It can either be pushed or pulled and its position helps with clinical diagnosis.

10 Tension Pneumothorax: Air under tension between the chest wall and the lung, causing it to collapse. The patient gets too little oxygen and treatment is urgent. It is due to a 'ball valve' effect from injury—air can escape from the lung into the chest around it and cannot get back in. It rapidly causes severe tension. This quickly becomes a problem if the patient is placed on a ventilator without having a chest tube in place.

11 Clavicle: Collarbone. On the right side, air was compressing the lung away from the chest. The needle went well below the collarbone, straight into the air, allowing decompression of the pneumothorax.

12 Tweede Nuwe Jaar: Afrikaans, lit. Second New Year.

13 Boot: English form of 'trunk.'

14 Rands: Unit of currency. From Witwatersrand, where gold was discovered. It became the financial center.

15 Ectopic pregnancy: A pregnancy outside the uterus, usually in the uterine tubes, but possibly in the abdominal cavity. It is commoner in abnormal tubes, as after infection. The first sign is often collapse from severe blood loss. Urgent surgery and blood transfusion are lifesaving. The tube is usually removed.

16 Gigli saw: A rough braided cord of metal, which was passed beneath a bone and then pulled and rocked back and forth, like lighting a fire by twirling a stick. The friction sawed through the bone.

17 Bovie: An electro-cautery machine, with a pen-like applicator, which applies a modified electric current to both cut and seal tissues at the same time.

18 Tape: An umbilical cord-tying tape or a flat tape like a shoelace. These were placed around blood vessels to pull them out of the way. They could be double-looped and pulled tight to stop blood flow in an emergency. In later years silicone rubber 'vesseloops' replaced them.

19 A-V fistula: Arterio-venous fistula, or opening between the artery and the vein. This 'short-circuits' the blood, allowing a huge flow to go through, starving the limb beyond the hole, and often sending the patient into 'high output' heart failure.

20 Four 0: The size of a fairly fine suture. A thick one would be above 'one' and an eye suture 7 0 or 11 0.

21 Esophageal varices: Varicose veins in the esophagus from cirrhosis of the liver, usually from alcohol abuse. See # 3.

22 Esophagoscope: A tapered brass tube with lights at the thick end. Two feet long, it was passed down inside, to view the esophagus. A slot was cut in one side, through which the varicose vein bulged, to allow injections.

23 Sengstaken-Blakemore bag: A rubber bag assembly, named for its inventors. It was a thick, two-foot long catheter, with three tubes reaching the tip. A long balloon, like a condom, with a round balloon below it, surrounded these catheters. The tube was passed through the mouth into the esophagus and stomach. The bags were inflated and some upward traction applied. This stopped the veins bleeding, but after 24 hours of pressure definitive surgery had to follow immediately. This was all complex, dangerous and time-consuming.

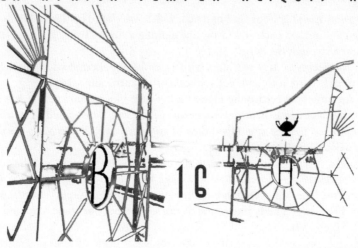

'There is always something new from Africa.' This was already true at the time of Pliny the elder (A.D. 23-79), who penned those words in his book *Historia Naturalis*.[1] Visitors and most white South Africans could always find something new and strange going on in the country and at Baragwanath Hospital in particular. No matter how many amazing, amusing or shocking incidents occurred, no one had ever seen or heard them all.

One afternoon I was helping out another surgical unit on a 'sessional pay' basis, because they were short of house staff. For a change, everyone was relaxed, sitting around telling stories. Then came news of a train wreck. A gasoline tanker rail car shunting on a branch line had become uncoupled. The rail car ran down a slope into the coaches of a mainline commuter train packed with homebound Soweto residents. A spark from the crash or a burning cigarette ignited the escaping gasoline, causing a huge ball of fire that engulfed and destroyed several passenger coaches. Hundreds were injured.

I only had time to alert the Superintendent, the Chief of Surgery, Professor Mason and the Surgical Admissions Ward, before the casualties arrived in droves. While the surgeons saw the patients, Professor Mason, the administrators and the Matrons worked on the big picture. They arranged for some victims to be held overnight at NEH—the Non-European Hospital in Hillbrow, Johannesburg. Others would go to Coronation Hospital, smaller but closer to the crash site. They knew that most of the cases would come to Bara, but delaying any of them would ease our burden. They planned to take over the Bara YMCA building, fill it with mattresses and bed linen and convert it into a burn unit, staffed and equipped like a regular ward. By a Herculean effort, this was achieved by nine the next day.

The first patient I touched in the Resuscitation Room clearly had no chance of survival. He was burned black from head to toe, his skin crisp, leathery and hard. His eyes alone were not burned, since he could close the lids. The crinkles at the outer corners had some living skin preserved in the depths, with the color burned off. This gave his face a startling 'sunray' appearance; white and black wrinkles radiated from his eyes. I gave some instructions for dressings and found a spot where I could give a large dose of intravenous morphine. As the drug took effect the patient said: "You are a good doctor."

I could have wept, both for the patient and my own frustration and guilt at my inability to save him. Being a 'good doctor' would mean only easing pain until death gave release from suffering. A houseman cut through dead skin at the wrist to find a vein for an IV, to give minimal fluids and plenty of morphine. There was no point in prolonging death.

The other Unit's chief now arrived in Casualty, and we decided to split duties. He took charge of the Emergency area and Resuscitation Room with half the unit. I took the others down to Surgical Admissions, where I organized the fluid therapy and dressing care for the patients. I also got the nurses to arrange for large supplies of dressings, drugs, fluids, giving sets[2] and plasma to be stockpiled before the patients arrived.

The surgeons did the triage in Casualty. Dead people went straight to the morgue. Minor burns were treated and sent home. The Resuscitation Room was used for setting up IV lines on moderately severe burns. Most of the bad patients were sent 'Urgent Direct' to the Admissions Ward. I walked around the ward with a houseman and the sister, who carried her large notebook. We looked at each patient in turn and made an estimate of the burn depth and its area, using the 'Rule of Nines.'[3] The housemen posted these numbers on the head of the bed and wrote appropriate fluid orders.

Patients with large surface area burns needed huge amounts of IV fluids, far more than most of the housemen or nurses had ever seen used before. Some patients would need over twelve liters of fluid (3 gallons) on the first day, whereas the staff had previously given no more than three liters in a day. I had to keep on assuring them all that the numbers were correct. There were no automatic pumps for IV solutions at the time, and the nurses had to count the drops per minute, do the calculation, and set the drip rate by hand. They did this by using a small finger adjuster that compressed the tubing.

The house surgeons and students each took a patient, selecting the most serious first. They did brief histories and examinations and then set up large-bore IV cannulas to cope with the fluids. They quickly referred problems to me or to the registrar.

The first problem was a man with difficulty breathing. He had severe face and neck burns and singed nasal hairs. He would need an urgent tracheotomy.[4] I called the theater while the registrar rushed the patient up the short corridor and into an open operating room. I reached the theater with them and we started surgery immediately. There was a great sigh of relief when the tube was in place and connected to oxygen. The registrar suctioned the patient's lungs with a curved tube. The man's color improved dramatically. There was no ICU yet, and we sent him to the side room of Unit Five for 'special' care.

Quite early in the evening one of the housemen asked a young woman where she was burned. She denied burns and said she had vaginal bleeding. Her card showed she had been on a stretcher in Casualty, on her way to see the gynecology registrar. The porters had swept her up in the general excitement and taken her off to Surgical Admissions. She was politely sent back to Casualty, very glad she didn't belong in this group of patients.

After the surgery, I returned to the ward and made sure that the sickest patients with the larger and deeper burns received optimal treatment. I made the reasonable assumption that the bad ones would be deeply shocked and acidotic, so I empirically[5] added bicarbonate to their fluids. The Pharmacy stocked several fluid formulations I had devised. There were no facilities for checking the patient's pH levels, so we had to watch their blood pressure and urine flow to govern therapy. By the end of the crucial first two days, I was delighted to see that, except for the first patient I saw, there had been no deaths. No one went into irreversible shock, and there were no cases of kidney failure.

There were seventy burn admissions that night and over twenty came in the next day. In the morning the five surgeons met with Professor Mason. We each agreed to take one fifth of the patients, as one or two surgeons could not have coped with them all. The cases were fairly allocated using the burn sizes recorded on the beds. Some units had space for a few patients, but most of them went to the YMCA, where many stayed until their discharge.

Dressings were done according to each surgeon's preference, since there were many possible methods but no single acceptable standard. With so many patients the dressing changes took all day. So, the simpler, the better. The surgeons did weekly rounds together to assess and compare treatments. After a week, I abandoned the antibacterial cream I was using, as the results were inferior. Another surgeon used silver nitrate solution and it also failed by comparison with other methods. It was extremely uncomfortable as it was then being used. It also stained bed linen, floors and furniture permanently black.

The two winners were simple daily Vaseline gauze dressings or frequent dressing changes with Eusol hypochlorite solution, an old Bara standby. Daily tub bathing was clearly very helpful, but there were not enough baths to use it on everyone. Patients with more superficial burns entered the healing phase quite rapidly and were discharged as soon as their dressings could be done at an outpatient facility.

The day after the disaster, I asked Professor Mason to push the Superintendent for a new device to aid skin grafting. The purchase had been refused by Pretoria the year before, because of expense. The instrument was an innovative 'mesher,' like a miniature version of an old-fashioned clothes 'mangle.'[6] There were special knives on the upper roller. After a sheet of skin had been harvested, it would be passed through the mesher, which would cut a pattern in it, allowing the skin to be stretched open like chicken wire or expanded metal. The graft could then cover a much larger area of raw burn surface.

Miraculously, the mesher was delivered in a few days. I could use it on the first case I took to the theater. All the other surgeons used it, making the operations much quicker and reducing the number of times patients had to return to surgery for more grafts. For big burns this could often be six or seven operations, so any reduction was welcome.

Burn care is time consuming, a benchmark being 'one day per 1% of body surface area burned.' Many patients had over 40% burns, meaning six weeks of care. The YMCA 'Burn Unit' stayed open for about six weeks, until the patients were healed or the surgeons took them to their own units. The nurses who worked there had done a most remarkable job.

Very early in my career at Bara I planned to do a cholecys-
tectomy and bile duct exploration on a sixty year-old man with
obstructive jaundice, thinking he had gallstones. At the time there
were no methods for making a better diagnosis than that. Since
gallstones were rare in blacks and in males of all races, I had done a
barium meal to see if a cancer of the pancreas was perhaps invading
the duodenum and bile duct. Nothing showed up, so I proceeded
with the surgery as planned.

To my great surprise, I found the cause of the jaundice to be a
tiny cancer in the head of the pancreas, surrounding the common bile
duct. I had not previously done a 'Whipple Pancreatico-duodenectomy,'[7]
but had to do one now to cure that patient. This is a complex, major
procedure, but it went very well because the man was slender and the
tumor small. There was no need for blood transfusion, and the operation took only two and a half hours. I was delighted and watched the
patient's progress with great interest. Pathology reported very favorably
on the small size of the tumor. The patient should have been cured.

When I thought he should be able to eat and I was ready to
remove his IVs, the man refused food or drink and said he had been
bewitched. He wanted nothing more done and put the blanket over
his head, where it stayed for the rest of his life. He remained in that
state until finally dying some weeks later. His relatives couldn't help.
Fortunately, they gave consent for autopsy, and I had it done. There
was absolutely nothing physically wrong with him to cause his state
and the operation had healed perfectly, with excellent continuity of
all the organs where they had been joined and no evidence of other
cancer deposits.

This was just one more example of the hold witchcraft had over
these people.

Cancer is mostly a disease of older people. When it occurs in
the young it seems more sad and shocking. I once had two teenagers
transferred from nearby African states with large muscle or bone
sarcomas.[8] At that time, such tumors were fatal, unless small enough
for curative removal or radiation. Chemotherapy for such cases was
experimental.

The bone tumor was in the lower end of the boy's thigh, the size
of a moderate watermelon, covered in shiny skin, with large visible

veins. 'Witchdoctor marks'[9] on the skin over the tumor showed that Bara was the last resort. The tumor was so heavy that this weak and malnourished youngster could barely move his leg in bed. He was bound to have blood-spread tumors elsewhere in his body, which would cause his death. His treatment was amputation high in the thigh and speedy mobilization with crutches and a prosthesis, so that he could go home and enjoy the rest of his short life—probably under a year.

The other boy, of fourteen years, had as big a tumor in a similar place, arising from the muscles in his lower thigh. The cancer was even more advanced, since two areas of spread were clearly visible. One was a round lump on his head the size of a tennis ball, under his scalp and hairline. A smaller lump was present on the back of his head. These were most unusual places for a cancer to produce secondary tumors, but showed its highly malignant nature. All three tumors had 'Witchdoctor marks.' I amputated his leg and sent him for palliative radiation,[10] but he wasted away and in a few weeks he went home to die.

Another terribly advanced cancer was in a sixteen year-old girl, with vaginal bleeding and constipation. Examination showed a huge tumor mass, starting in the rectum, and also invading and blocking the vagina, the bladder and the urine tubes leading down into the bladder. She was untreatable because of both the local disease and the distant spread. After tests to find the extent of the disease, I told the family, who elected to take her home.

Esophageal cancer was endemic in Bantu males aged over fifty. More than 150 cases a year came to Bara. According to my research, the occurrence correlated with both smoking and alcohol abuse. 'A man who drinks a lot, smokes a lot and loves them both,' described most people with this cancer. My youngest patient with the disease broke this rule. She was a pretty and educated 24 year-old woman who neither drank nor smoked. I made the mistake of getting emotionally involved with her care—treating her as if she were family and losing objectivity. I was 'mad at the cancer,' as Dr. Ackerman used to say about a surgeon in St Louis. I just could not bear it that I might not be able to help her.

This state of mind caused me to operate, when I had knowingly or subconsciously ignored some signs that she was beyond surgical help. I opened her chest in an attempt to remove the tumor, only to discover the hard way that this was impossible, as it was very advanced and fixed to vital organs. I had to swallow my pride, back out and conclude the surgery. I knew that she probably had only three months to live, with increasing difficulty swallowing, and I would have to put a plastic tube inside her esophagus for her to swallow through. I recognized the reasons for my error of judgment. In the future I tried to avoid similar situations. I promised myself I would never look after my own family.

Unusual diseases sometimes demand unusual cures. Bantu patients were prone to getting black skin cancers, called melanomas,[11] on the soles of their feet, which are usually non-pigmented. The cancers usually developed in 'nevi,' or areas of abnormal pigment on the sole. It was not known why the tumors developed there, rather than the rest of the body, except for poor or absent footwear and walking barefoot.

The patients regularly came in with huge tumors, at least the size of golf balls. The usual treatment would have been leg amputation, but the patients invariably refused this measure. A friend of mine, Andrew, in charge of another unit, and I decided to use an unusual method to treat these people. Dr. Creech had pioneered it in Louisiana.

The procedure was called 'Isolation-Perfusion' of the limb. It involved temporarily cutting off all connection between the leg and the body and using the heart-lung pump to circulate blood through the leg to keep it alive. A very high and otherwise fatal dose of a chemotherapy drug called Melphalan[12] was then given into the arterial side and allowed to circulate for an hour before the procedure ended; we drained the limb and the normal circulation was re-established. The patient's bone marrow was thus protected from the high dose of chemotherapy.

The tumor was locally excised and a skin graft put on the wound. Often, we removed the lymph nodes in the groin at the same or a later sitting. The results of treatment were excellent, with most patients keeping their limbs, without recurrent cancer in the leg. Since general chemotherapy for the cancer was not available at that time, these patients sometimes died of melanoma spread elsewhere after a few years. In view of the advanced nature of their disease, the success of perfusion in these patients at Bara certainly validated its use.

Another very unusual tumor seen quite often in the Bantu throughout Africa was 'Kaposi's sarcoma.'[13] This was felt to be an almost exclusively African disease. It was slow growing, patients living many years, with gradual progression of the tumors up the limb. It was usually treated by radiation therapy, with only moderate success. The two of us tried Melphalan isolation-perfusion in these cases also. The treatment seemed to arrest the disease, but because of its long natural history, results were harder to assess.

This same tumor has now come to the forefront in AIDS patients worldwide, presumably related to their immune suppression, but also suspected of being virus-induced.

Some young women I saw with tumors had lumps in the breast. Luckily none were cancers. Older British surgeons called them 'breast mice,' or technically, fibroadenomas. These were smooth, rubbery, benign lumps that slipped around in the breast, like a mouse escaping from a cat. They were removed through small incisions, producing happy patients.

One day I had as a patient a sixteen year-old girl with the 'grandmother' of all breast tumors. Her right breast was of normal size, while the left one was at least a size 46 C cup, hanging down to her navel. The tumor felt smooth and rubbery, like the 'breast mice,' and was not hard or irregular, like cancer. I removed it, being able to leave the nipple in place but there was not much breast left behind. Pathology called it a 'giant fibroadenoma,' possibly a 'cystosarcoma phylloides.'[14] The patient was pleased to not have cancer, but none too happy with her new small breast.

In my early years at Medical School, I had a vacation job with the local Health Department. I rotated through meat inspection and the laboratory and worked at Sharpeville Clinic. One day I finished testing the butterfat content in milk from the dairies—a really useless occupation. I walked out of the door for some winter sunshine and saw an African man sitting patiently on the step outside. As I asked him his business, I noted many blisters and pustular lesions on his face. They were the reason he had taken the train from Evaton, half way to Johannesburg. He had been in contact with many people *en route*.

Though I had never seen such a case, I knew immediately from my books that this was smallpox. The patient had never been vaccinated and came from a religious group that did not believe in it. I immediately alerted Dr. Bernstein, the Medical Officer of Health, and everyone else I could think of. This was an emergency, particularly among the blacks, who were less likely to have been immunized. The Health Department notified all the local industries and the coalmines, put notices in the paper and broadcast on the radio. The patient was vaccinated for his own safety and sent to 'Fever Hospital' in Johannesburg.

The Health Department had soon mobilized several teams to go out and vaccinate the population. Workers went out in every direction to anywhere they could find groups of people. I was on the job daily for weeks, playing a full part. I well remember one coalmine where my team immunized hundreds of migrant workers from the country. In Evaton the local authority also set to work to control the situation. Only a few people developed smallpox, and they were isolated and vaccinated as soon as they were located, while the town was fully covered. Further spread of the disease was stopped, but the vaccination program went on, far and wide. That was a very good reason to have a Public Health Department.

Another religion that often compromised good medical care was the Jehovah's Witnesses. They are devout, evangelistic people, but from the medical viewpoint they take one sentence from the Bible and use it out of context to refuse blood transfusions for their children and themselves, often with fatal results. Apart from media horror stories, my first encounter with the problem was during my training in England. The father of a twelve year-old boy was bleeding heavily from a gastric ulcer and in danger of dying from hemorrhage. I talked seriously with the patient and his wife, explaining the high chance of death without blood transfusion, even before surgery could attempt to stop the bleeding. I mustered all the logic at my command and must have been persuasive, as the man finally agreed to receive 'as little blood as possible.' The operation was successful. The family thanked me and hoped 'I did not think too badly of them for taking the blood.' I could reassure them on that score—it was surely better for the wife to keep her husband and the son to still have his father!

Daniel Ncube was a forty year-old man with the earliest and hence the most curable cancer of the esophagus I had ever seen. I was practically salivating at the thought of doing the operation and getting a real cure. When I went to get consent for surgery I saw the word 'Watchtower' on the chart. I had a problem—the patient was a Jehovah's Witness. I would never have attempted an esophagectomy without enough blood available, and I knew the anesthetists agreed. As I spoke to Ncube I thought of a plan.

"Daniel, I cannot do your operation without giving you blood," I said. "The anesthetists will also not put you to sleep without blood, so we have a problem."

"I understand," Daniel replied. He was educated and was a lay minister in his church.

"I have an idea," I said. "I can take a pint of your own blood every week for two weeks and keep it for you and then give it back if we need to during the surgery."

After some thought and further debate, Daniel agreed. I drew two pints and stored them in the Blood Bank. After the second unit was drawn, the patient had a visit from his bishop. He spoke to me on ward rounds the next day, and handed me a booklet titled 'Medicine, God, Blood, and You.'

"I'm sorry, Mr. Hunt," he said. "My bishop says that what we are doing is no good. Please give me back my blood. I must sprinkle it all on the ground."

"Well, Daniel, I tried to help you," I replied. "I'm very sorry. You must understand that I cannot do the surgery without blood, because it could kill you. We can only give you X-ray treatment and hope that works for you."

The blood was duly returned and sprinkled. The patient received high dose radiation and was 'cured' for five years—something not previously achieved at Bara. He then came back with 'constrictive pericarditis,'[15] due to the heavy radiation to the sac around the heart, which had been in the path of the X-ray beam. The Thoracic surgeons removed his pericardium without using blood, and Daniel was fine.

Ironically, Plasmalyte B, one of the fluids arising out of my shock research, became known as 'Jehovah's Blood' by one of the Cardiac units in South Africa. They used it to prime their heart-lung pumps when they worked on Jehovah's Witnesses. I later in life had cardiac surgery done without the use of donor blood, in a center that did great surgery, but also specialized in treating Jehovah's Witnesses.

Doctors also became ill at times. Some of the Bantu doctors practicing in Soweto and other townships on the Rand[16] used Baragwanath as their hospital in time of need. A couple of them came in repeatedly with pancreatitis[17] caused by alcohol overuse. Staff members who knew them said they consumed only the best brands and vintages, but the disease process did not care about the quality of the liquor! In fact, one of them also developed cirrhosis of the liver and its complications, leading to his death.

One doctor from Soweto developed renal failure and was placed on dialysis. He was offered a kidney transplant. He could not make up his mind and went to the witchdoctor for care. He never came back to the hospital. Later I heard that he had died of his disease.

One of the previous Bantu housemen in Unit Five was a much older man. I always admired him for what he had achieved. He had worked in asbestos mines for many years, then gone back to college and become a schoolteacher for a while and finally he completed the six-year medical course. He certainly showed dogged determination. After a decade of medical practice his work history caught up with him. He became ill and was admitted, at his own request, to my care. Workup showed that he had asbestosis of the lungs, causing the rare tumor called 'Mesothelioma.'[18] This was extensive and in both lung cavities. It was untreatable, and quickly led to failure of his breathing and death.

Lumps and bumps of all kinds occupied much surgical attention, and will probably do so far into the future. One of my most memorable cases was a lady who had walked halfway down Africa from Malawi, because of a large lump in her neck. She had heard of Baragwanath and thought she might get help. She was indeed grotesque, with a goiter[19] protruding forward from her neck by at least six inches and occupying the whole space between her chin and her chest. She could barely breathe or swallow. She agreed to surgery and I did it as soon as I could. The patient did well. Her major problem lay in returning to Malawi and getting the thyroid tablets she would need to take for life. The social workers found her the train fare and the pharmacy gave her ninety thyroxin tablets.[20]

Dr. Jonas, the gynecologist, referred me a young woman for a lump in her belly. She had just had a baby boy who came over with her, to lie in a crib at her bedside, for ease of care and breast-feeding. The lump, almost as big as a pregnancy, was situated in the upper abdomen. It seemed to come from the pancreas, but did not affect her blood sugar, she had no jaundice and it was not painful. She was in good physical condition, so it was not a cancer, or she would have wasted away to nothing. I worked hard to find a cause.

Finally, the moment of truth arrived and I had a long talk with her about doing exploratory surgery in an attempt to remove the tumor. She signed the operative permit and made arrangements for the baby's care. Blood was taken and cross-matched for possible transfusion. Her bowel was emptied and sterilized with antibiotics. Everything was in great shape. The night before surgery, she bathed in antiseptic soap and was about to be weighed.

While standing on the scale, she crumpled and fell on the floor, stone dead, in front of the whole ward. Attempts to resuscitate her failed. Even modern techniques would not have helped. I was heartbroken and requested an autopsy, which the family granted. The cause of death was a 'Pulmonary Embolus,'[21] a clot in the lungs, arising from a long clot in the vena cava[22] behind the tumor. This had probably formed because her pregnancy, lying on the tumor, produced unusual pressure and blockage of this large vein. By sheer chance the clot had chosen that moment to break off and move to block the pulmonary artery.

The tumor weighed thirteen pounds. It was U-shaped, with a dent in the center, where the pregnancy had been. It was a benign, non-functioning Islet cell tumor[23] of the pancreas. It would have been irremovable, because it wrapped round so many structures. Research showed it was the biggest such tumor in the world, but I never published the case.

A man came to Dermatology clinic with a rash. The doctor noticed (it was hard to miss) that under the rash there was a huge tumor below the jawbone, the size of a grapefruit, round and rubbery. After his skin cleared up I removed the lump. Luckily the pathology was a benign tumor of the salivary gland, with only a small chance of becoming malignant. The patient needed no further treatment and could be carefully watched.

A man of forty years presented with an equally large 'tumor' a little lower in his neck. 'Tumor' means 'swelling' in Latin. This one seemed to be pulsating, but it lay over the division of the carotid artery in the neck, so it was hard to tell. An arteriogram X-ray[24] showed it to be an aneurysm of the carotid artery (a large hollow swelling full of blood and clot.) The cause of aneurysms is usually arterial disease due to age, or injury to the artery from an injury. Neither of these was the case. The man was tall and had long fingers. He also had a high arched palate. This was probably a case of 'Marfan's syndrome,'[25] in which the connective tissues are defective and give way or stretch to cause aneurysms, usually of the aorta. These often rupture and are fatal, because the young people are not aware of their presence. I removed the aneurysm, replacing it with a synthetic vascular graft. Though the young man needed careful follow-up, it was doubtful whether he would come back.

Albinos are people or animals born without protective coloration in the skin. This trait is of course, less obvious in white people and I can't recall having seen too many 'White' albinos. In the Bantu it is very obvious, since the skin is pinky-white and the hair is yellowish white, with the characteristic tight soft curls of black people. In addition, albinos have nystagmus, a sideways flickering of the eyes, with inability to fix the vision on one spot.

A number of albinos lived in Soweto, so they were often seen at Bara. They got other diseases, but the main reason I saw them was the presence of skin cancers, due to sun exposure. These cancers also occur in whites without sun protection, but they are absolutely inevitable in albinos. Many times they would come in with two or three dozen cancers at the same time. These were usually small enough to be curable by surgery or radiation.

The tumors were sometimes large and affected vital structures, causing severe deformity or death. I had one albino patient like that. The cancer lay on the left side of her face and invaded deeply, destroying the facial nerve, causing an ugly facial nerve paralysis. She was unable to smile on that side or close her eye. It was hard to persuade the albinos that they needed absolute sun protection, with large hats, long-sleeved shirts, etc. Since many of them had outside laboring jobs, the requisite protection was hard to enforce.

Among my more impressive lumps and bumps were three patients with giant *hydroceles*[26] and one with a cancer of an undescended testis.[27] They were all in the ward together, and graciously allowed a group photo to be taken of their genital regions. The largest hydrocele hung down almost to the man's knees. It was bright and shiny in the sunlight. The patient with the undescended testes had almost no scrotum, but he had a lump in the belly. The contrasts between the cases were striking.

The man with testicular cancer was aged fifty and had two children. I did not disillusion him that they were not his own, since neither of his testes had come down normally. The heat in the abdomen makes such testes infertile. There was a large lump on the left, just above his groin. At surgery this was a large cancer which was removable, but with no chance of cure, because of distant spread. He also had chemotherapy and radiation.

The surgery of very big hydroceles was difficult, because the extensive raw surfaces produced by cutting out the large bag often bled post-operatively. Both patient and surgeon ended up with a bigger problem—a bag of blood—that could not be emptied, and took months to resolve. The logical but worst way to try and solve that problem was to put in a drain. The groin harbors many bacteria, which would soon track in along the drain and infect the hematoma. The patient then had a bag of bloody pus, and nobody was happy!

I had slowly learned to deal with this problem. I excised the bag of fluid and dried the bleeding points carefully with electro-cautery. After stitching the skin I applied a 'Crepe bandage'[28] firmly to the slack scrotal skin, forcing the testicles to the top of the scrotum. This compressed the lax scrotal tissues and prevented bleeding and swelling. It produced a long tube, larger than the penis. Many patients were amused when I told them they now had two penises! The end-result was worth it, as the slack scrotum soon shrank to normal.

SOME PATIENTS WITH IMPRESSIVE HYDROCELES—
OR "BAGS" OF WATER AROUND THE TESTES.

[1] Historia Naturalis: From the Oxford Dictionary of quotations.

[2] Giving sets: Prepackaged plastic IV tubing with an integrated drip chamber, filter and blood pump.

[3] Rule of nines: A 'rule of thumb' for estimating burn size. Used to predict survival rates and govern fluid therapy, the most vital part of burn care in the first 48 hours. The head was 9%, arms 9%, thighs 9%, chest and belly 18%, back 18%, neck 1%, palms 1%, perineum 1% and so on. Accurate enough for the purposes.

[4] Tracheotomy: Placing a plastic or metal tube through the neck skin into the throat to help breathing.

[5] Empirical: Relying on experience alone. In this case, I was also relying on my research experience.

[6] Mangle: A machine with two rubber rollers, seen on early washing machines. The rollers were turned with a handle and clothes were fed between them to wring out the water. Commercial machines with heated rollers were used for ironing laundry. The skin mesher also had two rollers, made of metal, one carrying sharp knife blades to cut the skin. Various models worked in slightly different ways. Their use revolutionized burn care.

[7] Whipple Pancreatico-duodenectomy: Removal of the head of the pancreas and the lower end of the common bile duct, plus the duodenum, which wraps around both of them. It is major surgery, needing a complicated 'hookup' to rejoin the stomach, small bowel, pancreas and bile ducts.

[8] Sarcoma: A type of cancer starting from 'connective tissues,' or bone, as opposed to 'Carcinomas,' which arose from the skin surface or the inside lining of organs like the stomach, colon or lung.

[9] Witchdoctor marks: Rows of tiny one-centimeter long scratches made by the Witchdoctor, usually marking the obvious limits of the disease process.

[10] Palliative radiation: Non-curative radiation given to slow disease progression and increase patient comfort.

[11] Melanoma: A type of skin cancer, often developing in white people from pre-existing nevi or freckles in the skin. Very common in heavily sun-exposed areas. Common on Bondi Beach in Australia. The tumor is not common on body or limb skin in Bantu people, but occurs on sole and palm skin, often associated with nevi.

[12] Melphalan: Phenylalanine mustard—a derivative of Nitrogen mustard, the first chemotherapy agent.

[13] Kaposi's sarcoma: A blackish tumor of the skin, usually of the feet and limbs, common in Africa and a few other places. Its cause was unknown. It is now common in people with AIDS and is probably viral in origin.

[14] Cystosarcoma Phylloides: A giant breast tumor of doubtful malignancy, similar to a fibroadenoma, but best treated by complete removal of the breast.

[15] Constrictive Pericarditis: The bag around the heart gets stiff and scarred and narrows down, constricting the heart and making it unable to pump adequately.

16 Rand: Short for 'Witwatersrand,' the ridge of hills on which Johannesburg and many gold-mining towns are built. The name was also given to the S.A. currency that replaced the Pound. Also in the gold 'Kruger Rand.'

17 Pancreatitis: A very painful abdominal condition, in which the pancreas becomes swollen and inflamed. It has two causes—gallstones, which are rare in the Bantu—and alcohol abuse. It often recurs in alcoholics unless they quit drinking. The chronic pain becomes quite crippling.

18 Mesothelioma: A fatal cancer due to asbestos exposure. It involved the inner surfaces of the chest and the adjacent outer surfaces of the lung. It was usually widespread when first seen and could not be treated.

19 Goiter: A swelling of the thyroid gland in the low neck. Often due to a lack of iodine in the soil and the crops in certain areas. It is why iodine is added to salt in modern times. Very large goiters need surgery.

20 Thyroxin: A purified drug that is the same as the hormone put out by the thyroid. After thyroid removal it is vital to take the drug for life. The body cannot function without adequate circulating thyroid hormone.

21 Pulmonary embolus: A large clot of blood moving to the lungs from the legs or elsewhere. Frequently fatal.

22 Vena Cava: The main vein of the body, running up in front of the spine, next to the aorta. It is often about an inch in diameter. A large clot detaching from this and moving to the lungs would understandably be fatal.

23 Islet cell tumor of the pancreas: The pancreas has some small areas of cells, called the 'Islets of Langerhans,' which produce insulin in the feedback loop that controls blood sugar. They may form small tumors, which produce too much insulin and cause unconsciousness from low blood sugar. In this patient, though the tumor was huge, blood sugar was not affected, so the tumor was non-functional.

24 Arteriogram: A needle is placed in the carotid artery and radio-opaque dye given while X-rays are taken.

25 Marfan's syndrome: A hereditary disease. The connective tissues are weak, causing aortic aneurysms. They are usually tall people, so basketball players may be affected, causing sudden death on the court.

26 Hydrocele: A bag of fluid collected around the testicles, in the scrotum. These can become very large. There is a historical picture in a textbook of one being carried in a wheelbarrow.

27 Undescended testis: A small number of boys are born without one or both testes in the scrotum. During development, the testes 'descend' from below the kidney to the scrotum. Some fail to get down all the way. Such a failure, if left alone, can cause sterility and/or cancer of the testis. Such cancers are more common in blacks but also occur in whites. All undescended testes should be brought down by surgery in childhood.

28 Crepe bandage: A lightly elasticized bandage, similar to the US 'Ace Wrap.'

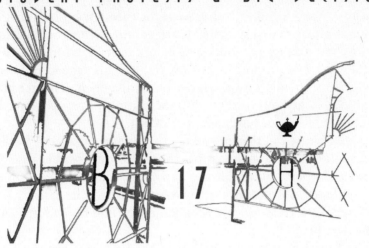

The 16<sup>th</sup> of June 1976 was different. It was a Wednesday, usually slow for the surgeons. Discharge rounds were followed by a quick tea break, with Martha's excellent little sandwiches. There was the usual cheerful banter and gossip with other units in the tearoom and exchange of consultation cards. After tea I returned to Ward Five for bedside student teaching rounds. The rest of the team went to Outpatients, led by the Unit's new assistant surgeon, Joel Moroka, who was related to an African royal house. Joel had recently finished surgical training with an Irish F.R.C.S., of which he was rightly proud. He was the only qualified black surgeon in South Africa, and likely in sub-Saharan Africa.

I had my group of fourth-year students gathered round a bed, starting to examine a patient, when I was paged over the PA system.

"Mister Hunt. Casualty. Urgent, Mister Hunt please!"

This was an unusual call, and I rushed to the phone in Ward Five's office, returned and spoke briefly to the students. They would have to amuse themselves until the 11.30 a.m. Bara bus took them back to town. I hurried out of the ward, knowing only that there was trouble in Soweto. I was going to see a bad gunshot wound. Perhaps more than one.

When I reached Casualty, a whole new experience unfolded. The patient was in the Resuscitation Room, nurses all around him. He was barely alive—the first of many such people I would see that day. The young man of about 18 years groaned feebly. His breathing was rapid and forced. His clothes, the blankets and the gurney were

soaked in blood. A bullet had gone right through him, causing a horrendous injury. It first shattered his right arm, then passed through his right chest and upper abdomen, before it emerged from a two-inch diameter exit wound in his left flank. This ragged hole was surrounded by an angry, swollen, red-black, five-inch diameter blast injury. Blood leaked out steadily onto the mattress. I set up a large IV line and took blood for type and cross-match.

"Sister, please call theater and tell them what to expect," I called out. "A major laparotomy, possible thoracotomy, possible vascular damage, and open fracture of the arm. They should have a blood pump and blood warmers ready. Say there may be more cases!

"Staff Nurse, please get Mr. Moroka and the unit from Outpatients to come over here."

The Outpatient Department was not far away, and the team soon came in running.

"Joel, there's terrible trouble in Soweto, with a lot of shooting," I said. "I don't know any details. Will you do this man, while I look after things here? I've told Theater.

"As you can see, he was shot by a high velocity bullet, right through his arm, his chest and belly and points in between—probably his liver and who-knows-what else. That's a good few hours of work for you. Ask the orthopods to fix his arm. I'll come by soon, but I must first see what's going on out there. Call me if you have a problem."

I soon heard there had been demonstrations at a high school in Soweto. The police first used tear gas to try and stem the riots and then started using live bullets. Many people were injured or killed, including some children. The violence spread to other areas and the army was called in. Many more gruesome details filtered in during the rest of the day.

A stream of gurneys now flooded in, each one with its bloody burden. The wounded were writhing, cursing, groaning and yelling in pain. The higher voices of crying children could be clearly heard above the general hubbub. Some people had already died, and their porters only needed a doctor's confirmation before heading to the morgue.

I saw one boy who had a number of small, tender bumps under the skin of his chest and abdomen. I turned the patient over and found several matching holes in his back. I realized that buckshot from a shotgun, coming from behind, had gone right through the patient's chest and abdomen and everything in between, such as his heart, lungs and intestines. There was no time for an X-ray. I rushed the boy straight to the Resuscitation Room for placement of large IV lines and chest drainage tubes on each side.

I soon realized that my unit, and indeed Baragwanath, would have to totally revise our concepts of trauma. I felt sick, as the enormity of the situation dawned on me. Despite all my years in surgery, my strong stomach felt quite queasy. I walked out of Casualty for a while, leaving the team to handle the constant stream of patients.

Outside I stopped and breathed deeply, felt a bit better and walked briskly up to the top floor of the ICU, the only multi-storeyed building in the Hospital. I looked through a window, over the ten-foot hospital wall and across the main road. I could see the bus and taxi terminals across the highway and the huge area of Soweto beyond, stretching far into the distance, covered as usual in its almost impenetrable midwinter blanket of smoke.

My gaze dropped to the foreground. I was horrified by the carnage I saw. At the bus shelters many bodies lay still on the sidewalk, some wrapped in blankets, several surrounded by crying relatives. Hundreds of people milled around, yelling and gesticulating angrily. Heavily armed white and black policemen and soldiers were everywhere, shouting instructions, ordering people around, but unable to create any semblance of order.

I looked up again from the chaotic scene below me. Through the smog, I could now see palls of thick black smoke rising over the townships. As I discovered later, these came from burning schools and administration buildings or wrecked and overturned buses. The ICU nurses by turns gazed out of the same small windows and gathered in groups, heatedly discussing what they had seen and the little news they had already heard.

"Mister Hunt, this is terrible!" one said. "Why do they have to shoot the children?"

"I don't know, Sister," I replied. "We're all working in Casualty and theater to do what we can to save them. We can't do more."

"There will be much more trouble," she said. "It's not over yet."

I returned to Casualty and resumed triage. I examined every victim myself, sending porters with their charges on to the Resuscitation Room, the operating theaters, X-Ray, the morgue or elsewhere. I ran back and forth to the Resuscitation Room, but my staff looked after the patients and did the surgery. Later, after consultation with the Chief Surgeon, Professor Mason, and the Superintendent, a second surgical unit was co-opted to help.

The atmosphere in the emergency area became increasingly tense. The black nurses and interpreters, usually friendly and voluble, became terse and non-communicative. The orderlies rushed a black policeman into the Resuscitation Room. He was bleeding heavily from a head injury caused by a rock hurled by one of the demonstrators. The nurses refused to look after him, saying he was a collaborator. I put on a pressure dressing and got one of the housemen to clean and suture the wound and do other necessary care.

"Whatever happened to your 'Hippocratic Oath,' or whatever you nurses agree to when you graduate?" I asked the nurses in general.

They shrugged their shoulders and looked away. After that, with injured policemen or soldiers the Casualty officers and surgeons had to do the nurses' work as well as their own.

· During a small lull in the stream of trauma, I walked out through the front door with the elderly white Chief Matron (head of nursing), and we viewed the chaos together. A passing black man turned his head and, without saying a word, spat a long stream of tobacco juice onto her uniform.

Another man, in a venomous tone, said: "You white people! You should not be here. You will get what you deserve."

"You black people are the ones who will be sorry if we get out," I replied.

In the courtyard out front, dark green armored cars full of soldiers drove through the grounds of the hospital, while black people yelled racial insults angrily at their white occupants. The soldiers and policemen replied in similar vein. The crudity, venom and raw racial hatred expressed in these exchanges were quite terrifying. The hospital gates were unsuccessfully attacked on three separate occasions. No one could ever explain why.

I returned to Casualty, but was soon called to surgery because of the complexity of one of the operations. Fortunately, I could now leave triage to the second surgical unit for a while and go to the theater. There I could solve my own unit's problems and set up plans for handling the large volume of serious trauma that was still coming.

I changed into theater scrubs and surveyed all the rooms. I stuck my head in each one to see how they were coping. The Unit had to 'crash' three of the routine operating schedules of other surgeons. These men graciously agreed to end their schedules. They promised to help Unit Five cope with the work, an offer that I gladly accepted.

Joel Moroka was working with a houseman and a senior student. They had the toughest case—the 18 year-old patient whom I had seen first in the morning. They had placed a right chest tube and connected it to an underwater drain bottle, which contained only a moderate amount of blood. The lung was functioning and appeared to be fully expanded, though the X-ray showed it was badly bruised. The orthopedic registrar was seated behind Moroka, with a second scrubnurse, working on the right arm. The fracture was under control. I looked inside the belly and decided to scrub up and help Joel.

He had the abdomen open via a long midline incision. A large expandable self-retaining retractor held the wound wide open for good access. Moroka had placed large packs of gauze cloth both above and below the liver to help control the bleeding from star-shaped bullet-holes in the reddish brown organ. This maneuver had so far been successful.

The big problem, however, lay beyond the liver. The entire left side of the colon, some 18 inches long, had been burst apart. It was torn to shreds and was purplish black. Its foul-smelling contents were splattered all over the abdominal cavity and other organs. We removed the dead colon and tied off a few big blood vessels. Joel brought the two open ends of the colon out through the abdominal wall, as separate colostomies, one in the upper and one in the lower abdomen. We washed out the foul-smelling mixture of blood and stool as best we could, using three liters of saline containing an antibiotic solution.

Moroka now surveyed the further path of the bullet. The left kidney was smashed wide open, bleeding freely, and reduced to mush. He removed the pieces and tied the large blood vessels. Mercifully, the bullet missed the spleen and passed below the stomach. Even though both organs were heavily bruised, they looked viable. We left them alone.

We now saw that a large hole had been blasted in the thick flank and abdominal wall muscles. It was about five inches in diameter, with shaggy, half-dead edges of muscle all round. I demonstrated 'Hunt's Test,' in which I touched any doubtful piece of muscle with the electro-cautery. If it twitched rapidly, it was probably alive, and I left it alone. If it responded weakly or did not twitch, I assumed the muscle was dead, and we cut it away.

"Hau!" Moroka exclaimed, in his native tongue. "A good trick. I will use it again."

Joel continued trimming the muscle. Then, at my suggestion, he plugged the hole in the abdominal wall with a piece of the omentum, which is a large sheet of fat that normally hangs inside the peritoneal cavity. Fortunately, it was not badly damaged.

"The omentum is the 'policeman' of the abdomen," Joel told the student. "It always seeks out trouble and sticks on to the problem area, to try and fix it. It also provides a good blood supply for healing. We often use it in surgery for the same purposes."

I now spoke seriously to everyone in the room: "We must all realize that this is a whole new ballgame. We normally deal with knife or .22 pistol wounds, which produce very little tissue damage. Today that all changed. The police and the army are using combat weapons, with high velocity ammunition. You just saw what one high velocity bullet can do. It devitalizes a huge volume of tissue, due to a shockwave from the high kinetic energy that's released when the bullet hits something solid.

"A knife blade does no damage to the surrounding tissues, and a .22 pistol, with a short barrel and low muzzle velocity, does very little. A handgun needs a really big slug to have much stopping power. That's why both the police and the gangsters prefer pistols with big bullets, like .38 Specials or .45s. Hollow pointed bullets and the like, which are illegal, do their harm by bursting open on contact and so creating a lot of damage.

"Though modern high power bullets for assault weapons or rifles are not much bigger than a .22, their powder charge is far greater. This produces muzzle velocities of around 3000 feet per second, against 7-800 for a pistol. Why does this matter? Well, according to the laws of physics the kinetic energy released when a moving object hits something is equal to the mass (weight) times *velocity cubed*, (3000x3000x3000.) so the *weight* matters very little.

"I've done the math, and taking a high velocity bullet of maybe ten grams, versus a pistol bullet of say thirty grams, the relative kinetic energy levels are about 270 billion against only 1.5 billion. Thus the tiny high velocity bullet releases 175 times more destructive energy than the big one, or than anything we've ever really met with before.

"We now have to consider the nature of the weapon when deciding on treatment. If it's a rifle or semi-automatic assault weapon, we can assume the higher values, with colossal injury potential. So, if the tissue looks bad, it's probably dead, and it needs to come out. There's no place for just repairing holes in bowel in these cases. Cut out the bad bit, no matter how big, and bring out the ends of what's left."

When I was satisfied with the progress of the case, I scrubbed out and left the room. I now continued my tour, first to the theater where my senior registrar was operating. This patient had a relatively simple injury, through the flesh of the abdominal wall. The bullet hit no vital structures. There was none of the blast effect I had just seen. I thought the police must have also been using their revolvers.

"Roger, they're using high velocity guns out there," I said. "I don't think you've seen any of these injuries yet."

I repeated my recent speech. I would do so frequently during the next few days.

"If you get into one of those cases, call me or get one of the other surgeons. We can talk about it later, if there's any lull in the work."

In the next room I found my junior registrar being helped by another surgeon. I greeted them and thanked my friend. They had already figured out what type of weapons were in use, since their case was much like Mr. Moroka's patient. They were removing a large piece of lacerated small bowel and preparing the good ends to exteriorize.

I now headed upstairs to the tearoom for a short break. I went to a small office and tried to call home for the second time that day. There was still no line. I knew that by now Ann would have heard about the riots and would be worried out of her mind.

I came back into the lounge and started to discuss the day's events with the surgeons and anesthesia staff in the room.

"Has anyone heard what's going on?" I asked. "Is there anything on the news?"

"There was a riot at a high school in Soweto, over the compulsory teaching of half the school subjects in Afrikaans," said Professor Sarah Levin, the chief anesthetist. "As you know from *The Daily Mail*, the people of Soweto are none too happy about that—they know that Afrikaans is useless anywhere else in the world. They regard it as the language of their oppressor and have no wish to learn it. There are also not enough qualified people to do the teaching. Their school facilities are awful. The authorities are unwilling or unable to do anything about it. Some petty officials would not bend the rules. Today it all reached a head and boiled over, causing demonstrations at several high schools."

"Yes," another anesthetist chimed in. "They're forming 'bull's horns' formations, like in the days of Shaka. The adults are at the back and the kids in front. So the police shoot the kids—good publicity for the organizers' cause. I don't think these riots are spontaneous. They're too well organized. I can see it now in the overseas headlines: 'In South Africa they shoot children.'"

Sarah Levin spoke again: "That may be so, but the police are very quick on the trigger, like in Sharpeville 16 years ago. I don't think the soldiers are really sympathetic either."

"Well, it sounds pretty awful, whatever the facts may be," I said. "I just hope this is a brief incident and doesn't escalate or drag on too long. Today's trauma in Casualty and the 'Pit' is absolutely horrible, with a load of deaths and some really dreadful injuries."

Professor Levin spoke again: "The authorities have closed all the schools and won't open them till this is all over. Meanwhile, the blacks refuse to go to school at all."

"They will cut off their own noses," said her assistant.

Sarah took me aside and led me to her office. She shut the door.

"John, I didn't want to inflame any more passions," she started, "but one white person has already been killed in Soweto. His name was Mark Adelson, a social worker there. He was also a member of our congregation."

"My God! I knew him. How terrible," I exclaimed. "He'd done a thesis for his master's degree: 'What the Young Black is Thinking.' I guess his widow just found out."

The usually cheerful and upbeat Sarah sobbed quietly.

I embraced her and said softly, "I'm desperately sorry."

We were old friends and stood looking at each other for a long time. We could each remember a happy past and see a clouded future. I patted Sarah's back, shook my head and broke away. I changed the subject as we left the office and returned to the tearoom.

"I've just been round the theaters to make sure my boys are doing a good job. Luckily a lot of surgeons who were pushed out of their theaters have stayed to help, so we have plenty of staffing at the moment. How is your anesthesia coverage?" I asked Sarah.

"We're OK, nobody is going home until we see how things sort themselves out here."

I now ran into Arthur Mandel, head of the orthopedic department. We discussed the handling of bone and muscle in the new era. Arthur agreed there should be little implantation of metal plates, due to extensive tissue damage and potential infection. But it might be unavoidable and lifesaving. They would need to think it through and draw up new plans. Arthur said that in order to save lives we might need to do primary amputation in some bad cases, judging by experience in Vietnam and other recent conflicts.

We had earlier called the thoracic surgeon for the boy with the shotgun wounds of his chest. His unit was already at work. The neurosurgeons and all other specialty units were also on full alert. The theater sisters and staff nurses had made their own plans. I was now satisfied that the operating rooms were well staffed and prepared for anything.

I left the theater block and went to the medical superintendent's office, where a conference was in progress, with most of the senior medical staff, including Professor Mason, the matrons, administration, security, and officers of the police and army all present.

They made plans to staff the hospital at a high level, with accommodation available for on-duty nurses so that they need not go into Soweto if they were afraid. A report had come in that some white doctors' wives and children, trying to go home by car, had been attacked with stones on the road back to town. They had just managed to get through to Johannesburg. The 'Bara bus' was unable to leave through the hospital's front gate.

The plans would allow doctors, other staff, the 'Bara bus' and anyone needing access to Baragwanath to use a different highway, and enter through the back gates of the hospital, past a police post and an army barracks. This arrangement would continue for six months.

The day remained exceedingly busy. Cases came in steadily, sometimes singly, often in bunches. Packed 'Soweto taxis' would screech to a stop in front of the hospital and disgorge five or six injured, bleeding people at the door. They were picked up on gurneys by waiting porters and wheeled quickly into Casualty. I was always amazed at how many passengers could be crammed into one of those old vehicles.

The onslaught of deaths and terrible injuries persisted. Several teenage children were among the dead. The patient load was higher than that of a Saturday night. Many hundreds of cases were seen, and over a hundred were admitted to the surgical admissions ward. Three operating rooms worked full steam till after dawn.

I often scrubbed in, to help with major abdominal or vascular trauma. The thoracic surgeons, neurosurgeons and orthopedic surgeons all played their part during both day and night. Everyone had to learn the lessons of high velocity assault weapons.

Towards evening, we noticed that some of the young men showed the scars of prior stab heart or great vessel surgery. I thought they were 'Tsotsis,' or Township thugs who were involved in the general violence and were likely injured by their 'friends' or enemies, as on a Saturday night. Such people did not go to school, so were clearly not legitimate student protesters. Perhaps they were part of the organization staging the riots.

Nobody slept that night. I started 'post-intake' rounds early, to let the unit get home to bed, as I could not read the future. They might easily be needed before the next intake.

I went to Ward Five to make discharge rounds. After I finished, the ward sister took me aside:

"Mister Hunt, I'm so worried about my son."

"Why, Sister?"

"Well, he's going out there today, and I'm frightened he will be killed."

"Sister, then he knows what to do. He shouldn't go."

"Doctor, he has to go. The organizers have told him that if he does not go, his family will all be killed. I believe them! The 'Tsotsis' will kill us. "

"I'm very sorry, Sister," I said. "I guess he has to do what he has to do—but talk to him—try and stop him, Sister."

I left Ward Five, to set out for home. It had been the worst day of my career.

As I drove home through the barracks, I reflected on the events of the last 36 hours. I had seen and heard some of the most horrifying and upsetting things of my entire life. This was plainly the dawn of a new and terrible era in my beloved South Africa.

I also thought about something that had often troubled me during my career at Bara. I had not experienced the 'Sharpeville massacre' as I was overseas in training. Those victims of police and army violence had also come to Baragwanath hospital. The emotional scars had taken years to heal, or at least to be covered over. I had brought my family back from Britain shortly after Sharpeville, mainly because of parental and family ties. I had thought long and hard before deciding to return to South Africa. Now I seriously questioned the wisdom of that decision.

Sharpeville was the fairly new black dormitory town for Vereeniging, situated a mile from my childhood home where my mother still lived. The township had been built while I was in medical school. It was named after a friend of our family, who carried out the idea for the Vereeniging town council. The 'Old Location,' where the black people had previously lived, was dangerous, overcrowded, and an eyesore, with few essential facilities. During my summer vacation after high school, I took part in a housing survey there and soon learned of the appalling conditions under which these black people existed.

The students doing the survey could not count how many people lived in the sordid overcrowded conditions we encountered. The houses were crammed together and had been repeatedly extended with lean-to additions of cardboard, corrugated iron and other makeshift materials. Many people occupied the same space, often sleeping in shifts. We could only count the houses and shacks and such facilities as we could find. This survey formed the basis for planning a new Township to help satisfy the needs of the black people of Vereeniging. The plan was well under way before the Nationalist Government developed the concept of Apartheid, so they could not be blamed. With the insights I had, I felt that the creation of the new township of Sharpeville was necessary and represented enlightened slum clearance and the relocation of severely disadvantaged people to a much more favorable environment.

Though the new township provided a far better lifestyle for the residents than the extreme squalor of their old location, many people who had to leave their homes were upset by the move. As a white outside observer; however, I empathized with them but felt they would soon realize the advantages presented by Sharpeville. They now had new, much better, single-family housing, together with clinics, proper schools, playgrounds, and sports facilities. I also worked in Sharpeville during later medical school vacations. I knew it was clean, uncrowded, and properly laid out. It had always bothered me that some of the first signs of racial unrest unfolded there.

Racial tensions in the country appeared to have slowly simmered down since the Sharpeville riots. I had been pleased to see a softening of white attitudes, which I thought was leading to the elimination of some of the worst aspects of Apartheid. I had begun to feel more secure. Yesterday's events were a nasty shock, both to me and to South Africa.

I cudgeled my brains, trying to find a course of action. I knew that I loved the people of Soweto and the Africans generally. I loved my job. I loved the land of my birth; Africa was in my blood. But Ann and I had our children to consider. I reflected on the patients I had seen that day, particularly that first young man and the children and adults I had sent to the morgue. I considered the attack on the doctors' wives and children on the road to Johannesburg. I vividly remembered my trip to the front of the hospital with the Matron and the racial hatred so obvious there. I was concerned that there were indeed outside organizers of these demonstrations and the implications of their threat to my ward sister's son. And I thought long and hard about the fate of my friend, Mark Adelson, an innocent victim of senseless violence.

I could reach only one conclusion: I would not be saved for having been 'Mister Baragwanath,' or even the White Witchdoctor, for the last 16 years. I would probably be killed just for being white. In time, so would my loved ones.

As I got home, the family was waiting at the door and the children ran out and hugged me before Ann even got a chance to greet me.

"What's going on? We were worried stiff. Why didn't you call us?" Many questions came from them all at once.

"I think the lines were down. I tried to call several times," I answered. "I'm sure you've seen it all on TV by now. There was police shooting at a school in Soweto, because the students were demonstrating.

It was a really hard day, just like a bad Saturday. Some people think these riots were organized from outside, but nobody really knows yet."

I did not want to alarm the children, so I did not go into the gory details. I tried to keep the tone light for the rest of the day. When Ann and I had a chance to be alone, we could discuss things more openly.

"I told you Dan and Heather were right, leaving when they did," Ann said.

"I can't argue with that, but I really thought things were getting better and the Nats were getting some sort of message," I answered. "It looks like they never do."

"Well, you've tried Canada and there's no job there. Where else is there?" Ann asked.

"I'm not sure yet that I want to go, but you know me—always resistant to change. I'll certainly keep my eyes and ears open. At least we have contacts in the States and both Australia and New Zealand."

We talked for hours, round and round, examining every aspect of the situation, until I stifled a yawn.

"You look exhausted," Ann said. "You need an early night. Why don't you sleep in the study?"

I was grateful for the offer and soon climbed into bed. Despite my exhaustion, I just could not sleep. My brain was far too active, repeatedly going over the recent events. My mind always came back to the new era of high velocity weapons, and the horrors of their use by the police and soldiers. Even worse would be if such weapons reached the wrong hands, as now seemed likely with independent and unfriendly territories on South Africa's borders. I decided that neither my family nor I should ever be in front of guns like that. I did not want us to be behind such weapons either.

I got out of bed, went to my desk, and typed one-page letters to my old boss in St Louis and to several other professors I knew in America. I told them about the traumatic events of the last 36 hours and their implications. I asked for their help in finding a job and in emigrating. I slept solidly for the rest of the night.

My efforts to leave South Africa would occupy me for the next two years.

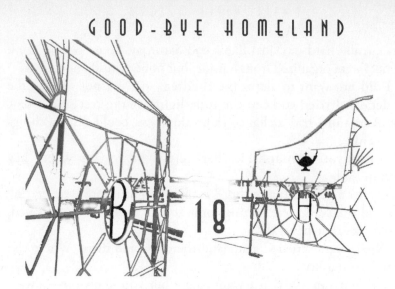

The disruption to life in Soweto and in the rest of South Africa persisted for months after the initial protests. Turbulence spread to many other areas by turns, suggesting the uprisings were organized rather than spontaneous. Riots continued in Soweto and other cities in the Transvaal and other provinces, with more people being injured, but nothing like the mayhem of the first two days; nine children had been killed in Soweto on the first day alone. There was much sympathy in the Black and Colored communities for the cause of the students.

The Government set up the Cillié commission to investigate the riots. They attributed the protests to agitators. There was uncertainty as to the organizations responsible, but there was clearly a Students' Representative Council involved, consisting of real students. In their report, probably conservative, the commission recorded 575 deaths and 2389 people injured around the country during the first eight months after the riots. Most of those killed were under twenty-one, while 104 were children under seventeen.

Property damage was enormous—notably the Library and Administration buildings at the black university of Zululand were burned down, as was the Legislative assembly building in Bophutatswana, a black 'Homeland.' The black University of Fort Hare was temporarily closed, due to attempted arson. Three hundred and fifty schools were ruined. In addition, 200 private homes of Africans, and hundreds of beerhalls, bottle stores, and shops, were also destroyed. Many administrative buildings, clinics, post offices, libraries and banks were also ruined. Over 300 PUTCO buses were burned out or severely damaged.

Following these disturbances 374 black people were arrested or detained by the police without trial. At least ten black consciousness groups were banned, including students' and parents' support organizations and a society of Black Journalists. A couple of newspapers were closed down. The leader of the Black Consciousness Movement, a young man called Steve Biko, was detained in April 1977 and subjected to proven brutality by the police, leading to his death from injuries in September 1977. The Soweto riots and Biko's death as a martyr became symbols of the African struggle against Apartheid. Many young blacks continued to join and belong to resistance movements underground in South Africa, in other African states, and overseas.

The education authorities made some concessions about language teaching, but the schools needed to be rebuilt. Students did not return to classes for months or years—many refused to go back at all. These children received no more formal education, joining the ranks of the unemployed. Some became 'Freedom Fighters,' or in many cases 'Tsotsis,' or township thugs. A whole generation was thus doomed to illiteracy and rootlessness.

At Baragwanath the atmosphere remained tense and unpleasant. The distinct deterioration in doctor-nurse relationships took many months to regain any semblance of normality. For the next six months I received a daily reminder of the problems when I drove through the police and army barracks to enter the hospital.

One day, during the week after the riots, I noticed a surgical colleague in the ICU bending over a bed, his unbuttoned white coat revealing a large handgun—a '.38 Special'—in a holster, exposed to full view. I felt that was inappropriate and likely to be somewhat inflammatory. At the same time, I clearly understood why he carried the weapon. This added to my personal discomfort and emotional conflict. It was certainly not the way I wanted to spend the rest of my life.

Daily papers and other news media were full of the riots. The *Sunday Times* carried graphic color pictures of many horrors from the week before. These included images of overturned and burning buses, destroyed schools and administrative buildings, corpses lying on the ground surrounded by wailing relatives, and rioters being chased and fired on by police or soldiers. The Government-owned television carried much more restrained (and probably censored) official versions of the traumatic events, with far less emphasis on army and police involvement. Debate in the media was constant and vociferous;

allegations and counter-claims were bandied about. Many solutions were offered, which the authorities were loath to accept.

The troubles soon spread to Alexandria Township, a squalid, poverty-stricken black area only a few miles from my home. People we knew lived on a secluded four-acre property situated in sight of the township, across less than a mile of open land. We visited them the following week and discovered to our horror that they had gone out to dinner on the weekend, leaving their teenage daughters at home with no protection. It clearly had not occurred to them that their children could have been in any kind of danger, nor did they accept that the risk might still be present. Discussion of the topic led nowhere and was soon abandoned due to rising tempers. That friendship was never quite the same again.

The incident reinforced my view that even educated white South Africans knew or cared little about what happened in the black communities. We remained unshaken in our beliefs and the plans we were making for the future.

The next week I took the family to visit my mother in Vereeniging and we discussed the situation. She was fluent in Sotho, one of the African languages, and often talked to her servants and their friends. She thus had a better grasp than most white people of the current situation and of how the blacks were thinking. She understood and agreed with my position. She was supportive, then and always, of our decision to leave the country. She was 76 years old and knew she would be lonely. She said she might move to another city, to be near her younger sister, but at her age she would not emigrate.

My brother and several of our friends were neither sympathetic with our views, nor enthusiastic about our plans to leave the country. Several were downright nasty. At the same time, many white people were planning to emigrate, resulting in much discussion and bitter humor. What some called 'white flight' and a 'brain drain,' others referred to as 'the chicken run,' or 'rats leaving the sinking ship,' depending upon their own viewpoints. Sadly, there was at least a grain of truth in each of the four analogies.

There were many Jewish people in the medical field, and they were prominent among those wishing to leave, but the desire to do so was neither confined to Jews nor to doctors. Ever able to make jokes about themselves, they would ask each other the question: "What's the definition of a patriot?" Answer: "A Jewish doctor who can't sell his house in Houghton." (One of Johannesburg's most expensive suburbs.)

Many South African whites made overseas journeys, known as 'LSD trips,' a word play on the effects of the hallucinogenic drug and the acronym for British money—LSD or pounds, shillings and pence. The trips were meant to 'Look, See and Deposit' (money).

Many young white people with the brains or special skills and some capital were planning to get out of the country as soon as they could. Others, on the other hand, appeared complacent, and did not openly acknowledge any danger to themselves or to their fellow whites. Some would stay in the country for truly patriotic reasons, and some for lack of appropriate English language skills or of sufficient capital to start a new life elsewhere.

Many people who might have preferred to go were bound by family ties or business investments, or just could not get jobs elsewhere. Most English-speaking countries, including the USA, had restrictive immigration policies, requiring applicants to possess job skills that were needed or to have capital for starting a business. So the topic of emigration was on many lips, resulting in acrimonious discussions and some strained friendships.

Fairly soon after the riots an old medical school friend, Dan, returned from Australia for a visit. He had emigrated several years before, having felt anxiety for the future at that time. We spent some time discussing the situation and Dan finally said: "You know, John, it's surprising, but you're the only one of my friends talking like this."

"I'm sure you're right, Dan," I replied, my voice slowly rising. "The reason is simple. *They just don't get it.* Most of our mutual friends don't even know where Soweto is, or even Baragwanath. They also don't work at Bara. They've never seen a real person with a bullet wound, *let alone a mangled sixteen-year old corpse with a hole blasted through it by a high velocity bullet from an assault rifle!*

"Our friends all live very comfortably in smart modern homes, with gardens neatly tended by their black adult 'garden boys.' They have one or more live-in black servants, who sleep in tiny backyard rooms and are paid a pittance, with minimal time off. They can't speak their servants' languages and they certainly don't know their last names, or those of their husbands or children."

"OK, OK, I believe you. I do see your point, John," Dan replied.

"Sorry for the outburst, Dan, but we're having a hard time dealing with the decision. *You know*—you've been through it. I've not had any replies to the letters I wrote to my professors in the USA. I haven't thought much about Australia, but I do have you there and Chris in New Zealand for advice and help. You know how tough England was job-wise when we left. I suspect getting a consultant post in Great Britain won't be any easier now.

"As for Canada, about a year ago, after I had spoken at a conference in Rio, I flew up there and took a trip across the country to assess the situation. It was only October, but it was already pretty cold. It was frozen solid in Winnipeg, and so was I. A Canadian Medical Society official told me that despite my double F.R.C.S. diplomas and my specialist status in both Britain and South Africa, I would have to re-do all my training. If I wanted to live in the habitable areas within 80 miles of the U.S. border, I would have to re-take my basic medical exams. But if I cared to work with polar bears and Eskimos in the frozen north, I could come right on in! A professor of surgery gave me an article showing the lack of need for more surgeons in five Canadian provinces. So I guess that rules out Canada."

"John, I really feel for you. I just hope for everyone's sake that you're wrong. South Africa is certainly in need of some changes, and I hope they'll be peaceful. You know you'll have our full support if you want to try Australia."

I arrived home one Monday and Ann handed me a letter from my old chief in St Louis, where I had done a surgical oncology fellowship ten years before. Dr. Bascomb was alarmed and sorry to hear the news, but had no jobs vacant at the time. He did suggest contacting Dr. Graham Harris, who was starting a new surgical program in West Virginia. I discussed the news after supper with Ann, who felt it was worth a try. It might not be too hard to persuade the children, since John Denver's mellifluous voice singing 'West Virginia, Mountain Mama' frequently reverberated through the Hunt household. I felt we were already halfway there. That thought was a bit premature.

Now started a busy time. As a first step I wrote to Dr. Harris, enclosing my CV (resume) and received a letter and a phone call expressing interest. That call, the first of many, came late at night, after I was already asleep. I was fascinated every time Dr. Harris' very polite secretary, oblivious to our differing time zones, told me to 'have a good day.' But I was still most grateful for the call.

Seemingly endless paperwork now had to be done. Meantime, I wrote to several other contacts I had made in the USA and Australia to try and set up visits. When I was ready, I bought a 'Round the World' air ticket, with the help of a pharmaceutical house that was obligated to me for the performance of much free work on their behalf during my years at Baragwanath. Amongst other things, I had designed one of their best-selling intravenous fluids and several others, receiving no royalty or other reward, except for intellectual satisfaction. I had also helped organize an intravenous fluid conference under their sponsorship, together with my anesthetist friend Jules Brobeck and a Cape Town doctor.

I started my own 'LSD trip' exactly one year after the Soweto riots. I planned to visit several places in America and return via Australia and New Zealand. My first stop was in West Virginia, to see Dr. Graham Harris. I was very hospitably received in Huntington and was clearly needed for the new surgery program in a brand new, community-based medical school. After several days I called Ann and said I was satisfied with the prospects for a job there and was sure Doctor Harris would do all he could to ease our immigration formalities. The community was suitable for bringing up the children, possibly far better than one of the big cities we had considered. My plan to visit half a dozen places in three countries now seemed redundant. I decided rather to rely on one person who really needed my services and was prepared to go to bat for me.

I cancelled the rest of the trip and spent a few more days looking around the area and taking care of a mountain of paperwork. I opened an account at a local bank and deposited most of what I had left of my travel allowance. Dr. Harris' wife, Elaine, was on faculty at Marshall Medical School as a researcher in the basic sciences. She gave me a list of textbooks I would need to prepare for the many exams I knew lay ahead. I returned home via New York City and stopped at Barnes and

Noble, where I bought a huge pile of books to take home. I wondered if this was 'Mission Impossible.'

Back at Bara there was still plenty to do, with the old five-day rhythm continuing unabated. I was also heavily involved with a research project in esophageal cancer that I had been working on for years. The hospital was admitting an increasing number of these cases; over 150 a year at that time. They mostly came for treatment very late in the course of the disease, when they could no longer eat or drink, with scant hope for successful treatment. This epidemic was unique to the African Bantu population, particularly those who lived in or came from the Xhosa-speaking area of Transkei in the Eastern Cape Province. The incidence of the disease was very low in whites and midway between the two races in the Colored population. There were other 'hot spots' in China and Iran, so this had become a subject of avid worldwide investigation, to find both a cause and a cure.

When I started the work some years earlier, I knew nothing about computers. At that time the data and programming all had to be entered on punch cards. A medical student with computer skills helped me set up detailed questionnaires and data collection sheets. I obtained a Cancer Society grant for a black social worker, Mr. Mokoena, to administer the questionnaire to both the cancer patients and an equal number of 'controls.' These were in-patients who did not have the cancer. Each one was matched for age, sex and race with one of the cancer victims. The five general surgical units collaborated in a clinical trial of treatment, with data entered on similar computer sheets.

This project had become my avocation, filling my spare time. My office was now crammed with large X-ray film boxes, each containing the data from a dead esophageal cancer patient or one of the controls. There was only room for my desk and a chair.

One line of enquiry was to study the amount and nature of the alcoholic drinks they used. Since the Shebeens served some badly adulterated brews, the surgeons felt these beverages might hold the key. This formed a detailed part of the survey. I asked Mr. Mokoena to bring me some 'Skokiaan,' one of the notorious drinks that many of my patients drank. He brought it one afternoon and Mokoena tried to open the bottle in my hot west-facing office. As he did so, the neck of the bottle broke, and the high pressure of the brew spewed the contents out like champagne, all over the two of us, the desk and many of the records. The strong, sickly, beer smell lingered there until I left the country.

The project was already past the data collection stage and I had to make sure the forms were correctly completed and then get them ready for punch card entry I also had to learn computer-based statistics, using the SPSS system, and how to punch the data onto cards. Some kind faculty members at Wits University statistics department helped me over these hurdles. I then proceeded with the real analysis, which was fascinating.

Each day, as soon as I could leave work, I took my stack of punch cards to the big IBM 360 computer on the University main campus. I stood in line to put the cards of the program I was going to run into the card reader, and I would return in a few hours for the results. If my printout was very thin, I knew I had made a mistake in the instructions and would have to track it down, re-punch the cards and begin again. If I got back a fat pile of paper, I had made a different error, causing the computer to print out reams of meaningless sheets. I soon learned the meaning of GIGO, 'garbage in—garbage out.'

But sometimes, like Goldilocks' bed, my printout was 'just right.' This was cause for great joy, like getting a surprise birthday present as a child. I spent many hours poring over the data and planning my next computer assault on the database.

Later that year there was an esophageal cancer congress in Cape Town. By that stage I had sufficient data to be able to present two papers at the meeting, which were afterwards included in the book of the proceedings. From the point of view of causation of the disease, the research showed that the patients with esophageal cancer were those who both smoked and drank a lot, statistically very different from the controls. I did not find any more exotic or ethnic-based cause.

When I went to the Cape for the Esophageal Cancer meeting, there would be an opportunity to write the E.C.F.M.G. exam, which was required of all doctors wishing to enter the USA, as evidence of their competence. This involved considerable burning of the midnight oil for many weeks, trying to come to grips with the pile of textbooks I had bought.

I first browsed through the biochemistry book. The subject had been reinvented in the 25 years since I attended medical school, with brand new terminology and concepts. DNA had been described by Watson and Crick a year after I graduated, and was now just a starting point for modern medical students. To master the field would have taken me years of hard work. I did not have the time available. So I closed the biochem book and studied the remaining subjects. Psychiatry was easy to learn because of my previous interests. Immunology was also fairly easy, since my year in the USA gave me a good grounding in what was now 'cutting edge science.' Surgery, of course, I knew well.

Though I had never previously *seen* a multiple-choice exam, I passed the test with good scores. It provided great experience for the two further examinations I would face before being able to work in the United States.

Every week that passed we waited for news on my application for an Immigrant visa, but nothing came. I had provided evidence that I was in the category of 'A person of International eminence,' having lectured at I.C.U. conferences in Rio de Janeiro and Giessen, Germany. Doctor Harris documented the need for my services in both the community and the V.A. Hospital, and his own inability to recruit someone in the USA. He was frustrated because he really needed help at Marshall, yet could not even get the INS authorities in Pittsburgh to take the paperwork out of their pigeonholes. He made repeated late night phone calls and wrote me many letters on the topic.

Dr. Harris finally appealed to West Virginia's powerful senior senators, Robert Byrd and Jennings Randolph. They quickly understood the problem and found a solution. They attached a mini-bill to other legislation. Its passage allowed Dr. John Hunt to enter the USA and provide needed skills at the Marshall University V.A. Medical Center Hospital. Doctor Harris called with the news. Both he and I were ecstatic. Things were moving at last.

It was now time to start talking to the children about the move. At ages 17, 14 and 7, they were all happily in school, involved with activities and friendships that they were not anxious to break up. So the discussions lasted for months, and included the fate of 'Rags,' our Jack Russell terrier. The children were adamant on that—'No Rags, No America.' Ann made plans for the dog to spend the required six months in quarantine. She also planned to take the children to America via Europe, to make the trip into an exciting holiday.

In April 1978, the long awaited visa arrived for John Hunt and family to enter the USA. It would be null and void if not used within three months.

We had not anticipated this deadline—it had been so long in coming. We had to sell the house and cars. There was a double garage full of 16 years' worth of treasures and junk. We had many 220-volt appliances that wouldn't work in the USA and had to be sold or given away. I had two transformers made for items we thought essential to take. We both worked day and night to accomplish the many tasks required before we could emigrate.

The children were excited about the change, but upset at the thought of losing their friends. Our black Xhosa servant, Beauty, was a favorite with the children and she loved them dearly. She lived on the property with her husband, her baby Trevor, aged 18 months, and his babysitter, aged six. She was terribly upset at the news, asking what would become of us without her to look after us and what would become of her and her family without her employer. She really wanted to go to America with the family and couldn't understand why this was not feasible.

The house was sold for a ridiculously low price, to lock in a suitable deal and transfer date. The cars would be delivered for sale at the last minute. I told all my black friends in the theaters and wards about my departure, and the need to sell electric appliances and the television set. By that time electrical supply had reached many homes in Soweto, so there was a lot of interest.

We arrived home at mid-afternoon one day to find that three of the black Sisters had come to see the appliances. Beauty had kept them all standing around in the lounge and would not allow them to sit down—her idea of the correct social order. Ann came in and asked them all to be seated and started to get to know the nurses. Beauty grudgingly went to make tea at Ann's request. The Sisters drank their tea and, after more pleasant conversation, made their choices of the appliances and took their leave. Beauty then said with disdain: "One

CHAOS IN THE RESUSITATION ROOM
ON MY LAST CHRISTMAS AT BARA HOSPITAL.

of those nurses asked me to work for her. I said no. I will never work for a black person."

We were flabbergasted at this insight into Beauty's concept of her world.

My duties at Baragwanath continued until two weeks before I left the country. My last night of intake was a Saturday, with the usual month-end plus weekend payday celebrations going on in Soweto. Both the 'Pit' and the Resuscitation Room were loaded with yelling, groaning, stinking, half naked, bleeding humanity. The staff was fully extended already and I was there, working as hard as I could to help.

Yet another dying 'Stab Heart' was pushed into the 'operating'-corner of the room, crammed next to other victims. I verified the man was dead as he entered the room. I called a houseman to start an IV line. I hastily put on a gown and some gloves while a sister opened a drum. She threw antiseptic solution on the chest and handed me a knife. There was not the time or space between the patients to draw the curtains round the gurney.

I slashed open the chest and was able to force the ribs far enough apart to get my hand in the chest and start cardiac compression. I grabbed the Finochietto and wound the ribs open, slit the pericardium and soon saw the hole, with blood coming out in a weak stream, since the heart was already responding. The anesthetist soon arrived and gave a muscle relaxant to control the patient's breathing, intubate him and give some oxygen.

The patient on the next gurney was an unlucky Bara Staff Nurse who had been stabbed by her drunken husband. At that crucial point, with blood squirting in her direction and pouring over the edges of the gurney, she woke up and looked into the open chest wound. She promptly passed out again. She must have really thought she was in Hell. A student took a picture of the chaotic scene. I will remember that night forever.

There was one more hurdle for me to leap. The U.S. immigration laws for doctors had been tightened in 1976, requiring visa candidates to have higher professional and educational standards than in previous years. A more stringent examination would not be designed for another two years, so I was initially told to write the E.C.F.M.G. By the time I had permission to enter the USA a new exam had been created, called the V.Q.E. or Visa Qualifying Exam. I would now have to take this exam. The first one would be held in Johannesburg in a few weeks. I pulled more all-nighters, trying to glean all I could from my pile of books. I again did not touch biochemistry, but boned up even more on my strongest subjects—Surgery, Immunology and Psychiatry.

The venue for the examination was the new Rand Afrikaans University. I was amazed to see there almost everyone I had ever known in Medicine, from all over South Africa. Scores of doctors were preparing to leave the country, as I was. They included many of the best and brightest faculty members of several Medical Schools—a sobering thought.

I finished all the questions I could answer. I felt I had done quite well. Then I looked again at the biochemistry questions. I couldn't even understand the words. For the fun of it I took a stab at each one, since there was no penalty for wrong answers. I knew I was unlikely to improve my score. In the foyer afterwards, a group of us gathered round a professional biochemist, asking about a particularly abstruse question. The man confessed that even he did not know what the examiners were talking about. He had barely understood some of the questions in his own subject. I felt fully justified in having ignored biochemistry.

A few weeks later I got the news I wanted: I had passed the V.Q.E. Ironically, they gave me a free E.C.F.M.G! My way to America was now clear.

It now remained to set a date for my departure, in order to beat the deadline for U.S. entry, to resign my job officially and to get tax clearance. We also had to arrange financial matters. Emigrants were allowed to take out of the country only a fixed, relatively small amount of money, as a 'settling-in allowance.' The rest of our capital had to remain in South Africa to help prevent a massive outflow of funds from the country at that time of instability. At least it was better than one of the independent African states. Emigrants from there could take only one hundred pounds and a bed!

Despite all our efforts, the garage was not yet empty by my deadline. Much more had to be done. Ann remained to take care of it before leaving for the European leg of her trip with the children. The packers, when they finally came, took 186 packages of all sizes and various shapes, all carefully numbered, for shipment to the USA in a container.

Ann and the children would say goodbye to Rags at the last minute. All arrangements had been made for his quarantine and his eventual flight to the USA in six months.

We visited my mother during my last week, and she was still bent on staying in South Africa. My brother also saw no reason to leave. Our friends were now about evenly divided between those who were envious and could well follow us in the future, and those who, for a variety of reasons, were determined, or forced, to stay in the country.

The parting from Beauty and Trevor was traumatic. She still did not understand why the family was leaving her. She promised to write.

I found it bitterly hard to say good-bye at the airport. To leave my wife and children was bad enough. But at least I knew I would soon see them again. Leaving South Africa was harder. I could not really believe that this was the end of the line. I felt part traitor, part unfaithful lover. I did not want to look back. I was determined not to return for at least two years, because I knew I would not be able to endure the emotional strain of leaving again.

After a tiring thirty-hour flight, on 18<sup>th</sup> July 1978, just two years after the Soweto riots, I landed at John F. Kennedy Airport. I passed through customs and then immigration. And there they gave me that most prized possession: my *green card*.

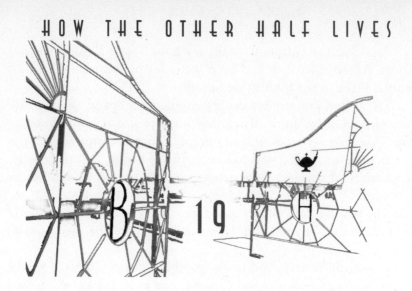

## A SOUTH AFRICAN BACKGROUNDER

### 1970s WHITE REALITY & PHILOSOPHY

In the mid twentieth century, apart from any lunatic fringes, relations between the races in South Africa seemed to be excellent. No one jostled in the streets or pushed anyone else off the sidewalk. Service in restaurants, stores and businesses was polite and efficient. People were civil and seemed friendly. White employers cared about their servants and looked after them. The servants, in turn, cared about their employers and their families. Many white children were brought up by black 'Nannies,' who loved them and cared for them, and the families loved their Nannies. In business, industry and the mines, similar relationships occurred, with some good workday friendships developing. In the gold mines, safety for all depended on everyone pulling together. There was no room for fighting.

Africans and Coloreds clearly lived on a far lower scale than the whites. Segregation, Apartheid and the political, financial and social realities under which they existed hurt them deeply, but they did not reveal this in everyday relationships with whites. In the minds of most white people, that was the way things were. Very few would go to bat for the blacks and try and correct social injustices. The status quo was very comfortable. The blacks 'knew their place' in society. Why rock the boat?

The African and Colored people knew far more about the lifestyles of whites than vice versa. This insight came from generations of working for and with white people in their homes, factories, farms and mines, buying consumer goods and dealing with bureaucracy and the law. American and other foreign films introduced a few to life in other countries. The differences in living standards between master and servant were painfully apparent to non-whites,[1] producing envy and frustration, together with higher personal aspirations.

On the other hand, white people, either at personal or corporate level, generally knew very little about their non-white employees or how they lived. They might have seen some squalid housing, shaken their heads, and said: '*They* should do something about it,' *they* meaning either the authorities or the inhabitants of the dilapidated houses. Few whites had ever been in a black person's home. Many whites failed to see either black poverty or poor housing as problems for which they should bear any responsibility.

Most white employers did not know their employees' last names. Whites had always called both Africans and Coloreds by their first names only. This patronizing habit was a sore point with black and colored people. Even though some Bantu last names were hard for whites to pronounce, this was no excuse for ignoring them. Only at the professional level were blacks properly addressed, e.g., Dr. Ngubane or Mr. Tshabalala. Even more humiliating, many whites called blacks or colored people 'boys' or 'girls,' even when they were grandparents with grizzled hair. For example, a young white 'madam' might have said to her friend over afternoon tea, which was served by a middle-aged black servant: "Did you see that nice new native girl who's working for me? She made the tea. Her name is Jane, sister of the girl who works next door. They're from the same tribe as our garden boy, so they all get along. Perhaps we'll have some peace around here now."

"You're so lucky," her friend replied. "My maid just left me in the lurch, with no replacement. I don't know what I'm going to do! Our boy's no good in the house. We'll eat burgers at the 'Doll's House' until I get help. Cooking and washing up without a maid is such a drag—and all that laundry!"

The most politically correct way to refer to a black person has evolved, however. While I was young, the term 'Kaffir,'[2] in colloquial and official use for centuries, was being phased out in favor of 'Native.' This gave way to the ethnologically correct word 'Bantu.' The word for a person, 'umuntu', comes from the same root. The positive words 'African,' and 'black' were also acceptable. Sensitivity among better-educated whites has gradually increased, with use of the less pejorative terms.

In my childhood home, servants were treated with respect. My mother was an English language teacher, who could also speak Afrikaans and two Bantu languages. She often employed black servants who spoke no English or Afrikaans, and who knew nothing about domestic work in a white household. She taught her servants both language and work skills, enabling them to take better-paying jobs. She used their languages for conversation and to organize work in the house. During childhood both my older brother, Llewellyn, and I learned a lot about the black people and picked up some of their languages. During our teens we played with many children of the Bantu farmhands on my uncle's ranch. I liked and respected them, and I thought they would work on the ranch one day. These experiences gave me a better understanding of Bantu people than most whites had.

Until I went to Medical School, the only black people I had met were in menial jobs. I was unaware they could achieve anything better. I knew black children also attended school, and assumed they would have jobs. I never gave it much thought, since everyone seemed satisfied with the status quo. That was just the way things were.

When I started the anatomy course in my second year at Medical School, racial integration at Wits University was in its early days and the authorities were being cautious. My class was asked if they would work with Bantu medical students in the lab, where six students used each cadaver. I agreed, but some classmates refused, missing a great broadening experience. I became firm friends with two black students. One graduate of the class, Nthato Motlana, became a physician in Soweto and a black political leader.

By comparison with America and First World countries, the living standard of much of the white population was upper middle class and above. Many suburban homes had in-ground swimming pools and landscaped gardens of half an acre or more. Often, tennis courts and two-car garages were standard. This lifestyle was boosted by the availability of cheap labor, both at home and at work. Even humble white households often had a black 'maid' to do the hard work. In more affluent homes a 'maid' and a 'garden boy' were *de rigueur*. Many upscale homes had numerous servants of both sexes. Most servants were housed in small back rooms, separate from the main house. Much of this luxury was offset by the need for high garden walls and burglar alarms. Despite my very modest government salary, Ann and I and the three children shared in the luxury, with a home, a pool, two cars, a maid and a gardener, two servants' rooms and a burglar alarm!

On the other hand, a number of upper middle class white people, including some of our friends, chose not to have black servants for a variety of reasons—philosophical, political, or just personal preference. Many poorer white homes had no servants.

A white housewife could easily justify the low wages of her maid, "because that's the going rate, and if she didn't work, her children would starve. In any event," the argument continued, "she gets a free room, eats from my table, gets a half-day off per week for church and she can buy all our old clothes. She gets free health care at Bara, and she can have a major operation for nothing. She's not educated, so she can't do anything else." This rationalization did have a certain logic.

Few whites accepted that it might be better to pay a living wage, so that employees could buy their own food and clothes, afford a home, educate their children and pay for their own health care. Sadly, many black women might then not have been employed, since their white madams could perhaps not have afforded to pay them enough to provide all the above necessities. That, unfortunately, was the South African scene in microcosm.

South African goods, such as gold, fruit, wine or wool, were only competitive in world markets because of low non-white wages. Employers could not pay their workers more under the existing structure. But poor productivity per man-hour made uneducated 'cheap labor' expensive. Modern Africa faced the alarming paradox that automation, with its great potential, had arrived when its burgeoning unemployed population lacked the education to learn the necessary skills. Labor-intensive industries would lose out in world markets to those that increased productivity by use of automation and a trained workforce. Bridging the education gap is expensive and slow, requiring much goodwill on all sides.

The legitimate aspirations of the majority black and colored populations could not be satisfied by revolution without causing chaos. Though natural evolution would be too slow for non-whites and too fast for the whites, it might be the only sensible solution. Violence and political instability would probably cause massive flight of white people, with their intellectual and monetary capital, and lead to worldwide disinvestment in South Africa. There were not enough blacks and coloreds with educational, administrative or financial skills to take over should the white population emigrate (or even be killed, for that matter).

The aim had to be universal education and vocational training and the advancement of all qualified people to positions of skill and responsibility in a racially equitable manner. Only interracial goodwill and political stability would allow the country to reach the goal of equality in all fields of endeavor. The whites would have to realize that the blacks and other colored people were their equals in every way, with similar rights and privileges. Equally, the majority black and Colored population and the outside world would have to realize that the whites were also South Africans, with nowhere else to go. They had to be seen as part of the solution—not made part of a new problem.

## THE PAST & THE PEOPLES
### 'A WORLD IN ONE COUNTRY.'

The history and complex relationships of the many peoples of South Africa are hard to summarize. Of the forty million population, about 75% are Bantu, 13.5% White, 8.5% Colored and 2.5% Indian, with smaller numbers of Jews, Greeks, Portuguese, Chinese and others. There are nine discrete Bantu language and ethnic groups. The white groups have two languages—English and Afrikaans. Both have been South Africa's official language. The Coloreds mostly speak Afrikaans. The other minority groups have their own tongues. The common thread is English, necessary for survival in the modern world. To borrow a phrase from the SA Tourism Industry—South Africa is truly 'A World in One Country.'

In 1602 the Dutch East India Company (VOC)[3] was chartered to trade with India and the East. By 1650 Holland was the strongest European trading nation. But these voyages cost many lives. On most passages nearly half the crew died of scurvy,[4] due to absence of fresh fruit and vegetables. The Company decided to establish a 'halfway station' at the 'Cape of Storms.' Passing ships had for decades traded with the local people and left mail under a 'Post Office Stone', for pickup by the next ship going in the other direction.

The Company found out that people could survive at the Cape. In 1647 a Dutch ship, the *Haarlem*, was wrecked there and the survivors waited a year for another VOC ship to pass and take them and the ship's cargo home. Jan van Riebeeck, a surgeon, was on the rescue ship. He reported to the VOC Company very favorably on the Cape, but emphasized the dangers of the local people. So in 1652 the VOC sent five ships, led by van Riebeeck, to the Cape to start a fort and a halfway and refreshment station. There they would produce fresh vegetables, fruit, meat and wine and provide care for the sick crewmembers.

The first humans the Dutch encountered were smallish, pale brown people, then called *Bushmen* and *Hottentots*. They are now known as San and Khoikhoi, collectively called the '*Khoisan*.' There were only about twenty thousand *San* people, who were hunter-gatherers, and they had a loosely organized society without fixed villages. They had amazing hunting, tracking and survival abilities. They hunted with bows and poison-tipped arrows. Once they had shot an animal, they could run for many miles in pursuit, waiting for their poison to work. They kept caches of water in ostrich eggshells hidden throughout their very dry territory. Many of their beautiful rock paintings have been found scattered in caves throughout South Africa, some dating back 26,000 years. They have helped provide details of San history, lifestyle and demographics. The San language was unlike those of the Bantu, but influenced some of them. It has many unusual 'click' sounds, similar to some used in Xhosa, which is otherwise totally different in grammar and vocabulary. Only a handful of the San people survive, largely in Botswana, a neighboring African country.

There were probably one hundred thousand *Khoikhoi*. They were more pastoral and lived in better-organized communities of up to 2,500 people. They had herds of long-horned cattle and fat-tailed sheep. They traded cattle, sheep, copper and iron with their Bantu neighbors and with the Dutch settlers. Their cattle gave rise to the 'Afrikander' strain, still bred in South Africa today.

The *Khoisan* were initially thought to be different from the Bantu on grounds of their languages and their smaller stature and paler skin color. They are now thought to be genetically related but to have 'developed independent gene pools under environmental influences.'[5] They lived in the southwestern Cape, where there were no Bantu tribes, near the Dutch colony and in areas to which the farmers later migrated. The Khoisan had a love-hate relationship with the settlers. They marauded and stole white-owned goods and cattle, all the while trading with and working for the whites and providing sexual partners.

There was a lot of interracial sex involving Khoisan women and white men. The VOC initially encouraged the mostly male white settlers to breed with the local people. Much miscegenation occurred with both Khoisan and slave women, before and after the arrival of Dutch wives and other women. A number of old white South African families have occult Khoisan and slave ancestry through the female line. Two reasons for freeing a slave were marriage to a white or conversion to Christianity.

The Company needed labor for farms, gardens, orchards and wineries. They did not allow the Khoisan to be enslaved, so they imported *slaves* from elsewhere. They employed some Khoikhoi to work alongside the slaves. Other Khoisan traded with the Company and the settlers. The marauding and theft by the Khoisan, and the law enforcement required, caused much racial friction. 'Straf-commandos'[6] were often sent out to punish the raiders.

White people's diseases, such as measles, influenza and smallpox, often decimated the Khoisan, since they had no prior exposure. As the white colony expanded, many Khoisan became more integrated into Cape life. But some migrated to the north and west, together with renegade half-breed people (called 'Basters'[7]) and formed a group called the Oorlams. They melded with Bantu tribes in those areas, such as the Griquas and Korannas.

The *VOC slaves* came from many countries, with a variety of ethnic and religious origins. Many were Muslims from India, Bangladesh, Ceylon and Indonesia or Batavia. There were also many blacks from West Africa,[8] Dahomey, Guinea, Angola, and from the East coast—Abyssinia, Mozambique, and the islands of Mauritius and Madagascar. Few of the earliest slaves at the Cape were of South African Bantu or

Khoisan origin.[9] There were usually as many slaves in the Cape as there were whites.

The Dutch farmers who migrated inland from the Cape took their slaves, Khoisan servants and 'Free Blacks' with them. During clashes with Bantu tribes the farmers killed many tribesmen, reclaimed their own stolen cattle, took more from the blacks, and often captured some women and children and indentured them as servants or slaves up to the age of twenty-one. These practices continued well into the 19th Century.

The 'Cape Colored' people arose from several sources—the remnants of the Khoisan, the progeny from early Dutch miscegenation with Khoisan and slaves, the freed slaves and their offspring, and the original Free Blacks—all the Cape underclasses. The present 'Cape Colored' community remains concentrated in the western Cape, though colored people live throughout the country. They are often of paler color and shorter stature than typically results from black-white intermarriage. They are frequently Muslims due to their slave heritage. Afrikaans is their home language and it contains many words derived from Malay and slave influences. The Coloreds have been regarded, and indeed regard themselves, as ethnically distinct from the Bantu. They have called themselves 'Bruin Mense' (Brown People), and justifiably regarded their race as the illegitimate children of the whites. Their understanding that their white forebears had abandoned them has left a residue of deep bitterness.

Bantu people moved south into the Transvaal between 300 and 1,000 A.D. By 1652 many tribes were already established in parts of South Africa. The Bantu cultures were mostly feudal in nature. The chiefs had many wives—each in a separate dwelling—and the most cattle. They maintained much of their power by marriage bonds and by allowing others to marry into the royal family. The most powerful chieftains delegated power to sub-chiefs. The Bantu had quite advanced systems of deliberation and justice.

Their languages had about 20,000 words, like basic English. There were no written languages or history, and thus there was no formalized academic education. Children learned by oral tradition, experience or apprenticeship. Witchdoctors had great power. The

Bantu had primitive metal tools. Some tribes mined iron and copper. They cultivated millet or 'Kaffircorn,' for food and making beer. In the 1700s they started growing corn. They did not have the wheel. Ploughing was done with a spike on a sled pulled by an ox. They were pastoral people, for whom owning many cattle signified wealth. They would move to a better area if the grazing deteriorated. The women worked the fields. The father of a bride received payment in cattle, 'Lobola,'[10] which he had to return in case of infertility.

There were hundreds of tribes of varied size. Their chiefs were hereditary rulers, but they often changed by conquest. Some tribes were powerful, with large armies. Shaka, Dingaan, Cetswayo, Mzilikazi, Dingiswayo and Moshweshwe stand out in history as leaders. In the early 1800s, starting around 1820, a massive upheaval and forced movement of people, known as the 'Mfecane'[11] (the Crushing), occurred. This was related in part to a prolonged drought on the east coast and the need for more land to support the Zulu people. The trouble began when Dingiswayo was murdered and Shaka took over as chief of the Zulus. He and his 'Impis'[12] went on a rampage amongst neighboring tribes, producing waves of bloodshed, slaughter and conquest. Entire tribes fled tens or hundreds of miles to the north, west and south and settled in new areas of the country. The eastern part of South Africa became unstable for many years.

Dutch farmers or 'Voortrekkers'[13] entered this changing milieu as they spread across the country in search of land and freedom (See section 3). The Bantu repeatedly attacked these white invaders. Much written white South African history revolves around these battles and the changes in power structure and land ownership that ensued. In 1838 the Boers[14] defeated Dingaan in the famous battle of Blood River. December 16th was set aside as a public holiday, called Dingaan's Day, and later named the Day of the Covenant. For black people this was a day of fear and loathing. Whites and blacks thus experienced their bitter separateness with each annual celebration.

South Africa's white population had two major groups: Afrikaans- and English-speaking people. The Afrikaners were the larger group, descended from the 1652 settlers—the officials and workers on the original five Dutch ships, who started the Cape settlement. Some then migrated inland and settled in among the Bantu tribes. They were of Dutch, German and French descent, bearing family names from those countries. Initially Dutch was the official language at the Cape. Over time a simpler language evolved, called Afrikaans, derived from all three mother tongues, mostly Dutch. It had strong influences from Malay slave words, English, Bantu, and Khoisan languages. It has been, with English, the country's official language.

The English started arriving at the Cape in the 18th century and took it over in 1806. They stayed in control through the 19th century, when their numbers grew by immigration, both from the 1820 and other eastern Cape and Natal settlers and from those people attracted by the discovery of diamonds and gold after 1860. There are fewer English than Afrikaners because of their later arrival and because the Boers favored larger families. The British were city-oriented and the Afrikaners more rural, producing different lifestyles and politics.

Other white groups came to South Africa. Jews, among the first, have played a major role in financial, commercial, professional and cultural development. They have integrated into their communities, aligning more with the English. Smaller numbers of other Europeans came and made contributions in many fields. These include the Greeks and, after the independence of Angola and Mozambique, the Portuguese.

Indians came to the country in two waves. They first came to the Cape as slaves in the 17th century. Most Indians were brought to Natal after 1860, to work in the cane fields as indentured laborers, with renewable five-year contracts. They initially suffered many problems and abuses but were finally encouraged to remain in the country, because of their acquired skills, and were given land. Indian traders followed and prospered, spreading countrywide. By 1900 there were 100,000 Indians in Natal. They have done well in commerce and in the professions. The famous Mohandas K. Gandhi came to South Africa as an advocate for the Indians and developed there his doctrine of passive resistance.

Sir Alfred Milner, the Governor of the Transvaal, in 1904 brought Chinese laborers to work in the gold mines. They played a major role in the development of the mines. They have subsequently done well in commercial and professional fields.

Thus the whites and other minority groups are now 'Native South Africans' of many generations' standing. They are neither 'Colonists' nor 'Settlers'—they are South Africans with no ties to their ancestors' lands. South Africa is their homeland. They have nowhere to go unless they emigrate to a strange country.

For example, my wife's family on one side is in its ninth generation since her Huguenot ancestor came from France via Holland in 1747 as a VOC bookkeeper. Her genealogical database now has over 6,800 names descended from this one married man. Another of her ancestors arrived with van Riebeeck in 1652 and became one of the first 'Free Burghers.' That line now extends over thirteen generations.

Clearly, such whites, Indians and other minority groups, together with Khoisan, slaves, Bantu and many others, have built South Africa into the colossus of Africa, with a higher standard of living, a larger Gross Domestic Product, more miles of tarred roads and rail, more airports and telephones than the rest of the African continent together. The world must realize that the whites and other minority peoples must be part of the solution for South Africa. Without them in the mix, the country's economic, political and cultural foundations would crumble.

### DUTCH-ENGLISH SCHISM. WHITE EXPANSION. GREAT TREK. MINERAL REVOLUTION. BOER WARS.

South African politics in the late 19th and first half of the 20th century focused on divisions between the Afrikaans and English racial groups. The minority whites had the political power, even though much legislation concerned the blacks and coloreds. It is important to understand the background and reasons for the white schism.

Afrikaner antagonism to the English started in 1795, when the British first took over the Cape after 143 years of Dutch settlement and control by the Dutch East India Company. When the VOC started their halfway station at the Cape in 1652, they had no colonial intentions. The Dutch Government was not involved. The Company soon found itself in control of a large and expanding colony. The Governors were always high-ranking Company officials. The system worked for 140 years, but during the 1790s the VOC was overspending and becoming bankrupt. The administration of the large settlement became inefficient. The Cape farmers suffered a severe drought. Those on the frontier were upset that the Governor could not protect them from the Bantu tribes, so they refused to pay higher taxes.

In 1793 France declared war on England and Holland and in 1795 they invaded Holland. Both Britain and Holland had extensive trading operations in the East, so the Cape was of great strategic value. It was vital to keep it out of the hands of France. England took over the Cape in 1795 at the request of the exiled House of Orange (Dutch Royalty).[15] They met minimal local opposition.

The British had control for only eight years on that occasion. They made few changes, except to make English the official language. Prosperity increased but frontier disturbances continued. The winds of social enlightenment were stirring in Europe, with talk about human rights and the abolition of slavery. Some of this fervor reached the Cape. Mission schools were established for slaves, Khoisan and Bantu. The Bantu languages were formalized and started being written down. These increasing missionary activities created division and more discontent among the farmers. This was partly due to the unwillingness of some farmers to have their slaves converted to Christianity, and thus freed.

In 1798 the VOC became bankrupt and the Dutch Government took over the Company. After the Treaty of Amiens in 1803, the Dutch Government took control of the Cape for the first time. They appointed General Janssens as Governor and de Mist as Administrator, to govern the Cape as the 'Batavian Republic.' These two did well; they introduced major reforms and gained the farmers' confidence. Afrikaans became the official language. Dutch rule lasted only till 1806, when war broke out once more in Europe and the British again took over the Cape. This agreement was finalized in 1815, when Britain assumed a Dutch debt of six million pounds, which they owed to other European powers.

Thus a foreign people again dictated the Government of the Cape. Though prosperity increased, significant differences arose between the British administration and the Afrikaans people, particularly concerning race, slavery, the rule of law, and the collection of taxes. English again became the official language, and English immigration increased. In 1807 Britain banned slave trading in its colonies.

By 1806, the frontiers of white settlement were about 500 miles east and 375 miles north of Cape Town. This expansion of the community had started in 1657, when nine VOC employees—'The Free Burghers'[16]—were allowed to leave the Company and start their own farms. In 1679 twenty more Burghers were allowed to settle even further away, starting the town of Stellenbosch.

Farmers called 'Trekboers'[17] then started to migrate further and settle many miles north and east and inland, wherever they found fertile land, good grazing and water. As they traveled they clashed with many Bantu tribes. The Trekboers established their farms on land the blacks were occupying. They captured many, whom they often kept as slaves or 'indentured' workers. Thus started decades of black-white warfare, known as the 'Kaffir Wars'. Frontier conditions remained unsettled for decades, with constant raiding and fighting. A major Bantu attack on Grahamstown occurred in 1819.

In Great Britain at the same time there was great poverty and social unrest. The Government started 'Assisted Emigration' schemes. Over four thousand English people immigrated to the Albany district in the Eastern Cape to create a buffer zone between the white farmers and the Bantu tribes. These '1820 Settlers' had no prior knowledge of the conditions there. They arrived in the middle of the 'Kaffir Wars,' many suffering ruinous losses of life, property and crops. Some failed as farmers and moved to the towns. They stayed to become a substantial and successful English-speaking community, the forebears of many South Africans, including my family.

The English Government in 1834 passed a law freeing slaves in its colonies. Release of the slaves was preceded by four years of 'Apprenticeship.' For this and other reasons Afrikaner farmers were unhappy and soon started trying to escape from British rule. They met in secret to lay plans, send scouting parties ahead and form groups with defined leaders.

In 1836, many of these parties of 'Voortrekkers' headed out of the Cape in what was called the 'Great Trek.'[18] By 1840, over 15,000 people had left the Cape. They went mostly inland, north and east, seeking freedom, new land and a new life. The families traveled in groups, often taking different routes. They formed trains with their wagons, each drawn by twelve or more large, red, long-horned oxen and packed with family members and household goods. They took grain, herds of livestock and their slaves.

The causes of Voortrekker dissatisfaction were complex and went well beyond the abolition of slavery, since many of the farmers who were most affected remained in the western Cape. Most of those leaving came from the frontier and the eastern Cape, furthest from British control. The Trek was also not entirely socio-economic in origin, since many farmers who left were wealthy and sold their farms for next to nothing. Some Voortrekkers were people in debt. One leader, Piet Retief, was in deep financial trouble. For many, it was the spirit of adventure; others sought to acquire land for resale.

The Voortrekkers spread out widely across the country, reaching areas that became Natal, the Orange Free State and the Transvaal. They had frequent battles with the Bantu tribes they met. They defeated some and came to an uneasy co-existence with others. Their farms and villages were interspersed between black tribal land, resulting in continued raiding and wars and the capturing and indenturing of servants. The Boers set up their own republics in 'Natalia,' the Transvaal and the Orange Free State. The urge of the Afrikaners to be free of the British yoke continued for many years.

The Cape administration did not want to run such a large and rebellious country, since most trade was already conducted through the Cape. So at first they left the Boers alone. In 1843 they annexed Natalia, following protests over the Boer handling of slaves and for other reasons. The British also launched military actions against certain tribes. Complex alliances were formed and broken among farmers, Bantu tribes and the British, who systematically took control of most Bantu tribes and their land. The British fought some bloody battles with the Zulus.

Finally the Rinderpest[19] epidemic in 1896 killed the cattle of many white and black farmers and caused the latter to capitulate. The Cape Government then controlled the whole country, except for Boer Republics in the Transvaal and Orange Free State. Black areas became sources of labor for the farmers and, after 1860, for the diamond and gold mines and early industry—the 'Mineral Revolution.'

The Afrikaners waged two wars against Britain in the late 19th century. The first 'Boer War' in 1880 involved only a few hundred men. The Boers won this war, and a treaty with Britain gave independence from Cape rule to the Zuid Afrikaansche Republiek (Transvaal) under President Paul Kruger.

The second one, in 1899, was known as the Anglo-Boer war. It resulted in part from bad treatment of the 'Uitlanders,'[20] by the government of the ZAR, under an intransigent and aging President Kruger. The 'Uitlanders' were mostly British who came to the diamond and gold mines in the late 19th century, particularly after the discovery of gold in the eastern Transvaal, in 1870 and 1884, and near Johannesburg in 1886. They felt they were unfairly taxed and treated unequally before the law and had difficulty becoming citizens. They also resented the fact that many Hollanders (also Uitlanders) were active advisors to the Kruger administration and had obtained lucrative government contracts from them.

At the same time the British realized the great value of the diamond and goldfields and that the Transvaal would be the most valuable part of their colonial empire. They feared growing German power in South West Africa and Portuguese influence in Mozambique. The world was on the 'Gold Standard' and the Bank of England had low gold reserves.

The Afrikaners felt that British diamond- and gold-mining interests were making a grab for power. The abortive Jameson raid, also involving Cecil Rhodes, confirmed the Boer view. Kruger soon squashed that strange uprising.

Instead of negotiation, a destructive war ensued, from 1899 to 1902. This hard-fought battle ended with the defeat of the Boers and the Peace of Vereeniging. The Union of South Africa was created in 1910 and consisted of four provinces—the Transvaal, Orange Free State, Natal and Cape Province.

Despite the peace, the Afrikaners remained extremely bitter about the Boer War. The two main reasons were the British 'scorched earth' policy and their concentration camps. The 'scorched earth' policy was adopted to prevent the Boers from hiding and to stop their women from helping them. It was estimated that 30,000 farms and twenty villages were burned to the ground and destroyed, together with crops and livestock.

The concentration camps were established for the protection of Boer women and children. Many inmates died, by one account 20,000 people, due to measles, dysentery and primitive health conditions. This was nearly half the 44,000 white people who died as a result of the war. By another account, 28,000 white people died in the camps, 6,000 women and 22,000 children under the age of 16. Of blacks in the camps, 14,000 died. Only 4,000 Boers died in battle. Of the British troops, about 8,000 died fighting the Boers, while 13,000 died of diseases like dysentery and cholera, from drinking contaminated river water.

After the war, Sir Alfred Milner, the British Governor of the Transvaal, understood the severity of the destruction that occurred. He spent considerable sums of money to totally rehabilitate Boer farms, herds and crops. He also rebuilt the severely damaged railroads.

Despite Milner's efforts, Boer bitterness continued. The huge losses of women and children, farms and villages, had a chilling effect. This has been a matter for legend and heated debate ever since. A monument to the women and children in the camps stands in the city of Bloemfontein, inscribed 'To the eternal shame of England.' Much South African white politics has revolved around reliving the Boer War and the concentration camps.

For years after the Act of Union, the political parties were divided along language and racial lines, between the mainly urban English and the rural Afrikaans people. The Coloreds had voting rights and some Africans in the Cape had a limited franchise, but they had no real power. The 'Native Question' was often debated and much legislation was passed, but no effective or just solutions were found. The blacks and Coloreds remained 'second class citizens', providers of cheap labor. Many laws were aimed at maintaining that status. The United Party (essentially English) dealt with some of the land aspirations of the Africans by purchasing White-owned farms, to be used as black reserves. The farms of both an uncle and a friend of mine were expropriated for black settlement. Since blacks were over 70% of the population, the small amount of land purchased was grossly inadequate.

## PAYBACK TIME & APARTHEID POLITICS.

In 1948, nearly half a century after the Boer War, the Nationalist Party defeated the United Party at the polls. My friends and I stayed up the entire election night, listening to the radio. This surprise victory of the 'Nats' seemed to be the end of the world, particularly as Jan Smuts, the revered leader of the United Party, lost his parliamentary seat. For many years the Nationalists only had a majority of seats, not of voter numbers. This changed when they had disenfranchised both black and Colored voters, many years later.

The Nationalists first confirmed their ascendancy over the English. The civil service was 'Afrikanerized,' causing many English people to lose their jobs or not be promoted. Afrikaans became the main official language, causing reprinting of all official paperwork.

They then addressed black-white relationships, producing vast shifts in policy. Blacks outnumbered whites six to one. They were seen as a threat to white jobs, security and 'national purity.' Many poor and uneducated, mostly Afrikaner whites, had migrated from the farms to the cities, and needed employment, government support and protection. They lacked job skills. Blacks could have filled any unskilled positions for much lower wages.

The Nationalists solved the problem by passing laws to reserve jobs for certain racial groups and force the races to live in separate areas. These were the notorious Job Reservation Act and the Group Areas Act. To prevent further miscegenation, the Mixed Marriages Act and the Immorality Act were added. A Bantu Education Act was also passed to define and limit the scope of Africans' schooling to that of permanent servant status. The Racial Classification Act was then needed in order to label people and enforce all the other laws.

These draconian laws and their many offspring formed the basis of Apartheid,[21] which was dreamed up by the erstwhile academic, Dr. H.F. Verwoerd. The Nats later proposed individual Bantu 'Homelands,' or 'Bantustans,' where the blacks would have political rights. They would have no vote in South Africa, their birthplace, but could vote or become Prime Minister in their 'Homeland,' which they might never have seen. Ten 'Homelands' were partially implemented, but only four completed.

The rationale for Apartheid, which simply means 'Apartness,' was the idea of 'Separate Development' or 'Separate Freedoms'—'equality of whites and blacks in separate areas'. But equality never occurred, since housing, schooling, social amenities and job opportunities for the blacks and Coloreds remained inferior. The blacks were subjected to frequent harassment and brutality by the police for alleged infractions of the many laws and regulations that governed their lives.

As in America in earlier years, blacks and Coloreds, and indeed anyone considered 'Non-White,' had to use separate toilets, buses, train carriages and almost every other amenity of civilization. Education for blacks was conducted at a lower level than for whites, fitting them only for a life of subservience. That was the avowed goal of the administration.

Three major issues concerned the black peoples. The first was the notorious 'Pass Laws.' When I was young, my hometown enforced a curfew for blacks at 9 p.m. That practice ceased, but all blacks in South Africa had to carry an identity document at all times; whites did not. The Group Areas Act of 1950 forced blacks to carry an identity book, or 'Reference Book,' showing where they were entitled to live. Allegedly, this was done for 'influx control' to prevent country people moving to town and taking the jobs of those entitled to be there and straining already inadequate facilities.

The police could ask a black person at any time for his or her 'pass.' Anyone not carrying a valid identity document would be jailed, causing great inconvenience, expense, anger and frustration. Some people were summarily returned to their places of supposed origin. In 1960, a peaceful protest of these laws in the black township of Sharpeville led to the police killing 69 blacks, with 180 being injured. The same day, a similar meeting was held at Langa in Cape Town. Police killed three people and injured 47. These events sparked many protests and caused a sustained intensification of the anti-Apartheid struggle. Their echoes were heard around the world.

Another inhumanity perpetrated in the name of Apartheid was the forced removal and relocation of black people from their homes in areas considered to be unsuitable for their continued occupation. In 1950, amongst the first such moves was the relocation of the people of Sophiatown to the new area of Soweto. This was often called 'slum clearance,' and that rubric was partly accurate. But usually the land was simply used for the settlement of another racial group—often white. Ironically the white area that replaced Sophiatown was renamed 'Triomf' (Triumph) showing a complete absence of official feeling.

The clearance was often done without warning or compensation. Usually, no other accommodation was provided for those removed. They were dumped, with their few goods around them, on a bare piece of land, with no sewage, running water, or other infrastructure. One of the most notorious such forced removals was that of the whole area of 'District Six' in Cape Town, the multiracial home for many people, who had all been living there quite peacefully side by side for generations. After the land was cleared, the community refused to have anyone develop the site, and potential developers also declined to build there. It remains vacant to this day, except for a government technical college.

The third major issue was poor education. Black schools and facilities were inferior, with too few qualified teachers. Many Bantu and Colored children left school early to seek jobs. This caused a serious lack of non-whites with higher education and the ability to do better jobs or contribute to the advancement of their people. Whites filled all the skilled positions, but there were never enough educated

Europeans to provide all the skills needed in the developing country. For example, health care in rural black areas was practically non-existent, except for mission hospitals, owing to a dearth of trained black doctors and nurses.

The Soweto riots in June 1976 were a direct result of the inferior educational system for the blacks. It was ruled that half their classes should be taught in Afrikaans. The students objected, both in principle and because there were not enough qualified black teachers. These riots started the last phase of the push by the blacks to end Apartheid.

## 1970s BLACK & COLORED REALITIES

The unique social and political situation in South Africa evolved from its unusual history. There was separation of the tribes and intertribal warfare long before the whites arrived in 1652. The Khoisan and the many Bantu tribes had ever-changing dynamics and relation-ships, but enjoyed simple agrarian and pastoral cultures, with no written languages and no access to formal education or first world advantages. Change occurred mainly through tribal battles, natural disasters and southward migration under population pressures.

White settlement brought many changes—first world contact, organized religions, culture, education, ideas and ambitions, allowing evolution into a first world country. The whites eliminated many of the Khoisan, brought in slaves from many countries and enslaved Khoikhoi and Bantu people, before finally abandoning slavery. A new race—the Cape Coloreds—rose Phoenix-like from the ashes.

The whites took most of their land from the Bantu, who initially attempted to drive them out, but failed under superior firepower. Blacks and Coloreds were relegated to second-class status, used as sources of cheap labor.

The racial separation existing before 1652 increased during white domination, creating a stratified society. As urbanization increased, blacks and Coloreds were collected into 'Locations,' away from the white areas, and with far worse housing and infrastructure. In the middle decades of the 20th century, town councils and other authorities attempted to ameliorate the poor housing conditions by building more modern 'Townships,' still separated from the whites, as for example Sharpeville for the town of Vereeniging. This attempt was overtaken by the Apartheid zeal of the Nationalists after 1950, with their attempts at total rearrangement of peoples' lives, and displacement of whole communities.

Apart from those blacks and Colored people living in organized 'townships,' many blacks came to the cities seeking work opportunities, but had nowhere to live. Others were displaced from their homes under the dictates of Apartheid. Such homeless people lived in sordid squatter camps on open land outside the Townships, with no infrastructure or civilized amenities. Such places were breeding grounds for crime, rape, drug addiction and prostitution. There were no health care facilities, and disease was rife. Intertribal and interpersonal violence was endemic and spread to the Townships. Allied with the socio-economic deprivation, alcohol-related crime became a major component of life and death in these areas. Black-on-black crime was deeply entrenched in all urban black areas.

The use of migrant labor caused many men and some women to be housed in 'Compounds,' as on the mines, or in 'Hostels' in the various black Townships near major cities. Ethnic hatred and fighting was rife in these huge single-sex dwellings. On the goldmines this often became so bad that the entire labor force had to be repatriated and the mine closed until replacement workers were recruited and trained.

In the black rural areas, life went on much as it had for centuries. They remained home areas for many, where they could live in peace, poverty and ignorance, eking out a living from the land or as migrant labor in the cities or mines, or even on the white farms.

The black and colored peoples have had to fight their own way up if they were to make any progress. Subsequently, the fight went underground and many black resistance groups operated, both in and outside the country, to cause the overthrow of Apartheid. These movements started in about 1910 and increased markedly after the Sharpeville massacre in 1960 and the Soweto riots in 1976.

[1] Non-whites: A general term used in South Africa for people who were not of European origin. It was used more in an official or legalistic sense. For example, public facilities were labeled: 'Whites' or 'Non-Whites.'

[2] Kaffir: From Arabic: Infidel. Used in South Africa in prior centuries for Bantu people, e.g. Kaffir Wars of the 18th and 19th Centuries. Used colloquially for black people till mid 20th century. Now regarded as archaic and pejorative.

[3] VOC: Acronym for the initials of the Dutch East India Company—Vereenigde Oost-Indische g'oktrooieerde Compagnie.

[4] Scurvy: A deficiency disease, caused by lack of vitamin C, found in fresh fruit and vegetables. It was essentially the reason the Cape was settled at that time!

[5] Developed independent gene pools: Direct quote from Davenport & Saunders. See # 9 below

[6] Straf-commando: Afrikaans: Punishment commando.

[7] Basters: From Dutch, lit. 'Bastards' or half-breed people. They moved further north and integrated partly with Bantu tribes on the western side of the country.

[8] Blacks from west and central Africa and the east coast: These people were from essentially the same genetic roots as the South African Bantu tribes. One theory has it that the central origin of all the tribes was an area of the Congo, at Ubangi Shari, and the peoples fanned out from there, eventually reaching South Africa.

[9] Bantu and Khoisan peoples: Originally, the Khoisan people—'Hottentots and Bushmen,' were regarded as ethnically distinct from the Bantu tribes. They were the first indigenous non-white people encountered by the Dutch settlers in 1652. The Burghers, who left on the Great Trek and migrated east and North, started to encounter Bantu tribes as they went further on their travels, resulting in the many 'Kaffir Wars.' Modern studies in many disciplines have suggested that the Khoisan are not distinct but come from separate gene pools developing in response to climatic and geographic influences. Perhaps DNA studies will solve this semantic problem. The black slaves brought in from the rest of Africa, such as Angola, Guinea or Mozambique, were thus essentially of the same ethnic origin as the South African Bantu people.

[10] Lobola: 'Bride Price.' A custom in many tribes. The bridegroom gave the father of the bride a gift of cattle.

[11] Mfecane: A Bantu word meaning 'the crushing.' It had different spelling by different tribes. It was essentially a huge and bloody upheaval, with many tribes fleeing or being conquered or killed. It was preceded by several years of severe droughts on the east coast of South Africa and was centered on the Ndebele and Zulu people.

[12] Impis: Zulu name for armies.

[13] Voortrekkers: Voor means 'front,' Trek means 'pull.' See # 18 below. The 'Voortrekkers were the leaders in 'Trekking' out of the Cape Colony in 1836. They were farmers who were on the move in their wagons, taking along their slaves, herds of animals, food, ammunition and all their other worldly goods. They lived wherever they chose to make camp. They finally settled across Natal, the Orange Free State and the Transvaal.

[14] Boers: Afrikaans, lit. 'Farmers.' The word later became used internationally for the Afrikaans racial group.

[15] House of Orange: The Dutch Royal House. They were related by marriage to British Royalty and were in exile in London at the time. The order to hand over the Cape came from them in London.

[16] Free Burghers: Free citizens. They were allowed to farm for their own account, but first had to fulfill the needs of the Company by selling their produce back at Company-established prices.

[17] Trekboer: A farmer who was prepared to move away from his home with his family and all his belongings and establish a new farm elsewhere, perhaps hundreds of miles away.

[18] Great Trek: 'Trek' means 'pull.' Trekking essentially meant moving away from somewhere in a wagon pulled by a span of oxen. An individual farmer's establishment on the trail was often referred to as his 'Trek.' The Great Trek was a large migration of farmers (Boers) and their possessions away from the Cape and British rule. See #s 13 & 14.

[19] Rinderpest: An infectious virus disease of cattle mainly, resulting in a swelling of the throat like diphtheria. It was universally fatal.

[20] Uitlanders: People from outside the country—foreigners to South Africa. They were largely English, but there were some Dutch, German, French, Jewish and other European people.

[21] Apartheid: Afrikaans, lit: Apartness. Designed by Dr. Verwoerd, who was born in Holland. The system put a very hard face on some traditional policies that had been on their way out and added new and far stricter laws to the statute books.

The Soweto riots on June 16, 1976 marked the beginning of the final push to end Apartheid. The disturbances continued for months, rotating round the country from one area to another. Both black anger and public awareness remained at high levels. Many resistance movements became even more active in South Africa, other African states and overseas. The government suppressed such organizations as it could reach. The ANC[1] found a home in Lusaka, Zambia. Many people were banned, imprisoned or placed under house arrest for months or years. Nelson Mandela, who had been arrested for 'treason' in 1962 and condemned to life in prison in 1964, was still confined on Robben Island.[2] It was made illegal to publish anything these people said or wrote.

The worldwide boycotts of South Africa, in sports like rugby and cricket and in the Olympic Games, and the oil, arms and trade embargoes, produced severe international isolation of the country. The rapid economic growth of the nineteen sixties and early seventies gave way to depression, job losses and severe reductions in real wages. This situation was aggravated by a prolonged reduction in the price of gold. These factors all took their toll on the nation's psyche. Many whites, particularly in commerce and industry, and their more-enlightened politicians, began to realize that the old patterns of white domination could not continue.

Thus the government under President P.W. Botha adopted a 'Total Strategy' for change. It was aimed at defusing both overseas and internal criticism of the Apartheid structure, while covertly attempting to retain white Nationalist party power. This strategy essentially involved increased security measures, removal of the more troublesome and obvious aspects of Apartheid, and social and educational reform and restructuring. They wanted to raise the workforce to the standards required by modern manufacturing and business practices, thus creating more stability.

They started to change the more oppressive aspects of Apartheid and eliminated many aspects of so-called 'petty Apartheid.' For example, public amenities were desegregated. The Immorality and Mixed Marriages Acts were repealed. In 1986 the Pass Laws were dropped. The government changed its attitude to education; racial integration was permitted at private schools. They also recognized that the technological age required a trained workforce and this would make unskilled workers redundant. They improved facilities for teaching and technical training of blacks at all levels. Black people were also allowed to own more businesses in designated black areas, and could receive government financial aid. Botha aimed to create a stable black middle class.

When KwaZulu[3] in Natal and later KwaNdebele,[4] in the Transvaal, refused to take their independence, the government realized that the 'Bantustan' concept was failing. They tried to create political allies by drawing up a new constitution, enfranchising the Coloreds and Indians and establishing a joint consultative assembly with three chambers. The majority of the new voters boycotted the elections, and those elected were regarded as 'puppets.' A further attempt was made to obtain more political allies by creating black local authorities and community councils, with elected officials. These attempts also failed to gain overwhelming support and in fact were openly undermined by activists and the people.

The government antagonized the blacks even more by excluding them from the new tricameral constitution, supposedly because of their political rights in the homelands and their community councils. It was widely regarded as the final insult. When discussing the situation Chief Gatsha Buthelezi, the leader of the Zulus, commented that leaving the blacks out meant that 'The night of the long knives' was coming closer. It seemed that nothing the Botha government did could produce a solution to South Africa's problems.

At the same time, during the 1980s, black activism progressively increased. The blacks were not taken in by the 'Total Strategy.' Many things were happening on a variety of fronts, with one leading objective:

to make the black townships and areas ungovernable. As anti-Apartheid activities increased, so did security force and police repression. The South African author Rian Malan in *My Traitor's Heart* eloquently describes the gruesome horrors of this period, which included the murders by 'necklacing' of political opponents and thousands of other incidents of violence and civil disobedience. The townships were indeed becoming ungovernable. On June 12, 1986, Botha appeared on South African Television, predicted revolution on the 10th anniversary of the Soweto riots, and ordered a massive crackdown on black activists and organizations. Extremely severe suppressive measures were taken, resulting in no Soweto riot commemoration on June 16th. Huge expenditures were made on internal defense. The result of these actions was essentially stalemate. Neither the blacks nor the Nationalist government could attain their objectives. Severe dissatisfaction continued amongst the non-whites. It was a state of poorly concealed warfare. The black tactic then became one of massive civil disobedience.

Meanwhile, change came slowly. The year 1989 was a watershed in South African white politics. President P.W. Botha, at age 73, had become capricious, irritable and dictatorial. He was unpopular, feared and hated within his own party. In January 1989 he had a stroke, which worsened his moods, but gave an opportunity for progress. In July, he met Nelson Mandela in captivity, the first President to see him since his incarceration in 1962. In August, on the other hand, Botha publicly rebuked F.W. De Klerk, a cabinet minister and leader of the Transvaal sector of the party, for making contact with the ANC in Zambia. The cabinet revolted, asked Botha to step down, and made De Klerk the acting President.

Meanwhile, the white political landscape was changing. A small but growing liberal Democratic Party and a strong right wing both challenged the Nationalist party. This period of turmoil ended with an election in September 1989, causing a vast realignment of the power structure. Though retaining a majority, the Nationalists lost power to both the right and the left. F.W. De Klerk became the new President. A lawyer by training, De Klerk was an affable man and a smooth talker. But he appeared to be an unlikely reformer, since he had his roots in the right wing of the party. He held his cards close to his chest.

On February 2 1990, speaking at the opening of parliament, De Klerk surprised the country and the world. He promised revolutionary changes in political dispensations for the blacks and at the end of his address announced plans for the early release of Nelson Mandela. The government fulfilled these promises and, after 27 years in prison, Mandela became a free man on February 11, 1990, to great worldwide acclaim. The die was cast.

Three years of negotiations and political wrangling followed, with rapidly changing positions, and alliances being hastily formed and readily broken, accompanied by constant politically motivated violence. Despite this chaos a carefully crafted democratic constitution was written and adopted in 1993. The first democratic one-man one-vote elections were successfully held in 1994. Nelson Mandela became President and F.W. De Klerk Vice President, with an ANC-dominated government.

But this transition to majority rule had been preceded by several years of indescribable political unrest and violence, largely due to the diverse ethnic make-up of the country. It had mainly involved the two most powerful black leaders and their supporters. The Zulus were the largest ethnic group, under Chief Gatsha Buthelezi, head of the Inkatha Freedom Party. The second largest group, the Xhosas, supported Nelson Mandela and the ANC. Repeated clashes occurred between these groups in many parts of the country. The government secretly allied itself with Inkatha, and there were frequent allegations that the police were also involved in these problems, often giving covert help to Inkatha, while selectively looking the other way when ANC members were being attacked. The government denied such allegations, but evidence before the Truth and Reconciliation Commission has proved their extensive involvement at many levels.

The horrifying carnage was mostly black-on-black. Between 1984 and 2000 there were 24,457 politically related fatalities, with 1993 yielding the highest total of 3,794 deaths.[5] A particularly horrible punishment called 'necklacing' was often used on political opponents. A car tire filled with gasoline was placed round the neck of the unfortunate victim, whose hands were bound. The gasoline was ignited, causing a hideous and agonizing death.

Horrifying as these figures were, general violence and crime were increasing far more, as the authority of the white government faded and criminals took advantage of the chaos. Blacks previously had no access to firearms, but now arms smuggled from Maputo (Mozambique) were freely available to all. Russian AK-47s became the preferred weapons for car-jackings and other crimes. Of the 15,100 murders officially recorded nationwide in 1990, between 11,000 and 12,500 were from criminal rather than political violence and 96% of the victims were black.[6]

Chris Hani Baragwanath Hospital, renamed for a black leader assassinated by two white extremists in 1993,[7] has expanded considerably during the intervening years. Since 1994 all hospitals have been open to people of every racial group. By virtue of its proximity to Soweto, Baragwanath has continued to serve mostly black patients. The population of Soweto has tripled from over a million to about 3.5 million people.

Bara is the biggest hospital in Africa and in the southern hemisphere. The 1997 Guinness Book of Records has it as the largest in the world. Professor Desmond Pantanowitz in 1988 described it well in his authoritative multi-author book *Modern Surgery in Africa—The Baragwanath Experience*. He recorded that in 1987 the hospital had 30 operating theaters, performed 39,848 operations, saw 1.75 million patients annually and had 124,000 in-patient admissions. Thirty thousand children were born there that year. There were 3,000 nurses in training and 700 doctors on the staff, half of them from overseas. The surgical load was 70% trauma, with some 3,000 chest injuries, including 100 stabs in the heart. There were 4,000 head injuries and 700 abdominal injuries.

Since then the numbers have continued to increase. The hospital currently has an annual budget of 765 million Rands and treats over two million people a year.[8] It has 3,300 beds, but only 2,600 are operating. It handles 3,000 Outpatients a day and double that on weekends. There are 35,500 births per year—a quarter of all babies born in the Transvaal. It has a staff of 4,885, including 565 doctors and 2,121 nurses.

The load of disastrous gunshot wounds, with multiple organ damage, is reported to be increasing rapidly, far surpassing knife wounds in frequency. According to recent reports, serious trauma now overwhelms the available staff and facilities and dwarfs the number of all other cases, to the serious detriment of care.

AIDS is now the major medical problem in the country and thus also at Bara. Seventy percent of the world's AIDS cases are in sub-Saharan Africa. This has sharply reduced life expectancy. By the year 2005 the average lifespan of an African will be only 47.5 years—a reduction of 15 years during the last two decades. In South Africa AIDS affects over 4.7 million people, out of a population of 42.5 million. That is about 11%, or one of every nine people. The 1999 figure for HIV infections from the Department of Health is double that, at 22.4% of the population. The other 11.4% will probably also develop AIDS. (Not everyone infected by HIV has AIDS, which takes time to develop. Both numbers are staggering.) Every day, over 25% of the patients in Baragwanath are HIV positive. The Government has no funds to treat AIDS. This is highly discouraging to the medical and nursing staff, who are accustomed to trying to cure people. No doctor would now consider doing any form of surgery, patient contact, or blood drawing without wearing gloves.

Tuberculosis, always endemic in South Africa, has increased alarmingly, particularly in HIV positive patients. Even worse, drug resistant strains both of TB and HIV are becoming increasingly common, putting the general population at grave risk. As in many other countries, there is insufficient money to treat either disease adequately, resulting in appalling rates of illness and death.

President Thabo Mbeki, who succeeded Nelson Mandela in 1999, opened the 2000 International AIDS conference in Durban. He horrified his audience and the world by declaring that the disease was not due to HIV infection but to poverty, malnutrition and socio-economic deprivation. He could thus justify withholding expensive drug treatment. Though there have been developments in this saga, Mbeki has never withdrawn his statement, which has harmed both his reputation and the cause of South Africa's AIDS victims. Ex-President Mandela spoke up and disagreed with Mbeki at the time, and is becoming increasingly vocal in his opposition to these views, issuing a major statement in 2002. After meetings with ANC top brass he has regrettably also toed the party line. One way of avoiding paying for treatment has been for the authorities to call the treatment both experimental and dangerous. They are thus saving their people from harm!

Small wonder that one perverted belief in South Africa is that the cure for AIDS lies in having sex with a virgin! This has expanded to sexual assaults on babies. In a recent case the infant had to have its bowel bypassed. African women are becoming militant in trying to prevent these assaults. Some Provincial health departments will not pay for HIV positive mothers to get an anti-AIDS drug to keep their babies from getting the disease. These attitudes have caused an uproar in the country.

Public hospitals in South Africa are starved for money, staff and equipment, with conditions constantly deteriorating. In 1999 many well-respected senior doctors from 18 hospitals in Gauteng Province,[9] the industrial and commercial heartland, publicly denounced the abysmal and dangerous conditions in the public hospitals for both patients and staff. They cited absent resources, limited budgets and staff shortages. There is constant pilfering of drugs, equipment, bed linen and supplies, with annual turnover of these items exceeding 300% in some hospitals. In the year 2000 Edenvale hospital completed construction of a new Casualty, operating suite, maternity and pediatric wards costing 40 million Rands. The new facilities could not open for lack of staff.

Professor Pantanowitz some years ago took charge of surgery at Helen Joseph Hospital, another major teaching institution in Johannesburg. In 1999 he also went out on a limb and publicly denounced conditions there. Operating theaters and departments were forced to close. Services were being reduced and highly skilled and respected doctors were leaving in desperation.

This type of situation was not confined to Gauteng province. At Cape Town's renowned Groote Schuur Hospital, the well-respected head of the trauma unit resigned and emigrated after five years in the job and a life dedicated to public service. Before leaving, he described conditions there as the 'Siberia of surgery,' where gunshot wounds account for 80% of all surgery. He also said, "We are looking at the total destruction of medical standards in South Africa."

Perhaps as a result of such protests, the Gauteng provincial administration announced in December 2000 that Chris Hani Baragwanath Hospital would be revamped into a multi-story building at a cost of millions of Rands. Computerization of the hospital is planned. The source of the needed funds in the cash-strapped Gauteng province was not revealed.

Sadly, an independent ethics study of the hospital, released in November 2001,[10] revealed Bara to be a 'Sick Hospital' with abusive medical staff, demoralized doctors, theft of linen and drugs and bribery to get services. This survey was based on a 20% sample of all levels of the staff and 200 patients. The study produced 26 recommendations, calling for improvement in management and leadership; human resources; material resources; admissions; discipline and ethics; patient care; and an increase in the budget from the Gauteng Department of Health and the Government Treasury.

At the same time, the annual budget of R765 million (about US $74 million) is set to decrease. In January 2002 it was separately announced that budget allocations countrywide would be reduced for the major teaching type hospitals, which get a big share of current provincial budgets. This was because primary care, a main focus of the government, is given chiefly outside these hospitals. The effects of this reduction on patients and doctors in the major hospitals such as Baragwanath, the Johannesburg Hospital and Cape Town's Groote Schuur are too horrible to imagine.

One good piece of health news for Johannesburg in January 2002 was that Mr. Donald Gordon had donated R100 million to work with the University of the Witwatersrand in Johannesburg, and set up a facility like the Mayo Clinic, on a commercial but non-profit basis, with retained earnings to be put back into the facility. This will improve standards of medical care and possibly keep more doctors in the country, but will be of scant use to most of the patients at Bara.

From the socio-political viewpoint, the transition to Black rule in 1994 was far more peaceful on an interracial basis than had been predicted by many, both within and outside South Africa. There is no doubt this was largely due to the immense stature and personality and forgiving nature of Nelson Mandela, the first black President. The black and Colored people are undoubtedly far happier with a properly democratic country. They can at last view themselves with pride. People of goodwill in all racial groups are trying to build a better future for South Africa. Many black entrepreneurs and others catering to the needs of the black population are thriving. Black middle and upper classes are growing. Some are moving to previously all-white suburbs, but many find they miss the old social life of the townships.

There are some more hopeful signs for the future. One is South Africa's realization that tourism holds a key to more money, foreign exchange and jobs. The country is becoming a leading tourist destination. For those visiting Johannesburg, tours of Soweto are major attractions. The public and private game parks are lures for many. Tourism has picked up further since the terrorist attacks on America. Secondly, the price of gold has increased in the last few months, due to political uncertainty and terrorist fears in the Middle East and elsewhere. This makes gold production more profitable and offers the possibility of increased employment on old or new mines.

The 'Truth and Reconciliation Commission,' established by Rev. Desmond Tutu in 1995, reported in 1998. The intention was for people or organizations to publicly confess their past political crimes committed against other people or groups between 1960 and 1994. They would receive amnesty, without penalty. Tutu said that there could only be national reconciliation in this way. Some horrendous confessions ensued, confirming many prior suspicions. The nation is probably better for this catharsis. But the commission was only partially successful in attaining its goals. Several people, such as President Botha, refused to testify. The ANC wanted the atrocities they committed in the struggle against Apartheid to be ignored. Many who requested amnesty received it after providing full confessions and cooperation. Several whites did not receive amnesty. They included the police and others responsible for the death of Steve Biko in 1977 and the two radical right-wing whites who assassinated Chris Hani in 1993. There has been no mass retribution as a result of the T.R.C. findings, but many victims of apartheid felt the absence of punishment to be wrong.

For the masses, change has been tardy due to lack of money, low educational levels, limited job opportunities, and a huge backlog of unmet needs in housing and infrastructure. Unemployment of blacks is still near forty percent. More than half the population, or 22 million people, exist below the poverty level, on an average monthly income of R144.00. (About US $14.00.) Vast shanty towns still exist. Seven and a half million people lack adequate shelter. Just 1.2 million houses have been built since the start of black majority rule in 1994, with a backlog of 2-3 million. The backlog on basic sanitation is three million households, while four million homes still have no electricity.

With that background it is easy to understand that South Africa and its provinces are short of cash for major capital expenditures, or even to pay for anti-retroviral drugs to fight AIDS. It is thus incomprehensible that President Mbeki still insists on spending forty billion Rands on arms purchases, when the country's social needs are so pressing and there is no likely threat to South Africa.

'Africanisation' of jobs is increasing, and has led to the promotion or hiring of many competent black people. Unfortunately, many unqualified blacks have also been given jobs ahead of well-qualified whites, Indians or Coloreds. This has led to a loss of hope in many whites, contributing to an aggravation of the 'white flight' or 'brain drain' of recent history.

Bribery and corruption is rife at all levels of society, with new scandals involving government members or officials erupting weekly. Organized crime takes novel forms, such as buying copper wire and scrap metal from poor people, who are only too willing to steal it in order to make some money. Recently theft of copper cable from a train signal line north of Durban caused a train crash. For R26 ($2.60) worth of copper, 24 people were killed and 112 injured. Countrywide, the direct costs of copper theft are many hundreds of millions of Rands per year. Far larger indirect costs include the provision of security for power and rail lines and the dislocation of transport services, traffic signals and electricity supply. Even bridge guardrails have been stolen for their scrap metal value. The theft of blankets, bed linen and drugs in hospitals has also been linked to organized crime.

An innovative method of robbery recently took place. Four Pakistanis were arrested for systematically following foreigners coming in from Jan Smuts Airport to Johannesburg on a highway, then turning on blue revolving lights like police cars, forcing the foreigners to the roadside, and robbing them of their luggage, personal belongings and money.

Violence has become a way of life, spreading to the white suburbs, where it was previously feared, but rather rare. The earlier political violence has stopped, while murders, gang violence and general gangsterism have taken its place. Someone is raped every six minutes—the highest rate in the world. The population has largely lost faith in the police, so there has been an upswing in vigilantism, particularly in black and country areas. This has itself become a problem, since the vigilante groups administer brutal and often fatal summary justice, especially a group called PAGAD[11] in Cape Town.

Murders of white farmers and their workers are frequent, with 800 dead since 1994, including 138 murders in 816 attacks that occurred during 1999 alone. The numbers are higher again for 2001.

Land re-allocation is an issue that continues to simmer in both black and white minds. The terrible events in Kenya many years ago and the current land grab and atrocities being encouraged and perpetrated in Zimbabwe by President Mugabe have many whites in a high state of anxiety. In May 2002 Mugabe's government gave 2,900 white farmers 90 days to permanently get off their own land. President Mbeki's failure to openly condemn Mugabe has not reassured many South Africans. In his 2002 State of the Nation speech President Mbeki said that in three years he would have completed the return of land taken from blacks by the Apartheid minority government. Time will tell how that scenario plays out.

Gated, limited-access communities are the norm in more affluent areas, with burglar alarms, huge garden walls and guard dogs, plus human guards or security services. Johannesburg is now Africa's most dangerous city, with 136 murders annually per 100,000 compared to Washington DC's 70 and 50 for the whole of South Africa. Life in the central city is intolerable. Both the Carlton Hotel and the Holiday Inn have been shut down, their windows boarded shut. Major banks are closed; vagrants make fires in their marble foyers.

Many large companies, previously based in Johannesburg, have changed their headquarters and stock exchange listings to the United States or Britain. The Johannesburg Stock Exchange and many other major businesses have left the city, to establish new headquarters in the elite suburb of Sandton, where they offer drive-in, guarded, gated parking in their own multi-story buildings.

Car-jackings occur daily, frequently accompanied by murder of the owners. People hardly dare to stop at traffic signals. An acquaintance of the author was killed in a car-jacking in his own driveway in suburban Johannesburg. As this page was being written, a 38 year-old white lawyer in suburban Cape Town was critically injured in his home; his car and household goods stolen, his young child left asleep in the house. In December 2001, Marike, the first wife of ex-President De Klerk, was stabbed and strangled to death, apparently by the security guard of her 'high security' apartment in Cape Town.

So, unfortunately, the predictions I made in 1976 have largely come to pass. Were it not for friends and family still in the country there would seem to be scant reason to even visit South Africa.

The heartbreak remains. Home is home forever.

AFRICA STAYS IN YOUR BONES.

[1] A.N.C: African National Congress. A banned South African black political organization; one of the oldest in the country. Widely regarded at that time as the 'Black Government in Exile,' it became the major party in the new 1994 Government of South Africa, with Nelson Mandela as its leader.

[2] Robben Island: South Africa's maximum-security prison, in Table Bay off Cape Town.

[3] KwaZulu: A projected 'Bantustan' or 'Homeland' for the Zulu people, situated within Natal province. Gatsha Buthelezi, its leader, persistently refused to accept independence. The Zulus are the largest ethnic group in the country, so this rejection carried tremendous weight.

[4] KwaNdebele: A similar 'Homeland' for the Ndebele people, situated in the Transvaal.

[5] Black-on-black violence: Figures from the S.A. Institute of race relations report 2001.

[6] General violence: Figures from David Ottaway's book *Chained Together*.

[7] Chris Hani: Leader of 'Umkhonto we Sizwe,' or 'Spear of the Nation,' a militant black anti-Apartheid organization, the military wing of the ANC. He was assassinated in 1993 by two right wing white extremists.

[8] Bara figures 2001: From *The Star* newspaper, November 8, 2001; 'Ailing Bara in critical condition.' Also the website of Chris Hani Baragwanath Hospital.

[9] Gauteng: The south central of the four provinces created out of the old Transvaal in 1994. It contains the industrial and financial heartland of South Africa.

[10] Ethics Survey: See # 8, above.

[11] PAGAD: 'People against gangsterism and drugs.'

# CODA

I see him now, my long remembered patient with whom I shared the front pages of international newspapers. We made medical history Zephania Ndlazi and I. I can see his face now. The open, honest smile around the missing teeth, the infectious humor beaming from his eyes, the absolute certitude invested in me that I could reattach his leg. The White Witchdoctor could do it…

But in that unique scheme of things all of the best intentions, all of the desire, all of the mustered skills that were brought to bear could not achieve Zephania's wish: to have his leg back again; to walk as before.

In so many ways we were different men. And yet, and yet…when I think about it, I see our common bond in a deep love for South Africa. Perhaps in the idealism and hope of his leg surgery, we can find in microcosm the idealism and hope for our beautiful and savage land. We tried for something new. We matched our hopes in a common venture to do something good and right. It was our lot in that place and time to see that medical sophistication could not keep pace with these journeys of the heart.

I'm sure Zephania joins me in hoping that South Africa can nurture her boundless gifts to overcome the daunting problems she faces. He smiles at me across the years, patient to doctor, man to man, black to white, friend to friend. I smile back.

Belfield, Eversley. *The Boer War.* 1993, Leo Cooper, London, and Barnes and Noble.

Breytenbach, Breyten. *Return to Paradise.* 1993, 1st Edition. Harcourt, Brace.

Davenport, T.R.H. & Saunders, Christopher. *South Africa. A Modern History.* 2000, 5th Edition. St Martin's Press.

de Villiers, Simon A. *Robben Island.* 1971, 1st Edition. C. Struik, Cape Town.

Gordimer, Nadine. *Burger's Daughter.* 1979, 1st Edition. Viking Press, N. Y.

Mackenzie, W.D.A. & Stead, A. *South Africa. Its History, Heroes and Wars.* 1899, George Spiel, USA. Out of print.

Malan, Rian. *My Traitor's Heart. A South African Exile returns to face his Country, his Tribe, and his Conscience.* 1990, Morgan Entrekin. Atlantic Monthly Press.

Mandela, Nelson. *Long Walk to Freedom. The Autobiography of Nelson Mandela.* 1995, 1st Edition. Little Brown, Boston.

Meredith, Martin & Rosenberg, Tina. *Coming to Terms. South Africa's Search for Truth.* 1999, 1st Edition. Public Affairs, New York.

Millin, Sarah Gertrude. *God's Stepchildren.* 1924, 1st Edition, Reprinted 1936. Constable, London & Macmillan, Toronto. Out of Print.

Ottaway, David. *Chained Together. Mandela, De Klerk and the struggle to remake South Africa.* 1993, 1st Edition. Times Books. Random House.

Pantanowitz, Desmond. (Ed.) *Modern Surgery in Africa. The Baragwanath Experience.* 1988, 1st Edition. Southern Book Publishers. Johannesburg.

Picard, H.W.J. *Masters of the Castle.* 1972. C. Struik, Cape Town.

Richburg, Keith B. *Out of America. A Black Man Confronts Africa.* 1997, Basic Books. Harper Collins.

Van Woerden, Henk. (Translated by Dan Jacobson.) *The Assassin. A Story of Race and Rage in the Land of Apartheid.* 2001, 1st American Edition. Metropolitan Books. Henry Holt.

Worden, Nigel. *The Making of Modern South Africa. Conquest, Segregation and Apartheid.* 2000, 3rd Edition. Blackwell, Oxford and Massachusetts.

# WEB SITES & NEWSPAPERS

African History                              http//africanhistory.about.com/library/weekly/

Africa Stage—General History                www.worldtrek.org.odyssey/africa/

BBC News Africa                             http//news.bbc.co.uk/

Business Day                                www.bday.co.za/bday/content/

Chris Hani Baragwanath Hospital             www.chrishanibaragwanathhospital.co.za/

Daily Mail and Guardian online              www.mg.co.za/

Dutch East India Co. (VOC)                  www.geocities.com/sa_stamouers/

Guardian U.K.                               www.guardian.co.uk/

Marula tree: ICRAF online                   www.icraf.cgiar.org/

News 24                                     www.news24.com/

S.A. Labyrinth                              www.sael.org.za/

Slavery at the Cape                         http//Batavia.rug.ac.be/slavery/

South Africa online (Govt)                  www.southafrica.co.za/govt/

South Africa (Describe)                     www.ancestry.com/learn/reference/country/
                                            southafric a.htm/

Third World Network                         www.twnside.org.sg/title/1976.htm/

Weekend Mail and Guardian                   http//web.sn.apc.org/wmail/

Star Newspaper, Johannesburg                Nov. 8 2001. *Ailing Bara in Crisis*
                                            by Sheena Adams.

DURBAN HOUSE

# EXCEPTIONAL BOOKS
## BY
# EXCEPTIONAL WRITERS

## Check out these other fine titles by Durban House at your local book store.

### AFTER LIFE LIFE    DON GOLDMAN
This murder mystery takes place in the afterlife. Andrew Law, Chief Justice of the Texas Supreme Court, is the picture of robust health when he suddenly dies. Upon arriving in the afterlife, Andy discovers he was murdered and his untimely death has some unexpected and far-reaching consequences—a world wide depression among others. There are all sorts of diabolical plots running through his hilariously funny, fast-paced whodunit with an ending that's a surprising double cross.

### BASHA    JOHN HAMILTON LEWIS
Set in the world of elite professional tennis and rooted in ancient Middle East hatreds of identity and blood loyalties, Basha is charged with the fiercely competitive nature of professional sports and the dangers of terrorism. An already simmering Middle East begins to boil and CIA Station Chief Grant Corbet must track down the highly successful terrorist, Basha. In a deadly race against time, Grant hunts the illusive killer only to see his worst nightmare realized.

### DANGER WITHIN    MARK DANIELSON
Over 100 feet down in cold ocean waters lies the wreck of pilot Kevin Hamilton's DC-10. In it are secrets which someone is desperate to keep. When the Navy sends a team of divers from the Explosives Ordinance Division, a mysterious explosion from the wreck almost destroys the salvage ship. The FBI steps in with Special Agent Mike Pentaglia. Track the life and death of Global Express Flight 3217 inside the gritty world of aviation and discover the shocking cargo that was hidden on its last flight.

### DEADLY ILLUMINATION   SERENA STIER

It's summer 1890 in New York City. Florence Tod, an ebullient young woman, must challenge financier, John Pierpont Morgan, to solve a possible murder. J.P.'s librarian has ingested poison embedded in an illumination of a unique Hildegard van Bingen manuscript. Florence and her cousin, Isabella Stewart Gardner, discover the corpse. When Isabella secretly removes a gold tablet from the scene of the crime, she sets off a chain of events that will involve Florence and her in a dangerous conspiracy.

### HOUR OF THE WOLVES   STEPHANE DAIMLEN-VÖLS

After more than three centuries, the *Poisons Affair* remains one of history's great, unsolved mysteries. The worst impulses of human nature—sordid sexual perversion, murderous intrigues, witchcraft, Satanic cults—thrive within the shadows of the Sun King's absolutism and will culminate in the darkest secret of his reign: the infamous *Poisons Affair,* a remarkably complex web of horror, masked by Baroque splendor, luxury and refinement.

### A HOUSTON WEEKEND   ORVILLE PALMER

Professor Edward Randa11, not-yet-forty, divorced and separated from his daughters, is leading a solitary, cheerless existence in a university town. At a conference in Houston he runs into his childhood sweetheart. Then she was poverty-stricken, neglected and American Indian. Now she's elegantly attired, driving an expensive Italian car and lives in a millionaires enclave. Will their fortuitous encounter grow into anything meaningful?

### JOHNNIE RAY & MISS KILGALLEN   BONNIE HEARN HILL & LARRY HILL

Johnnie Ray was a sexually conflicted wild man out of control; Dorothy Kilgallen, fifteen years his senior, was the picture of decorum as a Broadway columnist and TV personality. The last thing they needed was to fall in love—with each other. Sex, betrayal, money, drugs, drink and more drink. Together they descended into a nightmare of assassination conspiracies, bizarre suicides and government enemy lists until Dorothy dies…mysteriously. Was it suicide…or murder?

### THE LATERAL LINE   ROBERT MIDDLEMISS

Kelly Travett is ready with an Israeli assassination pistol and garlic-coated bullets to kill the woman who tortured and murdered her father. Then the CIA calls with a double warning: she ought to know about Operation Lateral Line and her enemies are expecting her. Revenge is not so simple in the ancient killing alleys of Budapest. There's a Hungarian Chief of Police and his knife and a smiling Russian Mafia boss who has a keen interest in her Israeli pistol…

### LETHAL CURE   KURT POPKE

Dr. Jake Prescott unearths a deadly secret that has one of the most powerful companies in the United States desperate to silence him. A botched attempt to assassinate him gets Jake's wife critically injured and his daughter is kidnaped. In a more successful attempt to get rid of Jake his enemies frame him for the murder of their own hit man. Hopelessly outgunned, Jake turns to a former patient, a retired PI, for help. Together they match wits with the cold-blooded assassin hired to eliminate Jake and his family.

### THE MEDUSA STRAIN   CHRIS HOLMES

A gripping tale of bio-terrorism that stunningly portrays the dangers of chemical warfare in ways nonfiction never could. When an Iraqi scientist full of hatred for America breeds a deadly form of anthrax and a diabolical means to initiate an epidemic, not even the First Family is immune. Will America's premier anthrax researcher devise a bio-weapon in time to save the U.S. from extinction?

## PRIVATE JUSTICE    RICHARD SAND
**winner of the Ben Franklin Award for Best Mystery 2002**
After taking brutal revenge for the murder of his twin brother, Lucas Rook leaves the NYPD to work for others who crave justice outside the law when the system fails them. Rook's dark journey takes him on a race to find a killer whose appetite is growing. A little girl turns up dead. And then another and another. The nightmare is on him fast. The piano player has monstrous hands; the Medical Examiner is a goulish dwarf; an investigator kills himself. Betrayal and intrigue is added to the deadly mix as the story careens toward its startling end.

## RUBY TUESDAY    BARON BIRTCHER
Mike Travis sails his yacht to Kona, Hawaii expecting to put LA Homicide behind him: to let the warm emerald sea wash years of blood from his hands. Instead, he finds his family's home ravaged by shotgun blasts, littered with bodies and trashed with drugs. Then things get worse. A rock star involved in a Wall Street deal masterminded by Travis's brother is one of the victims. Another victim is Ruby, Travis's childhood sweetheart. How was she involved?

## SAMSARA    JOHN HAMILTON LEWIS
A thrilling tale of love and violence in Post World War II Hong Kong. Nick Ridley is the survivor of a POW camp in Changi. After the war, he moves to Hong Kong and purchases several U.S. Army surplus C-147's. Years later his Cathay Airlines is a world-class company and he's about to realize his crowning ambition when suddenly his world begins to unravel. When the love of Nick's life is kidnaped, he must once again face the man responsible for the horrors of Changi. An unforgettable climax.

## SECRET OF THE SCOLL    CHESTER D. CAMPBELL
Colonel Greg McKenzie has unknowingly smuggled a first century Hebrew scroll out of Israel into the U.S. Someone wants it back. McKenzie's wife Jill is taken hostage: her life for the scroll. A Nashville wants to know why McKenzie hasn't filed a missing persons report on his "missing" wife. And the secret of the scroll has the potntial to turn the Arab-Israeli disput into a raging holocaust.

## SECRETS ARE ANONYMOUS    FREDERICK L. CULLEN
Bexley, Ohio is a quiet, unremarkable town in the heartland of American. But its citizens have secrets and amitions which they reveal in interesting ways: chat rooms, instant messaging, e-mails, hypnosis, newspaper articles, letters to the editor, answering machines, video tapes, eavesdropping, vanity plates and coctail napkins. All-American "unremarkable" Bexley is suddenly beseiged by The National Security Agency, the FBI, the Securities and Exchange Commission and a drug cartel—and the guy who runs the ice cream parlor lets them all use the restroom—at a price. What's going on?

## THE SERIAL KILLER'S DIET BOOK    KEVIN MARK POSTUPACK
**finalist in *ForeWord Magazine's* Fiction Book of the Year**
Fred Orbis is fat—very fat—but will soon discover the ultimate diet. Devon DeGroot is on the trail of a homicidal maniac who prowls Manhattan with meatballs, bologna and egg salad—taunting him about the body count in *Finnegans Wakean*. Darby Montana, one of the world's richest women, wants a new set of genes to alter a face and body so homely not even plastic surgery could help. Mr. Monde is the Devil in the market for a soul or two. It's a Faustian satire on God and the Devil, Heaven and Hell, beauty and the best-seller list.

## THE STREET OF FOUR WINDS   ANDREW LAZARUS

Paris—just after World War II. On the Left Bank, Americans seek a way to express their dreams, delights and disappointments in a way very different from pre-war ex-patriots. Tom Cortell is a tough, intellectual journalist disarmed by three women-French, British and American. Along with him is a gallery of international characters who lead a merry and sometimes desperate chase between Pairs, Switzerland and Spain to a final, liberating and often tragic end of their European wanderings in search of themselves.

## WHAT GOES AROUND   DON GOLDMAN

**finalist in *ForeWord Magazine's* Fiction Book of the Year**

Ten years ago, Ray Banno was vice president of a California bank when his boss, Andre Rhodes, framed him for bank fraud. Now, he has his new identity, a new face and a new life in medical research. He's on the verge of finding a cure for a deadly disease when he's chosen as a juror in the bank fraud trial of Andre Rhodes. Should he take revenge? Meanwhile, Rhodes is about to gain financial control of Banno's laboratory in order to destroy Banno's work

# Nonfiction

## FISH HEADS, RICE, RICE WINE & WAR: A VIETNAM PARADOX
### LT. COL. THOMAS G. SMITH, RET.

This memoir set in the Central Highlands of Vietnam, 1966–1969, draws on the intensely human and humourous sides of the strangest and most misunderstood war in which American soldiers were ever committed. Lt. Col. Smith offers a powerful and poignant insider's view of American soldiers at their most heroic who in the midst of the blood and guts of war always find the means to laugh.

## MIDDLE ESSENCE—WOMEN OF WONDER YEARS   LANDY REED

Here is a roadmap and a companion to what can be the most profoundly significant and richest years of a woman's life. For every woman approaching, at, or beyond midlife, this guide is rich with stories of real women in real circumstances who find they have a second chance-a time when women blossom rather than fade. Gain a new understanding of how to move beyond myths of aging; address midlife transitions head on; discover new power and potential; and emerge with a stronger sense of self

## WHITE WITCHDOCTOR   DR. JOHN A.HUNT

Dr. Hunt's skillful blending of emotionally charged events with dispassionate storytelling makes this a truly compelling and powerful memoire of one white surgeon's fight to help save his beloved country of South Africa. The reader is drawn in the by South African culture, folkways and mores, the political upheaval and race relations. It is a memorable and fascinating look at a turbulent era during the time of Apartheid.

## PROTOCOL   Mary Jane McCaffree, Pauline Innis & Katherine Daley Sand

For 25 years, the bible for public relations firms, corporations, embassies, governments and individuals seeking to do business with the Federal government.

*This book contains a wealth of detail on every conceivable question, from titles and forms of address to ceremonies and flg etiquette. The authors are to be complimented for bringing us partially up to date in a final chapter on Women in Official and Public Life.*

—Department of State Newsletter